AF773375

THE POLITICAL ECONOMY OF CAMEROON

OTHER SAIS STUDIES OF AFRICA:

The Political Economy of Nigeria (1983)

The Political Economy of Ivory Coast (1984)

The Political Economy of Zimbabwe (1984)

The OAU After Twenty Years (1984)

The African Military in Politics (1985)

THE POLITICAL ECONOMY OF CAMEROON

Edited by
Michael G. Schatzberg and
I. William Zartman

A SAIS Study on Africa

PRAEGER

PRAEGER SPECIAL STUDIES • PRAEGER SCIENTIFIC

New York • Philadelphia • Eastbourne, UK
Toronto • Hong Kong • Tokyo • Sydney

Library of Congress Cataloging-in-Publication Data
Main entry under title:

The Political economy of Cameroon.

(A SAIS study on Africa)
Bibliography: p.
Includes index.
1. Cameroon – Politics and government – 1960– – Addresses, essays, lectures. 2. Cameroon – Economic policy – Addresses, essays, lectures. 3. Cameroon – Economic conditions – 1960– – Addresses, essays, lectures. I. Schatzberg, Michael G. II. Zartman, I. William. III. Series.
JQ3521.P64 1986 306'.2'096711 85-20492
ISBN 0-03-003093-5 (alk. paper)

Published in 1986 by Praeger Publishers
CBS Educational and Professional Publishing, a Division of CBS Inc.
521 Fifth Avenue, New York, NY 10175 USA

© 1986 by Praeger Publishers

All rights reserved

6789 052 987654321

Printed in the United States of America on acid-free paper

INTERNATIONAL OFFICES

Orders from outside the United States should be sent to the appropriate address listed below. Orders from areas not listed below should be placed through CBS International Publishing, 383 Madison Ave., New York, NY 10175 USA

Australia, New Zealand
Holt Saunders, Pty, Ltd., 9 Waltham St., Artarmon, N.S.W. 2064, Sydney, Australia

Canada
Holt, Rinehart & Winston of Canada, 55 Horner Ave., Toronto, Ontario, Canada M8Z 4X6

Europe, the Middle East, & Africa
Holt Saunders, Ltd., 1 St. Anne's Road, Eastbourne, East Sussex, England BN21 3UN

Japan
Holt Saunders, Ltd., Ichibancho Central Building, 22-1 Ichibancho, 3rd Floor, Chiyodaku, Tokyo, Japan

Hong Kong, Southeast Asia
Holt Saunders Asia, Ltd., 10 Fl, Intercontinental Plaza, 94 Granville Road, Tsim Sha Tsui East, Kowloon, Hong Kong

Manuscript submissions should be sent to the Editorial Director, Praeger Publishers, 521 Fifth Avenue, New York, NY 10175 USA

To the Memory of James S. Coleman

Acknowledgments

This volume is the result of a conference on the political economy of contemporary Cameroon held at the Johns Hopkins University School of Advanced International Studies (SAIS) in Washington in April 1984. Presentations by Victor Le Vine, Ndiva Kofele-Kale, Wilfred Ndongko, Virginia DeLancey, and Peter Agbor-Tabi were heard at that time; the special speakers were Cameroonian Minister of State Youssoufa Daouda and U.S. Assistant Secretary of State Princeton Lyman. The conference was part of SAIS' annual African Country Day Program, which each year features a gathering devoted to an intensive look at a selected African country.

We are grateful to the Exxon Educational Foundation for support for the conference and the preparation of this volume, and to the Ford Foundation for support for the conference. We are also grateful to Ambassadors Paul Pondi, in Washington, and Myles R. Frechette, in Yaounde, for their help and support, and to Theresa Taylor Simmons for her fine technical management of the conference and volume.

Contents

Introduction

It is timely and appropriate to focus attention on Cameroon in the middle of the 1980s, as it celebrates its quarter century of independence. Born with the New Year in 1960, Cameroon opened the year of African independence during which a third of the continent's states ended their colonial rule. It then became the first (and, so far, only) state to bridge the two major colonial systems by joining the southern part of the British Trusteeship Territory with the French Trusteeship Territory in a federal republic. In 1972, following the experience of most African federations (notably excepting Nigeria), Cameroon became a unitary state, with a de facto single party regime. But it is the events of the early 1980s that brought the spotlight back to Cameroon. In 1982, the reign of founding President Ahmadou Ahidjo came to an unexpected end with his sudden resignation. For reasons that still require further analysis, Ahidjo then had second thoughts about resigning and began plotting a return, culminating in the events of April 6–7, 1984 when the country suffered its first—but unsuccessful—military coup. The year 1985 therefore marks the full consolidation of power of Cameroon's second president, Paul Biya.

It is therefore a time to take stock, from three perspectives—evaluating the performance and heritage of the past regime, assessing the prospects and challenges of the new regime, and analyzing the events of that transitional hinge between the two regimes when power shifted from the hands of Ahidjo to those of his hand-picked and then contested successor, Biya. The balancing of regional and ethnic pluralism in an integrative system of centralized, cooptive politics, which was the strength and heritage of Ahidjo, has established rules of the game for Biya. The moral matrix of this system, its elite actors, their ethnic sources of power, and their economic and entrepreneurial relations are examined in chapters by Schatzberg, Le Vine, Kofele-Kale, and Ndongko.

Surrounding and intermingled with the politics of stability and succession is an unusual African record of economic development—both growth and distribution. It began with a continuation of economic ties of trade, aid and investment with the former metropole, paralleled by an unusual record of progress in agricultural productivity, then capped by recent oil discoveries the revenues of which have been banked rather than squandered, all giving rise to a growing indigenous industrial sector that is gradually developing its own interests separate from both state and foreign capital. As in the area of political stability, which has known its injustices and repression, the economic stability has had its share of errors, inefficiencies, and exploitations that also comprise the Ahidjo legacy and constitute an ongoing part of the Cameroonian system. The economic program of the state and its relations with foreign and domestic capital, the problems of industrial investment, the impending agricultural challenges and the impact of the oil sector on the present and future economy, and the international economic basis of Cameroon's foreign relations are analyzed in the chapters by Ndongko, Willame, Virginia DeLancey, Benjamin and Devarajan, and Mark DeLancey.

The resulting record of the quarter century is one of mixed reviews, both a sound position of assessment and a natural reaction to the official optimism of the past regime. For the moment, the founding president has contributed to the consolidation of power of his successor by serving as the scapegoat for all ills of the past, with enough verisimilitude to make the role credible. In a country marked by such rarities as the defeat of an internal guerrilla movement, a minimally functioning single party, the near absence of military coups, respectable per capita economic and agricultural production growth rates, the absence of Dutch Disease from petroleum dominance of the economy, and the absence of French troops in one of the core areas of French interest, it is hard to suspect that the first president did everything wrong or that the society made all its accomplishments only in spite of him. In domestic economic decisions, in political balancing of followers and factions, and in international maneuvering to preserve both privilege and independence, Ahidjo has left a record of lessons that his successor can emulate as well as revise and improve. It is up to the new president to choose the mix.

Despite one's temptation to make judgments, a time of succession—particularly when succession occurs under conditions of uncertainty, as in Cameroon—is scarcely propitious for evaluating a succeeded president. That task needs more distance and perspective. The times are more propitious for assessment of context, conditions, accomplishments, and challenges than for official biographies or personality dissections. Therefore, the focus of the following chapters is on the relationship between the polity and the economy, and on the interrelationships of the many components of each of these two facets of society. Ahidjo will be seen wandering through the pages, with Biya following him, but it is the political myths and economic policies, social groups and leaders, economic interactions and institutions, and foreign impingements and influences that form the basic material for *The Political Economy of Cameroon.*

THE POLITICAL ECONOMY OF CAMEROON

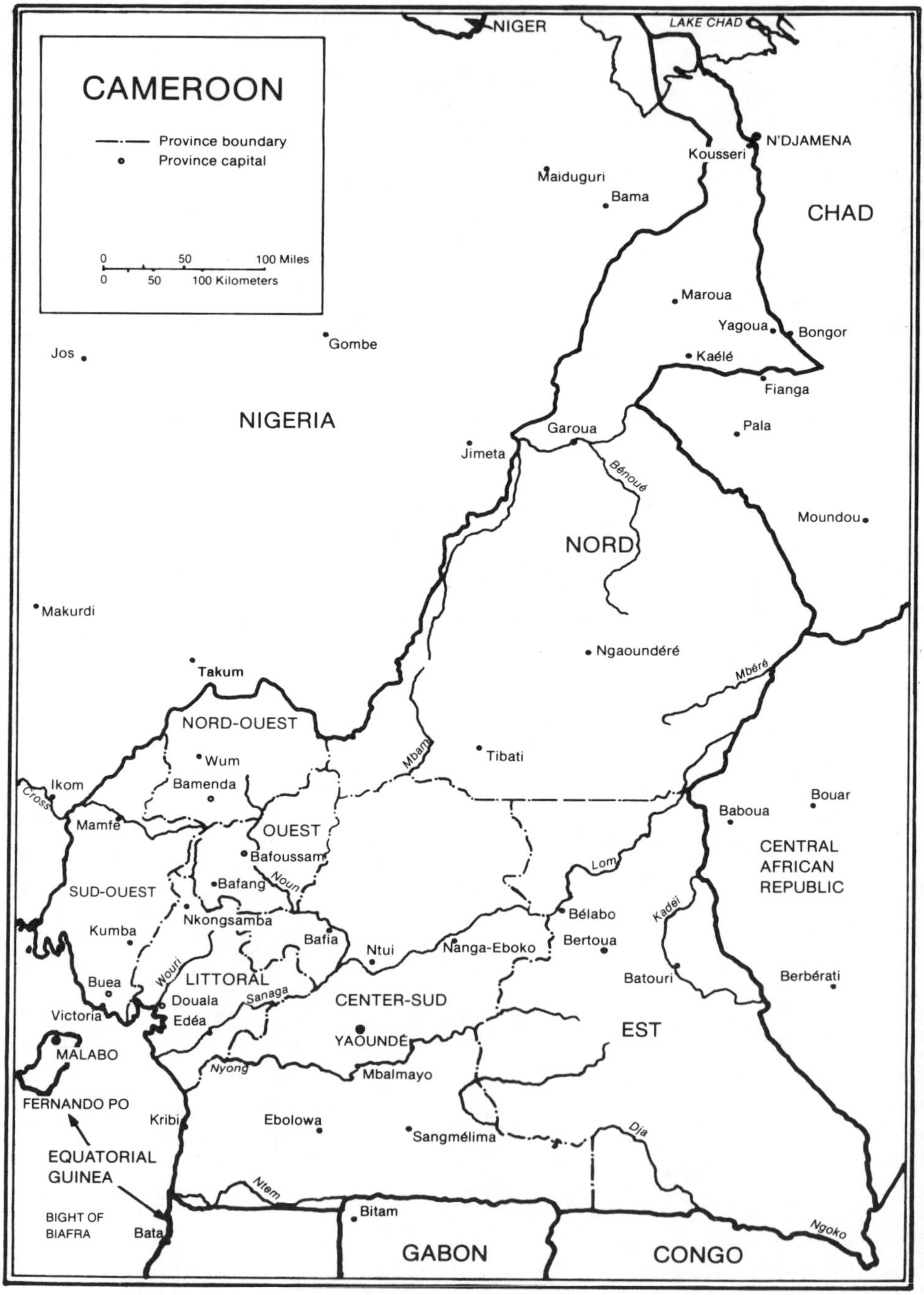
CAMEROON
Province boundary
Province capital
0 50 100 Miles
0 50 100 Kilometers
NIGER
LAKE CHAD
N'DJAMENA
Kousseri
Maiduguri
Bama
CHAD
Maroua
Yagoua
Bongor
Kaélé
Fianga
Jos
Gombe
NIGERIA
Garoua
Pala
Jimeta
Bénoué
Moundou
NORD
Makurdi
Ngaoundéré
Takum
Mbéré
NORD-OUEST
Wum
Mbam
Tibati
Ikom
Cross
Bamenda
Bouar
Baboua
Mamfe
OUEST
Bafoussam
CENTRAL
AFRICAN
REPUBLIC
Noun
Lom
Bafang
SUD-OUEST
Bélabo
Kadéi
Nkongsamba
Kumba
Bafia
Ntui
Nanga-Eboko
Bertoua
Wouri
LITTORAL
Batouri
Berbérati
Buea
Sanaga
CENTER-SUD
Douala
Victoria
Edéa
EST
YAOUNDÉ
MALABO
Nyong
Mbalmayo
FERNANDO PO
Kribi
Ebolowa
Sangmélima
Dja
EQUATORIAL
GUINEA
Ntem
Bitam
BIGHT OF
BIAFRA
Bata
Ngoko
GABON
CONGO

1

THE METAPHORS OF FATHER AND FAMILY

Michael G. Schatzberg

In seeking to understand Cameroonian politics, it helps to place the society in comparative perspective along at least one significant dimension of political life—the political and ideological use of paternal and familial metaphors. Conceived in a frankly speculative vein, this essay argues that the widespread presence and use of the metaphors of father and family in Cameroon and other African states both reflect and reinforce a deeply rooted and largely implicit comprehension of the polity that I shall call the moral matrix of legitimate governance. Although they are worthy subjects of study in their own right, I shall thus not be concerned with any of the Cameroonian regime's explicitly stated formal ideologies (planned liberalism, Cameroonian humanism).

My initial survey of this imagery assumes that such idealizations of father and family are both part of and, in turn, contribute to a widespread pattern of political authority in Cameroon and other contemporary African states. The notion of authority patterns derives largely from Eckstein and Gurr (1975, p. 22) who define it as "a set of asymmetric relations among hierarchically ordered members of a social unit that involves the direction of that unit," and their definition provides a useful point of departure. Elaborating part of a larger project on congruence theory, Eckstein (1980, p. 1; 1966, p. 234) posits that, in general, political stability, high levels of governmental performance, and—I would add—legitimacy, will result where patterns of authority in such social institutions as families, schools, and private enterprises are congruent with (that is, resemble in broad outline) patterns of authority in the formal political arena. Eckstein (1966) had applied his ideas to politics in Norway, while different scholars have studied patterns of political authority in other contemporary societies (Crozier, 1964; Isambert-Jamati 1965; Schonfield 1976; Bakvis 1978). In addition, Schatzberg (1979) has applied this concept to a study of social and political interactions in a Cameroonian lycee.

The concept of authority patterns directs attention to specific points of comparison between families, schools, state agencies, churches, and other private organizations. To what extent do relations between parent and child, for example, resemble those between teacher and pupil? Between principal and teacher? Between administrative superior and subordinate? Between president and citizen? The concept of authority patterns is also useful because it permits us to delve beneath the surface of the state's consciously created ideologies and symbolic constructions to see where these metaphors originate, how they are manipulated by those in power, and, importantly, whose interests they serve.

Starting from these paternal and familial metaphors, I shall try to make explicit a culturally valid and largely implicit comprehension of the limits of political legitimacy based on a complex moral matrix derived from idealized notions of patterns of behavior and authority within the family. This chapter will therefore elaborate these unstated assumptions and normative ideas that undergird both state and society and form the basis of a Cameroonian vision of legitimate governance. To accomplish this I shall first present an overview of the pervasive paternal and familial metaphors in question, comparing Cameroon to Zaire, Central African Republic (CAR), Gabon, Ivory Coast, and other states. Subsequently, attention will be paid to the historical and contemporary sources of this imagery. In addition, I shall then speculate on the significance of this pattern of political authority and symbolic moral matrix it represents. What does it mean and why has it been accepted so readily by the Cameroonian population? Finally, our analysis will lead us to comment on some of the ways that these metaphors are abused and manipulated.

PERVASIVE METAPHORS

The metaphors of father and family are widespread in more than a few African countries, and state-controlled media oftentimes present, deliberately and explicitly, the president as the father of the nation. In this vein, the father is usually described as kindly, loving, and generous; as a man motivated only, and constantly, by the thought of promoting the moral and material well-being of his children, the citizens of the country. To be sure, the chiefs of state in question encourage this image as part of a consciously propagated personality cult and will often describe themselves as the father of the nation, or as the father of the large national family (Badibanga 1980–1981).

To provide but one example among many, the Zairian press (*Salongo,* January 22, 1976, p. 6) has described President Mobutu in these glowing terms:

> In all times, the President-Founder of the Mouvement Populaire de la Revolution [MPR] has always preoccupied himself with the well- and better-being of the Zairian people. Of whom he is, moreover, the well-loved and generous father. His numerous actions taken for the benefit of the laboring masses testify to it. And translate in a convincing way the paternal love that the Guide [Mobutu] . . . manifests vis-a-vis his fellow citizens.

Although the image of the father of the nation is always reserved for the president, there are other "small" fathers as well. Ideally, each person in a position of authority is supposed to behave toward those under his control as would a kindly and loving paternal figure, one cut in the image of the president. So it is that agents of the territorial administration are exhorted continuously to be the "father" of those they administer (*Salongo,* January 31, 1976, p. 2).

In such cases as these it is but a short leap from father to family, and familial imagery is also quite common. The president is thus the father of the large national family to which all citizens belong from birth; the state, or single political party, is a family; and all citizens, regardless of their wealth, age, sex, religion, or ethnic group are brothers and sisters in the great endeavor of nation-building. When queried about the health of the MPR, one high-ranking party official assured his listeners that it was in excellent shape and then painted the following picture in familial terms.

> At a young age, the child overflows with vitality, with a boiling vitality. Toward the age of eleven, he no longer shows the same excitability. His effervescence is transformed progressively into a conscious energy, organized, fertile. The child is going to leave a phase of his life for that which must prepare him during several years, to assume validly the responsibilities of adulthood.
>
> The example of the child is somewhat applicable to the MPR (*Salongo,* November 22, 1976, p. 6).

On one level, this analogy is useful because it describes the political party in terms that all can comprehend easily. Families, as fathers, seem a "natural" part of the social order and are thus readily graspable and immediate notions that render complex political realities in a highly simplified form. On another level, however, the imagery of family applied to the political party is a subtle reminder that we are all "children" of the "family"/party and that it, too, is "natural."

President Mobutu and his mandarins are not the only ones who employ these paternal and familial metaphors. They were also regularly used in the CAR during Jean-Bedel Bokassa's turbulent period of rule. In the former emperor's own words, "That which counts the most in the Central African Empire is God, money and me, your papa"; and "In my country, everyone calls me papa" (Badibanga 1980–1981, pp. 104–105). When, in 1979, Bokassa was confronted with rioting students in Bangui, he summoned representatives of the parents of the rampaging students and addressed them in these terms:

> One cannot say to one's own child: "Go kill your country! go kill your grandfather, your grandmother, your sister, your brother. . . ." . . .
>
> The construction of a country is a difficult task, it is like raising a child! If you have given life to your child today, you need thirty years to make a man or a woman! But a country is the same thing, a country needs more than thirty years to emancipate itself, to be developed, a country is not raised in a day, in a month, in a year, in ten years, in twenty years, many years are needed to evolve a country (Bayart 1980b, pp. 91, 92).

The message being conveyed to the parents was simple: children cannot turn on their country, which is, after all, their parent; and one has to be patient with the country (and its president/father) because, in some respects, it takes even longer to raise a country than it does to raise a child.

Even after Bokassa's men had massacred scores of students and Amnesty International had publicized these events, he could still describe himself with a straight face as the "Father and Protector of all the children, who represent the future of the country" (Delpey 1981, p. 61). When faced with opposition from teachers, Bokassa was also reported to have said: "My daughters and sons, teachers, have lacked respect for their father" (Bayart 1980b, p. 93). There is more than just cynicism at work in the use of paternal and familial metaphors in times of crisis, for the hold of these metaphors on the public consciousness is so deeply rooted that even those who oppose the "father" often employ them. For example, in July 1979 the Mouvement de Liberation du Peuple Centrafricain (MLPC) issued a tract in Paris that called for the overthrow of Bokassa and the restoration of the republic. Their program for a new order and change of regime ended with a call for "the mobilization of all the sons of the country" (Bayart 1980b, p. 101).

Gabon is another state where the imagery of father and family reigns supreme. That nation's first president, the late Leon Mba, was usually portrayed as the father of the country. His successor in office, President Bongo, is the self-styled "Father of the Renovation" (Comte 1973, p. 56). Civics texts published during Mba's tenure in office explicitly compared the nation to a family and the president to its father. Similarly, when electoral campaigns rolled around he would actively present himself as the father of the great Gabonese family against whom opposition was simply unthinkable (Weinstein 1966, pp. 204, 246). An abortive coup against Mba in 1964 elicited the following presidential reaction after conditions had returned to normal.

> I have been called the father of the Gabonese country, now this father is reflecting in order to define what he must do in favor of his family, in favor of his sons, certain of whom have gone astray. All that I can tell you is that he will decide as a father, with firmness, but with justice (Comte 1973, p. 46).

There are two elements worthy of note contained in Mba's observations. First, political dissidents are presented as sons who have "gone astray" rather than as serious and committed opponents of the regime. There is thus a sense in which the metaphors may be used to project the notion that those who oppose their father, for whatever reason, are immature children rather than intelligent, thoughtful, and mature citizens who can no longer tolerate the deficient way their government is run. Obviously, only such thoughtless and callow youths could possibly question the rule of their father. Their father, after all, is generous, loving, wise, and has only their best interests at heart. The other side of the coin is that this imagery enables "the father" to depict political repression as necessary parental discipline. To be sure, errant children have to be punished so that they will not repeat their "errors." Such punishment, furthermore, is required not only for the good of the entire family, but also for the good of those who have wandered from the family fold. Second, there is the idea that the father has to be firm and authoritative, but also just and compassionate. He must know how to forgive as well as how to punish. From time to time such parental discipline can and does get out of hand. This was certainly the case in the CAR under Bokassa and in Equatorial Guinea under Macias Nguema. Even after losing power the latter could remark at his trial that "I don't think I have committed any offense. I regard all Guineans as my sons" (Jackson and Rosberg 1982, p. 249). Be that as it may, the court judged otherwise and the "father" was executed.

The states dealt with thus far—Zaire, CAR, Gabon—may be characterized, at least in some senses, as paternalist regimes. So, too, is Ivory Coast where Papa Houphouet-Boigny exercises the same type of rule, albeit perhaps more benignly (Medard 1982, p. 62). Although Houphouet displays a certain kind of charisma, Medard (1982, p. 63) notes that it evokes "more the authority of the father than that of the tribune, of the leader or mobilizer of the masses." Another observer argues that this paternalism robs Ivorians of their right to participate constructively in the task of governing their nation: "they are raised, surrounded [*encadre*] and oriented like children" (Toure 1982, p. 237).

In Ivory Coast, as in other states, the president portrays himself as the father of the nation. Since the father is, by definition, generous and loving toward his children, it is expected that the children, for their part, will reciprocate. In societies with prominent kinship systems, there is a cultural expectation that generosity will, sooner or later, be repaid in kind. There is thus a sense in which all that the father manages to extract from the population is merely the repayment of a never-ending and outstanding obligation (Schatzberg 1985). For example, when Houphouet decided to move the national capital from Abidjan to his home village of Yamoussoukro, the executive committee of the party's political bureau presented the decision to the population in the following way:

> All the members of the Executive Committee are happy to note that the work of the President meets the approval of a great number, for this transfer would not only answer economic and sociological imperatives, but would constitute an expression of the country's gratitude to the Father of the Nation (*Fraternite Matin,* January 21, 1983, pp. 14–15).

Here, then, we have the action not of a man who would merely like to see that his home village benefits enormously from the presence of the capital and its national institutions, but the action of grateful children who are simply repaying the father for all he has done for them in the past.

Although the examples chosen thus far demonstrate the use of the metaphors of father and family in predominantly right-wing authoritarian regimes, one should not assume that these states enjoy a monopoly on the use—or abuse—of these images. Paternal and familial imagery also figures prominently in the political rhetoric and discourse of left-leaning rulers. Somalia is a case in point as the rulers of that state actively portray their president, Siad Barre, as the heroic father of the revolution (Lewis 1980, p. 210). One of the socialist-inspired policies Siad has implemented is the creation of revolutionary youth centers throughout the country to house and nurture orphaned children. A song sung by these children speaks eloquently to the point.

> It is a time of pleasant surprises
> When one journeys from a place of
> drought and desolation
> to one of plenty and prosperity.

There was a time
When I did not know my lineage
Now I have a father in [President] Siad,
A mother in the October Revolution.

The flag is my uncle,
The land is my grandfather,
The soil is my grandmother . . .

As one observer (Abdi 1981, pp. 169–170) notes, "for all its naivete, this type of song does instill a spirit of oneness, of belonging to a larger community. It can also serve as a powerful tool not only for socialisation, but for indoctrination as well."

These same metaphors of father and family are also present throughout state and society in Cameroon. Moreover, President Ahidjo and other officials of the regime would actively propagate this imagery whenever possible. For example, when Ahidjo addressed the nation on the eighth anniversary of the creation of a unitary state, he took time to play the role of national father. After offering the nation his "brotherly greetings," the president delivered a paternal homily stressing, as was his custom, the key issue of national unity.

> Consequently, instead of regarding happiness only in terms of the accumulation of material wealth in a society of complaisance which attaches more importance to property than to human beings and instead of taking liberty for anarchy, we should work for a society governed by morals which must be crystallized through the respect of a set of norms at work, in life-style and behaviour. Priority should be given to the general interest over personal interests, sense of duty, good citizenship, spirit of collective discipline, moral rectitude, spirit of initiative, and generosity.
>
> The general ideal driving force is and should always be the search for national unity . . . (*Cameroon Tribune,* May 21, 1980, p. 2).

Similarly, when there appeared to be some "doubt" at the Third Ordinary Congress of the Cameroon National Union (CNU) at Bafoussam in February 1980 as to whether Ahidjo would again run for office later that year, the Congress's motion requesting the president to seek another term of office contained this passage.

> Ahmadou Ahidjo who, through brilliant victories won in various tasks of nation-building, has become the symbol of national unity and deserves the title of "True and authentic unifier of the country and Father of the nation" . . . (*Cameroon Tribune,* February 23, 1980, p. 2).

Ahidjo, of course, again consented to continue his heavy responsibilities and stand for reelection. As part of the electoral campaign, one of the official slogans of the CNU Central Committee was: "A vote for AHMADOU AHIDJO is a vote to renew your gratitude to the Father and the Tireless Builder of the Cameroonian Nation" (*Cameroon Tribune*, March 26, 1980, p. 3).

These extracts from Ahidjo's speech and the official party documents indicate that Ahidjo—as do Mobutu, Bokassa, Houphouet, and others—manipulates the same paternal and familial metaphors. He is the father of the nation and as fathers everywhere, he educates his children and shows them the path to follow. Within the imperative framework of national unity, discipline, morality, and generosity are the roads to take. To be sure, Ahidjo's emphasis on the importance of these themes sounds eloquent and appealing. Nonetheless, it should not be lost from view that such calls inevitably mask the fact that any opposition to the regime will be interpreted as indiscipline, will be severely punished, and that morality will be defined by those in power. In addition, a vote for the president is merely a way for the people to express their gratitude to Ahidjo for all that he has done for them. Once again, therefore, we see that people are called upon to reciprocate the paternal generosity of the national father figure.

Bayart's (1979, p. 253) superb study indicates that there is an important corollary to the presentation of Ahidjo as the father. Briefly, if the president is the father, then all Cameroonians are the children, and this image may well dominate the perspectives of the social and political elite. For example, on the tenth anniversary of independence the following poem appeared in the national press:

> The voice of the child-people resounds and implores your help and pardon.
> Breathless, ashamed and confused, we come to confess truly our demagoguery.
> We will have only you for the Heavans and Earth now know your vocation.
> Advise us like a father among his prodigal children.
> And above all, do not counsel us according to the degree of our abusive transgressions (Bayart 1979, p. 254).

To be sure, when children err, they have to be punished. Like Gabon's Mba and Zaire's Mobutu (Schatzberg 1985), Ahidjo always moved swiftly and decisively against pockets of opposition. These dissidents are not portrayed as mature and motivated individuals, but rather as children who have gone astray or as delinquents.

We have already observed that the metaphors of father and family are obviously related and highly compatible. Thus, in other Central African states the dominant single party is conceived as a national family. This is also true in Cameroon where political leaders maintain that the local cell of the CNU is the basic unit "where the members should live in a quasi-family relationship, on a permanent footing" (Bayart 1980a, p. 174). Similarly, shortly before the 1980 elections, Felix Sabal Lecco, the Political Secretary of the CNU Central Committee commented on the party's role in the upcoming contest (*Cameroon Tribune*, March 26, 1980, p. 3).

> Every parent expects his child to grow and the Cameroon National Party like a child born since September 1966 cannot be an exception. . . . The decision to hand over the campaigns for this year's presidential elections to the organs of the party is therefore a test of the maturity of the militants.

In addition, as in the other states I have referred to, the image of the father is replicated at lower levels of the social and political hierarchy by bureaucrats in various positions of authority. Taking the president as a model, they, too, are little "fathers" in their administrative circumscriptions. To be sure, such manifestations of paternal authority can be, and are, at times quite abusive. They are treated first in medical facilities; when on tour they are often given a young woman for the evening and generally conduct themselves as though such "considerations" are only their due because of their position in the social hierarchy. Their behavior is all the more significant since it is usually through their conduct that the population directly encounters the legal abstraction of the state, and impressions that villagers form of them determine how the state will be judged (Bayart 1979, p. 244; Ahidjo 1964, pp. 127–128).

There can be no doubt that the Ahidjo regime was remarkably successful in diffusing the metaphors of father and family throughout society. In early 1984 I received a letter from a Cameroonian student enrolled in a Nigerian university who wished to continue his studies in the United States. This letter was phrased in the usual paternal imagery and illustrates the point.

> It gives me great pleasure and honour at this moment as I write this personal letter to your humble self, notwithstanding the fact that we have never had any formal introduction. This letter is more of a letter from a son in need to a father from whom some help is expected (personal communication, January 23, 1984).

Although postindependence political leaders have done their utmost to spread these images through society, it would be shortsighted to assume that a consciously implemented personality cult is the sole reason for either their presence or their durability. The less proximate origins of these metaphors thus deserve attention.

ORIGINS OF THE METAPHORS

Throughout the preceding discussion I have alluded to the fact that there are certain norms and expectations of reciprocity and generosity present in societies with prevalent kinship systems. Although these and other values have been transformed significantly by the period of colonial rule through the diffusion of explicitly paternal role models by colonial administrators, teachers, and missionaries (Schatzberg 1985), as well as by the incorporation of Cameroon into the world economy, there is a basic sense in which they, and the metaphors that evoke them, are the direct legacy of precolonial patterns of political and social authority.

Cameroon, as are most contemporary African states, is a product of the colonial incursion and is therefore an artificial entity encompassing a diversity of indigenous ethnic groups. Although these cultures display a fundamental unity and basic similarities, extreme caution must still be exercised when generalizing about precolonial politics and society, for polities ran the gamut from decentralized villages to substantial kingdoms. Moreover, the task of trying to delineate the influence of precolonial politics and society on the metaphors of father and family is further complicated by the fact that "family," at least as we commonly understand the term in the West, is a category that had little precise meaning in precolonial Africa (Sabean 1983, p. 164; Vaughn 1983, pp. 275, 281).

The recent historical and anthropological work of Jan Vansina (1980; 1983) has forcefully called attention to the fact that lineage, long the basic building block of Anglo-Saxon anthropology in Africa, is certainly not an immutable aspect of African social structure, but a protean ideological construction that was consciously manipulated in the struggle for power and wealth in precolonial societies. As have all ideological concepts, the notions of lineage and family legitimized political rule, justified inequality and exploitation, and generally provided any given society with a moral charter. Lineage, then, was a political ideology that ultimately justified and "explained" why some had more power, influence, and wealth than others. But, in general, it is safe to say that political and family structures and terminologies were so closely interwoven in most Central African societies that distinctions between the two realms become almost purely analytical.

In many precolonial Cameroonian cultures the role of the chief was closely associated with the overarching family structure. Membership in a certain lineage, usually a senior one, was often crucial in determining who became chief—or even had the opportunity to become one. Here, too, political life and family structure were closely intermingled. But chiefs had different roles in different cultures. In some Cameroonian societies, like the Bamoum (Tardits 1980), chiefs were hereditary rulers in charge of established, ongoing administrative hierarchies; in others, such as the Bamileke, power was extremely decentralized and the chief may have been no more than a first among equals with circumscribed decision-making authority (Hurault 1962).

The Bamileke permitted men to rise in the social hierarchy on the basis of their personal achievements, and status was attained by becoming a member of certain title societies whose main requirements for admission were usually wealth and generosity. Political power was decentralized and subchiefs were often given important responsibilities in the realms of religion, politics, administration, and justice. Among some Bamileke groups it was possible for subchiefs, notables, and even the heads of compounds to compete with paramount chiefs for effective political power if they had managed to accumulate significant degrees of wealth and status (Brain 1972; Hurault 1970; Schatzberg 1979).

Among the Maka of southeastern Cameroon, paternal authority was an important building block of the system of governance. In this society there was, and remains, a distinction between two types of authority. *Idjouga,* or command, was restricted to the confines of the family structure and was exercised only by the father over his direct descendants and the women for whom he had paid bride price. *Ngoume,* or prestige, on the other hand, was an entirely different matter and a much weaker form of authority. In discussions in the village council a few elders enjoyed *ngoume* by virtue of their age and wisdom, but this type of authority had to be continuously asserted and demonstrated through force of rhetorical argument. None was willing to yield a point or accede to a command based on this principle without a demonstration of the elder's persuasive power. Leadership within the village, in other words, had to be proven, was based on performance, and could never be taken for granted since there were no permanent official positions within the village's decentralized political structure. Each man, however, reigned supreme within his own household, and the Maka system of governance was thus relatively open, egalitarian within limits, and extremely decentralized (Geschiere 1982, pp. 15–54).

In such cultures as these (Maka, Bamileke), generosity was incumbent upon a man wishing to advance in the society and be respected by his peers. In a fundamental sense these precolonial sociopolitical systems resembled a "Big Man" model of governance; a model that anthropologists have studied in Melanesia (Sahlins 1977). It was above all personal rule, based on the power and authority of an individual, and was not dependent on the possession of formal political office. In this type of system, influence was gathered and political followers created through the accumulation and subsequent distribution of wealth. In at least some regards, this system closely resembles what Price (1974), in an excellent analysis of Ghana, calls the "Big-Man Small-Boy" syndrome. Price (1974, pp. 175–177) argues that big man and small boy are terms that represent a pattern of normal behavior between people of unequal status, wealth, and power that is highly authoritarian. The big man looks after the welfare of his social inferiors and of those who are dependent upon him; makes decisions; and gives orders. He is conspicuous both in his generous distribution of largesse and in his exercise of power and authority. On the other side of this equation, the small boy, or social inferior, demonstrates an equally conspicuous gratitude for the bounty that the big man showers on him and behaves toward the big man in a way that publicly manifests respect and deference. The context of social relations is crucial in determining who will be the big man and who will be the small boy. It is entirely possible that a big man in one context (that is, vis-a-vis his own children) might well be a small boy in another social setting (for example, in relations with a superior in a bureaucratic hierarchy). Price (1974, p. 184) also notes, correctly, that although these patterns of behavior and authority were present in precolonial Akan society, their authoritarian aspects were further highlighted by the colonial system of domination in which the common metaphor for the relationship between African and European was paternal. Europeans perceived Africans as children and expected them to be obedient, respectful, and thankful for the "tutoring" they received. One student of the European colonization of Africa has noted that those sent to administer the outposts of empire "often extended overseas a system of rule . . . patterned after the relationship of authority which existed in the metropole between parent and child and school and child" (Cohen 1970, p. 427).

The big man model of politics illuminates certain aspects of political behavior in Central Africa and is obviously related to, if not dependent upon, the notions of paternalism and the metaphors of father and family. Vansina (1982, p. 67), for example, argues that Mobutu's style of rule derives from the model of the precolonial big man "who tied clients to himself by favors and expectation of favors, and dropped them whenever their stature or their power base acquired features that seemed to give them some independence of maneuver." But even when dropped from grace, they are usually given new positions fairly soon, and their loyalty thus remains constant. This aspect of rule is also present in Gabon (Weinstein 1966, pp. 182–183) and elsewhere. Bokassa describes well the contextual salience of relations between big men and small boys; and, in addition, his remarks indicate the basis of this phenomenon in the paternal orientation to politics as well as the relevance of the metaphors of father and family.

> I gave the name of "papa" to General de Gaulle and that seemed to have made numerous Frenchmen laugh, or smile. They did not know, therefore, that great affection and veneration are indicated by this term. Central Africans were happy to give me this name. Here [in Ivory Coast], I am myself happy to give this name to President Houphouet-Boigny. He is my father through his wisdom, his goodness, his experience and also the assistance and support he gives me. So it was for General de Gaulle. And it is for that that I cried on his tomb at Colembey-les-Deux-Eglises (Delpey 1981, p. 166).

What seems to have occurred, then, is a merging of precolonial and colonial perceptions and views of legitimate political authority and their subsequent application to contemporary political phenomena. Chazan (1978, p. 17) notes this well in the Ghanaian case. Values pertaining to power and authority in that state, and I would add in others, are deeply rooted in the local political culture and bear scant resemblance to Western ideas and constructs. In fact,

> attitudes towards the new political center not only do not differ or replace existing values, but can actually best be comprehended in terms of the application and elaboration of these local perceptions to new political objects and their reformulation in terms of new political structures (Chazan 1978, p. 17).

Although phrased using a different set of social science abstractions, Geschiere (1982, p. 205) notes essentially the same phenomenon among the Maka in Cameroon but refers to it as an "articulation of different modes of authority." The authority that state officials, such as the local subprefect and appointed chief, exercise is still conceived as *idjouga* (command). Obviously, however, it is a rather different and more far-reaching type of authority than that which fathers once held over their sons and others in their compounds. These officials, especially the subprefect, have little patience for the old norms of discussion and the value of rhetorical power. They decide matters quickly and can enforce their decisions by summoning the power of the state (gendarmes) if necessary (Geschiere 1982, pp. 46, 225). For better or worse, then, it is apparent that certain orientations have endured even as the specific content of notions of political authority have changed. Precolonial and colonial conceptions of idealized paternal authority have remained and help shape the way that Cameroonians and others perceive political legitimacy and authority in the contemporary political arena.

MORAL MATRIX

The major reason why the metaphors of father and family are so pervasive in Cameroon is that they strike a resonant and deeply embedded cultural chord. They form, in other words, part of a culturally valid and largely implicit comprehension of the limits of political legitimacy based on a complex and largely unarticulated moral matrix of legitimate governance derived from an idealized vision of patterns of authority and behavior within the family. At present, it will be possible to present the main aspects of this moral matrix only in broad outline, for there is still much we do not know.

In Meillassoux's (1981, pp. 47, 86) model of the domestic community in Africa, society is divided into elders, youth, and women. In this context, "father" does not necessarily mean biological sire, but rather he who nourishes and protects. The eldest man in the productive cycle usually plays this role and provides younger men with the subsistence goods necessary to continue economic reproduction. In addition, he also furnishes the women necessary for marriage and the continuation of social reproduction. The "father" thus "feeds" and "marries." Notions of kinship are used both to support an ideology of power and to legitimize dominance. Even if political domination is imposed from outside the community, it tends to be expressed in ordinary kinship terms. "The sovereign is assimilated to an elder . . . or to the father. He is entitled to 'eat' his subjects as his own children, i.e. to receive part of their labour or the product of their labour. Conversely he is expected to protect them" (Meillassoux 1973, p. 88).

There is thus a paternal premise of nurturance, and, if it is accepted, then people have a right both to be cared for and, importantly, to have individual relations with the powerful father figure so that conditions of nurture may be negotiated. As Sennett (1980, pp. 82, 86) points out, this right is assumed and exercised on a face-to-face basis in many non-Western societies and is a crucial premise of both the metaphors of father and family, and of the moral matrix on which they are based. Implicit, therefore, are the promises of protection, provision, and security. Fathers in Cameroon are providers. Implicit, also, is the assumption that the "father" must provide these benefits or else lose support and legitimacy. Recall the manifesto of the MLPC cited earlier that called on all "sons of the country" to work for the overthrow of Bokassa. The familial metaphor was not rejected as illegitimate, but the rule of the father was called into question because he had failed to fulfill his obligations to nurture and provide security. The moral matrix itself remains valid; the problem rests with neither matrix nor metaphor, but with the father who has failed to live up to his culturally defined responsibilities.

The metaphors are attractive to many because, first, they fulfill a universal psychological need for an assurance of security (Vansina 1980, p. 149). Second, the metaphors create an intimacy between rulers and ruled and thus succeed in representing complex political realities in a simplified form (Sennett 1980, p. 71). In one sense, this is the task of any ideology and Vansina (1983, p. 84) notes that lineage ideology in the precolonial forest area "reduced a complex reality to an elegant blueprint." Third, the images are "natural." Since we can all envisage the idea of father and family, the image of the ruler as father of a national family has immediacy and strikes a recognizable note. Fathers and families are indeed natural and in Africa, where family plays an even more important role than in the West, these metaphors are that much more compelling. Furthermore, such metaphors mask an exploitatively unequal flow of resources—an aspect noted earlier in the context of paternal "generosity" and the resultant "debt." Because the symbols shrouding such unequal exchanges are widely perceived as natural, exploitation and the extraction of resources appear that much more palatable.

By their very nature, metaphoric symbols of this kind are ambiguous. Moreover, the more they are ambiguous, the more they are flexible and the more they are powerful (Cohen 1974, p. 32). Ahidjo and other rulers can thus invoke the symbolism of father and family to evoke simultaneously several powerful, though partially contradictory, images. In the first instance, and on a corporate level, he is the father of the large and all-inclusive Cameroonian family to which all Cameroonians belong from birth. Second, and on a more personal level, he is the father of each and every Cameroonian. This imagery permits him to establish an intimate, individual relationship—at least in symbolic terms—with all citizens. This ambiguity in the level of the imagery and the relationship enables a shrewd leader to play off one symbolic level against the other. For example, since all that he does is, by definition, for the good of the large, corporate family, he is able to assert that all his actions are taken with the good of the whole uppermost in mind. But political actions and policies will obviously tend to aid some while hurting others. Such sacrifices that may result from these policies are perceived as necessary for the good of the national family and as a vital part of nation building. If, then, an unlucky or disadvantaged citizen should try to invoke his personal relationship with the father and request or expect nurture, the ruler can claim, in this instance, that he has acted with the good of the entire clan in mind. Similarly, there is a sense in which gifts and other manifestations of presidential largesse may be portrayed merely as the father taking care of his children. In this sense, the personal level of the symbolism dominates, and gifts to cronies, collaborators, kinsmen, and friends can be rationalized as the fulfillment of the promise of nurture implicit in the moral matrix. Others may well complain about this, but they also realize that the president is acting out the culturally legitimate role of the generous father.

These symbols are ambiguous in yet another context. Any attempts to question the prevailing political order are presented as efforts by ungrateful children who usurp the role of their father who, after all, has their best interests at heart. In this sense the metaphors of father and family are so powerful and immediate that I would guess that even those citizens who reject the present political order probably do so with considerable psychological reluctance and mixed emotions. While many of us rebel against our fathers as a normal part of the process of growing up, few of us are able to do so without significant feelings of guilt and personal insecurity.

I have argued that the metaphors of father and family enjoy a cultural legitimacy in Cameroon, but this should not blind us to the fact that valid symbols may be manipulated in illegitimate ways. As we shall see, some of the political and ideological uses of these symbols have a distinctly seamy side. Vansina (1980, p. 149) persuasively argues that precolonial lineages had marked ideological components and that under the guise of the legitimacy of family, gross disparities of wealth, income, and status were found. Certainly, many contemporary examples of the use of paternal imagery could be seen as cynical manipulations of a "natural" phenomenon designed to enrich those in political power and to legitimate the harsher aspects of their rule by presenting those with enough temerity to protest, or even revolt, against the present political and social order as wayward and misguided children. Similarly, as we have seen, the metaphors enable those in power to present political repression as firm "parental" discipline for prodigal "children" in need of a political spanking for their own good.

Ahidjo and others (Mobutu, Bongo, Houphouet, Siad) who currently employ the imagery of father and family have sought to freeze it. Ajami (1981, p. 131) makes the point cogently in relation to Sadat's Egypt. "Sadat's symbols—the community of love, the country as family, himself as the eldest of the Egyptian family—serve the same narcotic purpose: escape, a fake harmony of interests, a curious avoidance of politics. The myth of the family serves to freeze the society." Indeed, there is an implicit assumption in Meillassoux's model that one day the juniors, the youth, will become elders and thus come to enjoy more fully the fruits of society. While this did not always come to pass and the "youth" were often left in an inferior position as they grew older (Vansina 1980), people believed that they would, one day, "make it." In a related vein, Sennett (1980, p. 162) observes that in these kinds of societies illegitimate authority "would be precisely the attempt to freeze the conditions of authority into a single mold. Illegitimate authority . . . would be identified with permanence." A sense of movement and political rotation is thus central to a cultural understanding of the topic. In other words, the "children" have to be permitted to "grow up" and the "father" must not seek to remain eternally in power. This is the second crucial premise of the moral matrix of legitimate governance.

The question of the political leader's tenure in office is a particularly sensitive one in most African states. While there have been numerous examples of the peaceful and constitutional transfer of power, few reigning heads of state have willingly relinquished office when at the height of power and authority. In the 25 years since most of Africa achieved independence, there are only the examples of certain soldiers who have returned to the barracks voluntarily and Senegal's Leopold Senghor who have had the courage and foresight to arrange a peaceful transition. This sorry record notwithstanding, many African leaders do understand the implicit strictures and limitations placed on their tenure by the moral matrix of legitimate governance. Why else, for example, do most military leaders who seize power invariably issue a proclamation stating that after their job is done, after they have put things to right, after they have cleansed the political system of all that ails it, they will willingly return to the barracks and hand over the levers of power to a civilian government? In practice, of course, things tend to work a bit differently, and the return to the regiment is often accomplished only symbolically when khaki is exchanged for mufti. In general, civilian leaders have amassed no better a record on this point, and, even if they come to power through reasonably democratic means, they have a tendency to subvert the very processes that brought them to office and eliminate the possibility that others could benefit from the same procedures.

Ahidjo is at best a partial example, but one that proves the point. When President Ahidjo decided to step down in late 1982, his move was hailed as a statesmanlike gesture and was met with near-universal approval. Unfortunately, his alleged subsequent involvement in the attempted coup of April 1984 against his chosen successor, Paul Biya, raises the question of whether his initial action was sincere. Ahidjo's degree of involvement in these events may never be known with certainty, but the reactions of Cameroonians to stories circulating that he *was,* in fact, behind the attempt to oust Biya are noteworthy in themselves. As one man expressed it in Cameroonian pidgin, "*Why he done go then wan come back*?" (*West Africa,* July 9, 1984, p. 1388). Rightly or wrongly, people believed that Ahidjo had tried to return and that action was probably perceived as a violation of this second premise of the moral matrix. In other words, people may have felt it was an unjustified attempt by Ahidjo to retain power indefinitely and thus was behavior essentially devoid of political legitimacy.

The matter of succession also raises the question of whether the new leader will employ the imagery his predecessor has popularized. If the Father of the Nation is deposed, or retires voluntarily, will his successor choose new metaphors or rely on the old ones? Unfortunately, the number of applicable cases is far too small and not enough time has elapsed to be able to answer this question with any certainty. I would nevertheless speculate that the imagery will probably endure—albeit in slightly modified form. For example, we noted that in Gabon the Father of the Nation gave way to the Father of the Renovation. Similarly, we have also seen that the opposition movement in CAR was perfectly content to use the metaphor of family to try to rally opposition to Bokassa's rule. My suspicion is that these metaphors are deeply rooted in the collective consciousness and will probably endure, but this line of analysis remains conjectural.

CONCLUSION

This chapter began on a speculative note, and it shall end on one as well, for a precise weighting of the exact importance of each aspect of the moral matrix cannot be determined. These are cultural predispositions and implicit understandings rather than precise numerical variables. It is thus impossible to ascertain whether, say, a father who nurtures and protects but remains in power too long will have more legitimacy than one who fails to nurture but speedily departs at the expiration of his mandate. The only answer that can be offered at this point is that it depends on a whole host of other circumstances of the type usually studied by analysts of African political economy: economic conditions, degree of corruption, ethnic tensions, divisions within the ruling class, and the extent of exploitation, to name but a few. The culturally defined moral matrix should thus be seen as a background framework rather than as a major explanatory factor. But failure to comprehend these cultural understandings properly will result in vitiated and erroneous analyses of the other variables analysts commonly employ.

Throughout this chapter I have argued that the metaphors of father and family constitute a symbolic representation of an implicit, culturally enracinated moral matrix of legitimate governance that derives largely from an idealized vision of patterns of authority within the family. The distant origin of these symbols may be found in both precolonial patterns of governance and the kinship ideology that was used to justify significant inequalities in status, wealth, and political power. We may discern more proximate origins in the diffusion of paternal role models during the colonial period by both colonial administrators and missionaries. The precolonial heritage and the legacies of more than 70 years of colonial paternalism provided a fertile field on which politicians in the postindependence era could sow, yet again, these paternal and familial metaphors. As we have seen, Ahidjo and his collaborators in Cameroon, as well as their colleagues in other states, have consciously used and manipulated these images since independence with the result the metaphors of father and family now permeate state and society at all levels. But the presence of these metaphors, and the confusion of political and familial sectors that it produces, is far more than a footnote to contemporary Cameroonian history, for these symbols furnish the regime, and others like it, with a tough and durable ideological cement that renders some of the harsher aspects of political rule more acceptable. Exploitation and the extraction of resources can thus be presented, in culturally recognizable and valid terms, as the embodiment of kinship reciprocity and mutual obligation. Moreover, repression directed against political dissidents can be portrayed as stern, but necessary, parental discipline that is undertaken for the good of the entire national family.

Although Ahidjo and other heads of state have abused, manipulated, and misapplied the metaphors of father and family, it would be shortsighted to view these cynical manipulations *merely* as the ideological ploys of a corrupt and rapacious class intent on maintaining power. There are elements of that, to be sure. But even so, we still need to ask why this imagery has been chosen for ideological presentation rather than some other? The reason, I would submit, is that these metaphors are culturally relevant and strike a responsive chord; that legitimate governance in Cameroon and the other states we have examined in passing is based on the tacit normative idea that government stands in the same relationship to its citizens that a father does to his children. There is a substratum of belief that views paternal authority as legitimate as long as the implicit understanding of rights and duties contained in the moral matrix of legitimate governance is not violated. When Cameroonian political leaders behave as responsible fathers; when they care for, nurture, and provide security; when they do not seek to hold on to power indefinitely and respect the normal rotation of generations; legitimacy, and thus stability, are maintained. But when the implied cultural norms of political "fatherhood" are violated, tensions will mount and instability, repression, or both, will ensue. The problem in Cameroon and throughout much of Central Africa is not that these images are present, but rather that the unstated cultural norms and understandings that they imply have been ignored. The real tragedy is that the manipulation and misapplication of the metaphors of father and family may well discredit, over the long term, a culturally valid basis for the organization of legitimate political authority.

2

LEADERSHIP AND REGIME CHANGES IN PERSPECTIVE

Victor T. Le Vine

It was generally expected at the time that the peaceful—and constitutional—transfer of presidential power from Ahmadou Ahidjo to Paul Biya on November 6, 1982, would be accompanied by the gradual replacement of Ahidjo's people by Biya's in the top echelons of Cameroon's government. As Biya came to master the reins of power he would naturally wish to have around him people congenial to his style and philosophy of governance, and personally loyal to him as the new president of the country. Given the (seemingly) amicable circumstances of the event and the ex-president's apparent stake in a successful transition, I also argued shortly thereafter that Ahidjo and some of his *fideles* would stay on as a helpful presence to ensure calm passage to the new regime (Le Vine 1983).[1] I could not have been more mistaken.

It is now clear that, for whatever the reasons, Ahidjo soon had second thoughts about giving up the power he had held for at least 22 years and organized (or permitted to be organized) what eventually grew into a full-blown conspiracy against Biya. The plot/attempted coup failed, and that failure probably dashed any hopes Ahidjo might have had of returning to the dazzling new presidential palace in Yaounde. The point for our purposes is that, instead of a gradual and partial turnover of personnel at the top, Ahidjo's abortive 1983 coup and the failed military revolt of 1984 not only hastened but effectively guaranteed the country's first *wholesale* succession event, one in which not only virtually an entire leadership group (a *government,* in the classic sense) was replaced, but also one that has already yielded significant changes in the country's institutional framework and that presages policy directions substantially different from those of Biya's predecessor.

It is not unreasonable to argue that the Ahidjo plot and its denouement freed Biya from a number of constraints and uncertainties associated with the peaceful transfer of power itself: he no longer need worry about the continued (and problematic) presence of Ahidjo loyalists in the government; Ahidjo himself is no longer a constraining presence in the immediate background; and Biya's obligation to pursue most of Ahidjo's policies has been effectively removed. By October 1984, it was clear that Biya had taken advantage of these opportunities—including, most notably, the failed military coup of April 6–7, 1984—to assert himself in ways hitherto difficult or impossible. In the event, what took place in November 1982 and was unwillingly sealed by Ahidjo and his partisans in 1983 and 1984 was a change in "regime"—"the arrangement of authority, power, and political interests in a state" (Jackson and Rosberg 1982, p. 21).[2]

More broadly, and the political pyrotechnics of the November 1982–April 1984 period aside, the Ahidjo–Biya succession, while it was independent Cameroon's first wholesale leadership transition, was not the first but the sixth regime change since 1946 and was distinguished from the rest more by the sheer magnitude of leadership change than by its institutional/constitutional change which was only a secondary aspect of the transition. In each previous case, a significant alteration of the formal structures of government was also accompanied by changes in the composition of the ruling elite save at the very top.[3]

All of this raises a number of interesting questions about the nature of leadership circulation in Cameroon, not the least of which are those that focus on the interplay between national policy making and the structure of support for major political and economic changes in the country. It is the argument of this chapter that particular changes in the composition of the top political echelons of Cameroon can almost always be associated with attempts by the rulers of the country to crystallize, then legitimize, their most important policy initiatives. These personnel changes have not usually occurred as a result of popular pressures, or as a consequence of elections, though obviously important exogenous and (uncontrollable) internal events and trends have in the past and still do play a role in shaping national policy. The point is that the structure of power in Cameroon, as distinguished from the country's institutional/constitutional structures, has altered little in substance since 1946 and has made it possible for ruler(s) to be the main initiators and catalysts of personnel changes within the political elite. Before going on to elaborate the main argument, however, and to avoid definitional and theoretical ambiguity about its main terms, it is necessary to make a short digression into two closely related matters: the character of Cameroon's political elite and the structure of political power in the Cameroonian state. It need hardly be pointed out that without such clarification discussion of leadership and elite change in Cameroon can have little analytic validity.

WHO RULES AND HOW: THE STRUCTURE OF POWER AND THE POLITICAL ELITE

The literature on Cameroonian politics appears to agree at least that, on the national level, political power emanates from the state, which in turn is dominated by the president. This arrangement, which obviously suited Ahidjo and apparently suits his successor, reflects a structure of power with constitutional–political roots in both de Gaulle's Fifth Republic (on which Cameroon's 1960 constitution was closely modeled) and the colonial state created from an amalgam of the novel institutions of the Fourth Republic (1946) and the UN Trusteeship system. This structure of power is also based on Ahidjo's ability—at first before 1960, aided by the French, and thereafter, by himself—to create varying aggregations of elite support for his main policy initiatives.

It is often forgotten that when he became prime minister in 1958 Ahidjo was still a relatively marginal political figure on the Cameroonian political scene. His effective entrance into national policies came when he joined Aujoulat's Bloc Democratique Camerounais in 1951, but it was not until 1957 when he was named Andre-Marie Mbida's deputy prime minister and interior minister (posts appropriate to the 30 Union Camerounaise deputies he and Arouna Njoya brought to the Mbida coalition) that he could really begin to make his weight felt. Naming him prime minister, argues Bayart, suited the French, who saw in him someone they could easily manipulate. "The apparent mediocrity of the man had a good deal to do with his fortunes . . ." (Bayart 1979, p. 49. The translation is mine.) However, even if one concedes Bayart's scenario, to attribute Ahidjo's later success largely to active French patronage is not only to belittle Ahidjo's own political skills, but also to overlook and denigrate the sophistication and experience of Cameroon's politicians, many of whom had been active on the territorial scene since 1946 or earlier. It was not enough to simply induct Ahidjo into the circle of power; once in office, he had soon to prove himself by becoming his own man. This Ahidjo did once the country gained its independence; thereafter, almost every major national political event gave him opportunities to consolidate his position and to move people onto or off the national stage as they served his larger purposes.

At all events, the territory's structure of power was first cast in 1946 under the terms of the UN Trusteeship Agreement (which made France the administering authority in Cameroon) and by the Constitution of the Fourth Republic (1946) and its subsequent implementing laws, decrees, and ministerial orders (*arretes*). While it is true that the territorial legislatures as well as the local African politicians and the notables sent to France to represent Cameroon in the Fourth Republic's legislative and advisory councils all could and did affect the way executive power was handled in the territory, the statutory authority given the high commissioners made it clear where the final word lay: in Paris and with the high commissioners themselves.[4] Admittedly, the 1957 and 1958 constitutional changes did appreciably alter this situation. Nonetheless, despite the constraining presence of a Cameroonian government, high commissioners could and did intervene decisively when they (or the French government) deemed it necessary. The fact that High Commissioner Jean Ramadier was recalled for "administrative indiscipline" after Ahidjo replaced Mbida in no way vitiates the point; there is little question that it was Ramadier himself who forced Mbida's departure and put the official seal of approval on Ahidjo (Chaffard 1965, pp. 292–329, among others).

Cameroon's independence constitution, with its provisions for a strong executive president, obviously both continued and reinforced the mode of centralized decision making that had characterized the trusteeship period, with one important change: France was no longer the final locus of power, remaining in the background as part of Ahidjo's available support network. A whole series of Franco–Cameroonian conventions, both public and secret, testify to that relationship. The unpublished security conventions, for example, enabled Ahidjo to call on French military assistance to help put down the resurgence of the UPC rebellion during the years 1960–1966. Even more important, independence permitted Ahidjo to embark on the series of elite-building exercises that attended the amnesty and elections of 1960 and the subsequent creation of the federation, the single party, and the unitary state.

What is important to recall is that, despite the central position Ahidjo occupied in the country's structure of power, his own power was never absolute but rested largely on his ability to create supportive networks and coalitions that included, in varying combinations, major anglophone politicians, former opponents, leaders of critical southern and western ethnic groups, his own northern allies, businessmen, traditional chiefs and magnates, and members of the country's intelligentsia. His means were similarly diverse: alone or in combination, he used persuasion, cooptation, coercion, legislation, judicial action, constitutional revision, and elections and referenda to accomplish his ends.

It is, I think, a caricature of reality to liken Cameroon's structure of power, as does Bayart, to that of the court of a northern *lamido* and to argue that Ahidjo's main task was the construction of an hegemonic class responsive to his will (Bayart, 1979, especially pp. 183–232). For all intents and purposes, an indigenous Cameroonian political elite already existed at independence, and it was within that milieux that Ahidjo operated; whether it had class characteristics remains an open question (and one beyond the scope of this chapter), and whether Ahidjo strove to build an "hegemonic" class remains largely unproven, Bayart and Richard Joseph notwithstanding (Joseph 1978, Bayart 1979). The true picture is undoubtedly much more complex. For example, with some few conspicuous exceptions—*fideles* such as Moussa Yaya and Sadou Daoudou—the composition of the group around Ahidjo did change appreciably over time: younger men were brought in, old pols were retired or sent out to pasture in the legislatures or advisory bodies, people were moved out, put "*en reserve pour la Republique*," then brought back; others were moved up or down in the structure; and the top group was expanded or contracted as events and circumstances seemed to warrant. Granted, Ahidjo was always (after 1960) at the center of the enterprise and grew more authoritarian over the years, but he never had absolute and unlimited power. The system over which he presided was far too complex and always too potentially fissiparous for him to be able to accomplish that.

Who were involved in regime change, succession, and other events involving major personnel turnover? Given Cameroon's centralized decision-making structure, those most directly affected have generally been the top individuals in the country's national institutions: those attached to the presidency, vice-presidents, and prime ministers and their principal aides, cabinet ministers, the members of the single party's Political Bureau and Central Committee, and ranking bureaucrats such as secretaries-general of ministries, whose appointments usually have political implications. Of course, during the federal period, the affected groups included top state officials. Also at various times (notably in 1946, 1960, 1961, and 1972) the compositions of legislatures have changed significantly, not to speak of local and regional officials (prefects, governors, and the like); by and large, however, it has been the upper institutional ranks of policymakers that have mainly benefited or suffered during such events. The Biya succession was no exception; by October 1984, the top ranks had been almost completely replaced, and it was evident that the change had gone beyond the policy-making levels to such positions, for example, as the presidency of the Social and Economic Council, the directors-general of the parastatal corporations, the chancellorship of the University of Yaounde, and the chiefs of the police and security apparatus.

Those described above are most certainly members of what Mosca called a "governing elite." But they are only a part (albeit a large part) of Cameroon's political elite, which also encompasses various subelites who function (again, to use Mosca's formula) as mediators between the governing elite and the masses.[5] There is no question but that important or large-scale personnel turnover at the top impacts—to varying degrees, depending on the nature and scope of the changes—on the lower elite levels. However, tracing such impact, it need hardly be pointed out, becomes progressively more difficult as one moves down the elite ladder, mainly because there is no very good definition of the scope of Cameroon's political elite. A recent valiant, though partial, attempt is Pierre Flambeau Ngayap's *Cameroun, Qui gouverne*?

Ngayap's *classe dirigeante* (ruling class) comprises some 950 people, including (using Ngayap's own categories) ministers and prime ministers, senior civil servants (*hauts fonctionnaires*) in the presidency and the ministries, ambassadors, prefects, governors, members of the higher judiciary (*la haute magistrature*), top officials (uniformed and civilian) responsible for security and the military, members of the intelligentsia directly involved with government (*associee au Projet de societe du Pouvoir*), members of parliament, businessmen directly involved with government and the leaders of public or parastatal economic institutions, and "*apparatchiks*" (various top-level officials both in the UNC and the government) (Ngayap 1983, pp. 10–14, and passim). Ngayap himself admits excluding certain categories—for example, mayors, traditional chiefs, deputy directors in the administrative hierarchies—because they are not (by his definition) part of the "national ruling class" (Ngayap 1983, p. 12). One could argue with Ngayap that his categories are too restrictive; for example, a good case could be made for the inclusion of certain traditional chiefs demonstrably influential on the national scene (for example, the sultan of Bamoun), or certain religious leaders of similar standing, such as the archbishop of Yaounde, Msgr. Jean Zoa.

Nonetheless, one has to give Ngayap his due. His analysis is the first serious attempt to describe Cameroon's "governing elite," and though it fails to say much about the dynamics of elite interaction, or the way in which his "ruling class" rules, the picture he paints certainly agrees generally with what others, including myself, see in the country. Though Ngayap provides the first detailed analysis on the subject, a 1976 compendium of some 1,094 short biographies (EDIAFRIC 1976) appears to confirm Ngayap's outlines. Despite the presence of a few questionable inclusions (several notaries public, municipal councillors, consuls, lawyers, and lower-level functionaries), the bulk of the entries are drawn from the same national institutional, policy-making sectors. The fact that Ngayap and EDIAFRIC seem to agree on both the composition and the size of Cameroon's governing elite does not, of course, validate either claim. Yet it seems (at least to me) a pretty good approximation, particularly since Ngayap takes some pains to demonstrate that this elite has already achieved a considerable measure of integration and self-consciousness through its association with Cameroon's presidential center of power.

Within Cameroon's "governing elite," as defined above, two groups, the parliamentarians, and (Ngayap's) "governmental personnel," can be used in this analysis as surrogates for the whole. The unique position of both groups in Cameroon's political system justifies the choice. While it is true that, at least after 1960, both groups became subordinate to an increasingly powerful presidency, each functioned as useful sounding boards for presidential initiatives and as key parts of the visible structure of legitimation and national support for Ahidjo and his policies.

Moreover, before 1960, the legislatures and (after 1956) the governments of Mbida and Ahidjo, for most Cameroonian politicians, were *the* critical stages on which the territory's African politics could be played and pressure put on the French for the satisfaction of Cameroonian demands. If our image of Cameroon's structure of power is credible, therefore, it can be argued that, both before and after independence, regime changes and major succession events would find important reflections in the composition of both groups.

RULERSHIP AND LEADERSHIP CHANGE BEFORE INDEPENDENCE

The 1946 Trusteeship Agreement for Cameroon, as did its analogue for Togo, gave the territory special political and juridical status vis-a-vis France's other West and Equatorial African colonies. For one thing, given the supervisory role of the Trusteeship Council and the extraordinary access to UN and world opinion accorded Cameroonian politicians under the terms of the trusteeship, local political leaders could and did affect French policies in and for the territory much more directly and effectively than was the case in the other French African colonies. For another, trusteeship obligated France to move the territory toward self-government or eventual independence, a goal that the French government would never have contemplated in 1946 for its other West and Equatorial African territories (again, with Togo excepted). It remains, however, that the differences between Cameroon (and Togo) and the rest was one of degree, and the new 1946–1947 constitutional arrangements still permitted the French government to define the basic institutional arrangements and political rules for Cameroon, and Paris and the French high commissioners to exercise ultimate executive power in the territory.

Thus, as elsewhere in French Africa, Cameroon's first local assemblies found themselves

> . . . severely circumscribed; the assemblies could not discuss political matters, were permitted to deliberate only on what the French conceived as narrowly technical matters (guided by the resident French officials), and their ambit of consultation, though fairly broad, remained consultative, that is, the local governor could (if he chose) disregard any advice they gave. In addition, . . . elections to the assemblies were held on the basis of the dual "college" system. . . . Guaranteed seating in the assemblies, the local French citizens were expected to restrain any tendencies to undue political effervescence (Le Vine 1979, p. 134).

The new assemblies, including Cameroon's, were clearly conceived as little more than training grounds for Africans in the handling of some technical and economic aspects of public affairs. Robert Delavignette (1962, p. 128), a distinguished French former colonial civil servant, put the matter clearly. The typical local African assembly would be

> . . . Consultative at a first stage . . . (then) gradually awaken to deliberative responsibilities, but (only) to handle well-defined matters of local interest.

This narrow, even parsimonious view of the African assemblies' powers and functions was to last until 1956 and the Loi Cadre. To be sure, these restrictions did not prevent Cameroonian parliamentarians from broaching matters of political interest to them, or of making their weight felt in Paris and at the high commissioners' offices in Yaounde. Still and by and large, the Cameroonian politicians pretty much played the role assigned them, a result largely due to the fact that the French government, by controlling the agenda for political change and making the rules for political participation, could recruit a group of parliamentarians with whom it could deal and later negotiate.

> The members of that elite were the products of a system in which the French expected them to assume leadership, but not too soon. With few exceptions, the members of political elites of French-speaking Africa during this period (1945–60) were not revolutionaries—though a good many learned to express themselves in the language of the revolutionary—but were, for want of a better term, establishmentarians, formed within the French colonial system in its waning days (Le Vine 1968, p. 372).

One striking set of data confirms these observations. The 1968 study cited above reported that well over 50 percent of the members of the 1946–1959 assemblies in French West Africa were products of the colonial system itself—civil servants, administrators, educators. That is, they were those trained for and within it. By one set of rough calculations, perhaps 60 percent of the 1946–1958 and 70 percent of the 1958–1962 figures fall partially or wholly under the rubric of "government employees" (pp. 376–380). Given the fact that government increasingly became the principal employer in these territories, it is not surprising that expertise and political skill acquired *within* the system as it developed became the chief criteria of eligibility for recruitment to the legislatures. The African (second college) members of Cameroon's 1946–1956 assemblies follow the pattern almost exactly, as does the small number of Cameroonian "*evolues*" deputized to serve in the French National Assembly, the Council of the Republic, and the Assembly of the French Union. Of the 24 second (college deputies in Cameroon's (1946–1952) Representative Assembly, 14 had been "government employees" prior to standing for election, as were 18 of the 29 Cameroonians in the (1952–1956) Territorial Assembly.[6]

The first Cameroonian postwar regime, under which Cameroon (despite its special status as a UN Trust Territory) was ruled much like France's other African colonies, came to an end with the implementation of France's law of June 23, 1956, generally known as the Loi-Cadre Defferre, or simply the Loi-Cadre. Among the more important decrees issued under its terms were those that abolished the dual electoral college, introduced universal suffrage, and installed executive councils (for all intents and purposes, governments) in the individual territories. Cameroon was promised "institutional reform" in addition to the other changes, but in fact got its first important push to independence under a new special statute (Mortimer 1969, pp. 232–242; Ansprenger 1961, pp. 241–252; Le Vine 1964b, pp. 157–159, among others).

The circumstances leading up to the Cameroonian elections of December 1956 and the formation of Cameroon's first government under Andre-Marie Mbida are fully covered elsewhere and need not detain us here (Mortimer 1969, Chaffard 1965, Le Vine 1964a, Ansprenger 1961, Bayart 1979, Joseph 1977, etc.). Suffice it for our purposes to recall that by this time France had acquiesced to a grant of independence after a short transitional period and that the government of the territory operated, for the next three years, as a dyarchy in which the legislature and a Cameroonian executive council shared power with the last of France's high commissioners, Pierre Messmer, Jean Ramadier, and Xavier Torre. It is also important to note that though the last two Cameroon *statuts* gave the high commissioners enough latitude to intervene to affect the composition and policy direction of the executive council, the price two of them (Messmer and Ramadier) paid for doing so—recall by Paris—testifies to the fact that by 1957 the Cameroonians had become at least equal partners in the relationship.

It is hardly surprising, therefore, that the 70-member assembly elected in December 1956 (renamed Legislative Assembly in 1957 under the new *statut*) was admirably suited to both French and Cameroonian purposes. It contained not only most of the "establishmentarians" in the previous assembly and the most active politicians of the day, but also a new crop from both north and south specifically recruited to be supporters of the new constitutional arrangements. Ahmadou Ahidjo's 38-member Union Camerounaise group included all the representatives from the north and east; it quickly made common cause with Mbida's 20 Democrates, a combination more than enough to dominate the new assembly.

The Groupe d'Action Nationale (GAN) led by Paul Soppo Priso and Charles Assale had only eight members, all of whom came from regions near the coast. The (illegal) Union des Populations du Cameroun (UPC) was not represented at all, even by surrogates, having boycotted the elections, leaving only the moderates of the GAN to represent the political left and offer token opposition to the new majority.

The new assembly soon lived up to its promise by passing the 1957 Statute by a vote of 60 to 8 (Soppo Priso's GAN, which held out for immediate independence) and, on May 10, invested Mbida as Cameroon's first prime minister. High Commissioner Messmer undoubtedly would have preferred to see Soppo Priso at the head of Cameroon's first government, but having wasted Soppo's credit in an unsuccessful (and frustrating) attempt at reconciliation with the UPC during 1956, he had little choice but to call on Mbida, who had broken with Soppo (and Messmer) on the UPC question and then made a separate deal with Ahidjo and the UC. All things considered, Mbida was still a thoroughly acceptable choice: now like Messmer a hardliner on the UPC question and the senior southern (and Catholic) politician, Mbida had wholeheartedly backed the new statute and apparently had the trust of Ahidjo and his northern bloc. Besides, Mbida's 12-man cabinet was evenly balanced between Democrates and the UC, with Adhidjo appointed deputy premier and minister of the interior.

Mbida's government lasted until February 18, 1958,; when it was replaced by one headed by Adhidjo, now in coalition with the Group of Eight (Soppo Priso and Assale). Mbida and the Democrates went into bitter opposition. Again, the chain of events that precipitated Mbida's fall need not detain us here; what is germane is that they involved direct intervention by Gerard Jacquet, the French minister for overseas territories, who removed Messmer and sent in Ramadier, who in turn lasted only several weeks as high commissioner during which he nonetheless managed (by exceeding his instructions) to persuade Ahidjo's Union Camerounaise to desert Mbida's government and force the latter's resignation. Ramadier's replacement was Xavier Torre, who was content to permit Ahidjo the full exercise of his powers under the 1957 and 1958 statutes. Torre's arrival also marked the end of direct French intervention in Cameroon's internal political affairs.

THE AHIDJO ERA, 1957–1982

The First Ahidjo Governments, 1958–1960

The tasks before Ahidjo in 1958 were considerable ones: ensure (if possible) an orderly transition to independence, control the resurgence of

UPC-inspired violence (now shifted to the Bamileke areas), and consolidate his hold on the government. His first government (of February 20, 1958) simply reflected the new coalition, being drawn half (six posts) from the north and east (UC) and half from the Center-South (GAN and independent allies). With the 1959 statute firmly in place, however, his skill in putting together supportive combinations began to be apparent. His second government (of June 18, 1959) was almost a model for all those yet to come and for that reason deserves more than a passing glance. In addition to eight UC ministers (including such longtime allies as Arouna Njoya, Sanda Oumarou, and Jean Akassou), three posts went to ex-Democrates (including Andre Fouda, a powerful figure from the Yaounde area), and three to the GAN (including Assale). Charles Okala, the lone socialist maverick, was given justice, and Simeon Songue, a young Upeciste, was made secretary of state for popular education, information, youth, and sports. Songue represented the first ex-Upeciste coopted by Ahidjo under his new program of amnesty for and reconciliation with former rebels; Okala and the GAN were to represent the newly cooperative left; and Mathias Djoumessi (ex-vice-president of the Democrates and president of the Bamileke KUMZSE organization) was made "resident minister" in the Bamileke districts as a visible tender of Ahidjo's good intentions. Regional balance was also maintained: four ministers were from the North, one from the East, two from the coast, five from the Center-South, and three from the West. In the first two Ahidjo governments, only Ahidjo and Njoya had served under Mbida; to all intents and purposes, Ahidjo made a clean sweep and thereby, symbolically, prepared the way for his own regime.

The First Republic and the Federation, 1960–1972

Ngayap has already provided an excellent, detailed analysis of the composition, characteristics, and turnover of Cameroon's ministerial ranks from 1960 to 1982, so there is no need to repeat that discussion here (1983, pp. 18–94). For our purposes, what is notable in his analysis is the picture that emerges of a persistent and judicious mix of continuity and personnel turnover. From 1958 to 1982, Ahidjo presided over no less than 18 governments, some consequent to a major regime change (see Table 2.1), others the result of reshuffles and adjustments. The only clean sweep—or nearly complete turnover—occurred with Ahidjo's first governments. Thereafter every cabinet contained a core of *fideles* held over from previous cabinets (some, like Sadou Daoudou, Egbe Tabi, Yadji Abdoulaye, Enoch Kwayeb, Charles Onana Awana, eventually serving from 10 to 21 years) and the rest, for example, were brought in because they were rising stars deserving a tryout in the major league, because the presi-

Table 2.1. Major Regime and Leadership Change in Cameroon, 1946–1983

Type of Change	*Year*	*Nature of Change*	*Regime Type*
Regime (constitutional); leadership (partial)	1946	League of Nations mandate transformed into UN trusteeship under French administration; First Territorial Assembly	UN trusteeship under French administration
Regime (constitutional); leadership (partial succession)	1957	"Loi Cadre" reforms; Mbida is first Cameroonian Prime Minister	Dyarchy within trusteeship ("State under trusteeship")
Leadership (partial succession)	1958	Ahidjo replaces Mbida as Prime Minister	Dyarchy within trusteeship (autonomous "state of Cameroon," December 30, 1958–January 1, 1960)
Regime (constitutional)	1960	Independence; Ahidjo becomes President	Unitary republic
Regime (constitutional); leadership (partial succession)	1961	Federation; federal and states' governments; Ahidjo is Federal President, Foncha is Federal Vice President	Federal republic
Regime (constitutional); leadership (partial succession)	1972	End of federation; Ahidjo is President, Biya is Prime Minister (1975)	Unitary republic
Regime (institutional); leadership (full succession)	1982	Ahidjo resigns as President, is succeeded by Prime Minister Biya	Unitary republic

Note: This list includes only those instances in which a major change in government leadership or a regime change (plus leadership succession) takes place.

Definitions: Partial succession: leadership change below the very top. Full succession: leadership change including the very top. Dyarchy: considerable governmental power shared between French and Cameroonian officials; here, despite the appointment of a Cameroonian Premier and cabinet, final word remained with French High Commissioners. Regime: "arrangement of authority, power, and political interest in a state"; can involve a major leadership or constitutional change, or both.

dent needed their support for some new initiatives, because of their expertise, or because of the need to preserve the all-important regional (read ethnic) equilibrium within the government. Ahidjo's first independence government (May 16, 1960) reflected his new position as president: Assale became prime minister, but of the 18 other ministers, only four (Okala, Njoya, Sanda Oumarou, and Askassou) continued from the previous government. Ahidjo was now also able to bring in additional friends and supporters such as Sadou Daudou, Onana Awana, and Mohammane Lamine, as well as such individuals as Pierre Kamdem Ninyim and Victor Kanga, both coopted from the opposition. Kamdem Ninyim was a special prize: formerly a Bamileke chief and an active leader in the UPC *maquis,* Kamdem accepted amnesty and was one of nine "legal" Upecistes elected to the new National Assembly. That body, elected on May 4, 1960, included not only the nine who ran on UPC lists, but also 18 (mainly Bamileke) leaders with UPC sympathies willing to collaborate with Ahidjo. The Union Camerounaise won 52 seats, the Democrates 11, the Progressistes (ex-GAN) 8, and 3 were won by independents. In terms of ideological orientation, regional representation, age spread, and mixtures of experience and talent, the new 100-man assembly was probably the most representative legislature ever elected in Cameroon. More important, because it contained an alliance of old and newly converted supporters of Ahidjo and his policies, it gave Ahidjo the legitimacy and backing he needed to defeat the UPC insurgency as well as carry through his next project, the "reunification" of the country (Ansprenger 1961, extratextual Table 12, and pp. 392–404).

The period of the Federal Republic (1961–1972) was marked not only by the entrance of a number of important anglophone politicians onto the national political scene (Foncha, Muna, Jua, Egbe Tabi, Fonlon, Nzo Ekah Nghaky) and into the Ahidjo camp, but also by the simultaneous presence of three legislatures and three governments, of which only the federal bodies exercised decisive political power. The wisdom of hindsight now permits us to conclude that the federation was probably doomed from the start and that it was a necessary transition to the unitary state Ahidjo and his colleagues had wanted all along. A close reading of the terms of federation and of the political context in which it was consummated certainly supports such a conclusion (for details, see Johnson 1970a, Le Vine 1971, Rubin 1971, and Bayart 1979). Again, of relevance to our argument is the presence of three Anglophones in the first federal cabinet (Muna, Jua, Egbe Tabi), in addition to Foncha, who had become federal vice-president. Anglophones would remain a feature of every national cabinet thereafter. Moreover, the West Cameroon legislature of 37 members proved admirably supportive of the national government and Ahidjo throughout its ten-year life principally, I am inclined to think, because its members came to the unhappy recognition that no effective opposition could be mounted against the power increasingly centralized in Yaounde. The choice both in the western and eastern legislatures was between going along or being swept under. Certainly, the ten deputies from the western legislature who sat in the Federal Assembly never exercised the unusual collective veto granted them in the Federal Constitution (Le Vine 1971, pp. 88–89).

The federal period was also marked by the arrival of the single-party system in 1966. Along the way to what Ahidjo styled "the great unified party," the president used doses of coercion (the jailing of four main opposition leaders, Mbida, Okala, Mayi-Matip, and Beybey Eyidi in 1962; the forcible dissolution of the UPC party congress in 1962), vigorous persuasion (which resulted in most opposition deputies joining the Union Camerounaise), and various other forms of pressure on the country's several political parties and their leaders. By the end of 1965, nearly all had capitulated, and on September 1, 1966, the Cameroon National Union came into being.

> As for the UPC, its final act of submission came in September, 1968, when Theodore Mayi-Matip, out of jail and presumably reconciled, joined the CNU, Okala, Beybey, and Mbida . . . were also released in 1965. Okala quickly made his peace and assisted at the dissolution of his Socialistes. His reward was an ambassadorship. Dr. Beybey returned to his clinic in Douala, where he died in 1966. That left Mbida as the sole opposition leader of any note in Cameroon . . . who remained outside the embrace of the new party (Le Vine 1971, pp. 112–113).

It should be added that Mbida, then already terminally ill, reconciled with Ahidjo in 1967, and that Mayi-Matip, once in the *maquis* as Um Nyobe's lieutenant, is today the respected first vice-president of the National Assembly.

The effects of these events on personnel changes within the "governing elite" can hardly be overstated. For one thing, the termination of the federation in 1972 (styled Ahidjo's "peaceful revolution") was accomplished in an almost pro forma manner and, of course, without open opposition. Those state legislators who did not retire were subsequently rewarded with jobs in the administration, or with seats in the post-1960 National Assembly or on one of the consultative organs such as the Social and Economic Council. For another thing, and most important, recruitment to all elective positions thereafter came under the direct control of the CNU's Central Committee (also dominated by the president and his people) because by law no one could be nominated who had not received the prior imprimatur of the party's directing organs. After 1966, not surprisingly, the national legislatures became annual conventions with little other purpose than to ratify the government's legislative proposals; lend symbolic popular legitimacy to the government's actions; and provide prebendiary pasturage to old pols past their prime, party workers and officials deserving of reward for faithful service, and local politicians who were not deemed *ministrable* (eligible for ministerial posts) but needed recognition and status as representatives of some important social or ethnic group.[7] The fate of Cameroon's national legislature, it should be added, was hardly unusual, but similar to that of legislatures in other Francophone single-party states, confirming that in Cameroon, as elsewhere, critical political decision making had passed to other venues (Le Vine 1979). In Cameroon's case, it was to the presidency, the ministries of state, the CNU Central Committee, and the most senior civil servants, all, in any case, dependent on and responsible to the president himself.

The United Republic, 1972–1983

Evidence of the new directions in the elite recruitment process lies partly in the composition of Ahidjo's post-1971 cabinets. With the party now formally the supreme organ of popular representation, Ahidjo added legitimation of his ministerial choices to the functions of the CNU's governing bodies. Bayart reports that 12 of the 28 holders of ministerial office in July 1972 had also previously been elected to the CNU's National Political Bureau at the party's 1972 Garoua Congress: Messrs. Biya, Sengat Kuo, Yadji Abdoulaye, Andze, Sadou Daoudou, Ayissi Mvodo, Achidi Achu, Mongo Soo, Fokam Kamga, Kwayeb, Tessa, and Tonye Bog (in Joseph 1978, p. 77). The cabinets reformed or reshuffled in 1975, 1979, 1980, and 1982 received similar stamps of approval from the CNU's organs, though not necessarily at party congresses.

Ahidjo's 1972 cabinet was atypical in one important respect, in that it reunited the key technocrats and *fideles* previously dispersed among the national and state governments. Thereafter, however, the cabinets remained quite stable in the top ten positions (Ngayap's "*peloton de tete*"), but experienced considerable turnover in the lower, mainly technocratic ranks (18 to 21 positions). A superficial inspection of the five cabinets during the United Republic revealed some 16 new faces, all of them below the *peloton de tete* level. To be sure, during this period a major change occurred when Biya was brought in 1975 to fill the revived prime ministry (and later, to become the constitutional *dauphin*), several of the top group were retired, shifted elsewhere, or displaced (Onana Awana, Kwayeb, Keutcha, Muna), and the individuals themselves were from time to time moved from one ministry to another. On the whole, however, the cabinets reflected Ahidjo at the height of his powers and at his most secure; almost all of the changes were designed to improve performance or bring in personnel technically more competent to handle the increasingly complex tasks of government. Given the country's increasing prosperity, the relative absence of internal conflict, and the fact that the country's turbulent factions had been brought under control, Ahidjo was now free to devote his attention to developmental questions. The decade's relative elite stability—within governmental ranks—is a precise reflection of these circumstances. Biya himself testified to the degree to which elite turnover had become institutionalized during Ahidjo's last ten years in office: his first government retained most of the technocrats he had inherited from his predecessor.

That was, of course, before the events of June 1983 and April 1984.

THE BIYA REGIME, 1983–1984: CHALLENGE AND RESPONSE

At the beginning of 1983, Cameroonians had good reason to congratulate themselves on the state of their country. The economy, fueled by growing oil revenues, continued its strong growth, and a completely peaceful (and by all signs, benign) passage of power had been effected on November 6, 1982, from President Ahidjo to his legal *dauphin,* Prime Minister Paul Biya. The Ahidjo-Biya transition certainly could be viewed with considerable pride: it was only the third time since independence that an incumbent black African head of state had voluntarily surrendered his office according to constitutional rules of succession (the other instances being the Senghor–Diouf succession on January 1, 1981 in Senegal and the Osman–Shirmarke succession in 1967 in Somalia).

The events of the next 18 months, however, were to shake the Cameroonian system to its roots and, as was suggested earlier, permitted Biya to reorganize virtually the country's entire top leadership cadre. It would be beyond the scope of this chapter to trace these events in detail; but if they are seen as the matrix of elite turnover, then it becomes clear that they largely determined both the scale and the rate of that change. Biya may well have wanted to put his own people in the *peloton de tete* as soon as possible, but he was apparently willing to do so gradually in deference to Ahidjo and the amicable circumstances of the transition. All that changed radically as relations between the two men deteriorated, as Ahidjo began trying to assert the primacy of the party (over which he presided) over the government (headed by Biya), and as it became clear that Ahidjo was no longer willing to accept the role of elder statesman in which he had cast himself when he stepped down. Even the most cursory examination of the November 4, 1982, to July 1984 period suggests that as the challenge and, subsequently, the threat from Ahidjo grew so did Biya act with increasing forcefulness to replace or displace both the certified and nominal partisans of Ahidjo and his regime. (Table 2.2 proves a partial chronology of the events during this period.)

The course of events, again as they impact on personnel turnover, appears roughly to divide into five phases:

1. November 1982 through January 1983. These are, perhaps, the "days of amity." This phase begins with Ahidjo's announcement of his resignation, on November 4, 1982, and ends with the dismissal of Moussa Yaya, one of Ahidjo's oldest friends and collaborators, and three others from both the party and the National Assembly (January 10–12 1983). Apparently, Moussa and the others had openly and indiscreetly criticized the transition and Biya during a tour of northern and eastern areas of the country. On the same day that Biya took the oath of office (November 6, 1982), he designated Bouba Bello Maigari as the new prime minister, named Sadou Daoudou as the new secretary-general in the presidency to replace Samuel Eboua, who became minister of state for agriculture. The move of Sadou to the presidency was widely interpreted as a tender of Ahidjo's good intentions: Sadou was expected to ride disciplinary herd on top officials still dissatisfied with the presidential change. Moreover, Biya retained all the rest of Ahidjo's last cabinet in their former positions.

2. End of January to mid-June 1983. This phase, during which Ahidjo and Biya grew progressively estranged from one another, opened with Ahidjo publicly affirming the primacy of the party over the government on January 31 and ended with the dismissal from the government of six of Ahidjo's so-called "barons" (Sadou Daoudou, Samuel Eboua, Victor Ayissi Mvodo, Hamadou Moustapha, Guillaume Bwele, and Eteme Oloa on June 18). Also during this phase, Ahidjo attempted but failed to write the party's supremacy into the constitution. Finally, Biya's response was to begin his major housecleaning with six of Ahidjo's most powerful and prominent *fideles,* a dramatic move calculated both to bring the conflict into the open and to underscore Biya's command of the presidency.

3. Mid-June through August 1983. This period merits separate mention because the plot that Biya revealed on August 20 apparently (as later alleged) began to take shape on June 18 at secret meetings held by an enraged Ahidjo and some of his more fervent military and civilian supporters. Ahidjo himself left the country on July 20 but did not resign as CNU national president until August 24. On August 20, Biya also replaced Prime Minister Bouba Bello Maigari and Armed Forces Minister Maikano Abdoulaye. Though the two were not then inculpated in the plot, their dismissal on the same day the plot was revealed suggested their involvement.

4. End of August 1983 to the beginning of April 1984. This phase was marked by Biya's election as national president of the CNU (September 7), his confirmation as president by a general election (January 14), and by

the dramatic trial of Ahidjo (in absentia), Salatou, and Oumarou, resulting in death sentences for all three as well as new charges against Maigari, Maikano, and Wadjiri. On March 14, Biya commuted all three sentences. Biya also continued his housecleaning: on February 4 he again reshuffled his cabinet, dropping five (two of whom, Emmanuel Egbe Tabi and Christian Songwe Bongwa, were old anglophone politicians) and adding eight new faces (three of whom headed newly created ministries).

5. April to the end of August 1984. This phase begins with the attempted coup on April 6–7 and included the military trials (April 28 to May 7) and consequent executions, as well as important personnel changes involving the parastatal structures (May 15), the CNU Central Committee (May 24), and the cabinet (July 7). Various diplomatic posts were also reshuffled.

Table 2.2. Summary Chronology of the Key Events of November 4, 1982–September 1, 1984

1982	November 4	Ahidjo announces his resignation as president; Biya sworn in on November 6. Bouba Bello Maigari designated as new prime minister, Sadou Daoudou as new secretary-general in presidency.
1983	January 10	Affair of the "Band of Four": Moussa Yaya and three deputies are excluded from CNU by its Political Bureau. The four lose their parliamentary seats on January 12.
	January 31	In a *Cameroon Tribune* interview, Ahidjo asserts that it is the party (CNU) that "defines national political orientations" and characterizes the government as the "emanation" of the party.
	February 15–16	Questioned by the French press during an official visit to French President Mitterrand, Biya denies having problems with ex-President Ahidjo. During next three weeks, various breaches of protocol by Ahidjo signal the rupture with Biya. Foreign press speculates on possible presidential "bicephalism" in Cameroon.
	April 12	Light cabinet reshuffle: Young technocrats Bol Alima, Ntsama, E. Tankeu, Zambo, and Nkuete enter the government.
	June 18	Six Ahidjo *fideles* dropped from government: Sadou Daoudou, Samuel Eboua, Victor Ayissi Mvodo, Guillaume Bwele, Hamadou Moustapha, and Eteme Oloa Athanase. (Secret meetings are held by an angry Ahidjo at his residence and at home of Ibrahim Wadjiri,

		Delegate-General for Gendarmerie. Ahidjo demands the collective resignation of all northern ministers but is refused.)
	June 20–22	Official visit to Cameroon by French President Mitterrand. Privately, Mitterrand counsels peace between Biya and Ahidjo.
	July 20	Ahidjo leaves Cameroon for visit of indetermined duration to Europe; he takes "several tons" of baggage with him.
	August 20	Biya announces discovery of a plot "against the security of the State"; Commandant Oumarou and Captain Salatou, formerly military aides to Ahidjo, are arrested, charged.
	August 24	From France, Ahidjo announces his resignation as national president of CNU.
	September 7	At meeting of CNU Central Committee, Biya is elected CNU national president.
1984	January 14	Presidential election: Biya is elected president for a five-year term with (officially) 99.98 percent of the votes cast.
	February 4	Cabinet reshuffle: three new ministries created; new ministers enter the government, five depart.
	February 23–28	Trial of "August plot" conspirators before the Yaounde Permanent Military Tribunal; Ahidjo (in absentia), Commandant Oumarou, and Captain Salatou are charged with "revolution, subversion, and conspiracy to assassinate" President Biya. The three are found guilty, condemned to death. Bouba Bello Maigari, Maikano Abdoulaye, and Ibrahim Wadjiri are inculpated, remanded to civil courts.
	March 14	Biya commutes sentences on Ahidjo, Salatou, and Wadjiri to life imprisonment.
	April 6–7	Elements of the Republican Guard, the Gendarmerie, and police attempt a coup d'etat, which is put down by loyalist troops. Officially, 70 people are killed during the fighting (unofficial estimates put those killed at between 150 and 250, with at least 300 people wounded). Government announces 1,053 *putschistes* are taken prisoner, with 265 gendarmes missing, that is, presumed in flight. Ahidjo, in France, when informed of events, is quoted as saying, "If these (rebels) are my partisans, (I hope) they come out on top."

April 28–May 7	Military court tries rebels; various death sentences and terms of imprisonment meted out. More than two-thirds of those arrested are eventually released. (Amnesty International later claims that 120 people were executed, including most of the military officers involved. By end of September 1984, the identities of those executed had not yet been officially revealed.)
May 15	Heads of the most important parastatals are replaced.
May 24	The CNU Central Committee is reshuffled; eight of twelve in the Political Bureau are replaced.
July 7	The Cabinet is reshuffled; nine ministries are affected.

Sources: West Africa, November 1982–August 1984; *Africa Research Bulletin,* December 1982–September 1984; *La Gazette,* May 29, 1984.

Biya began his presidency with Ahidjo's last team virtually intact; it has even been suggested that Ahidjo's last cabinet reshuffle on January 7, 1982, which moved several technocrats into key positions, may have been undertaken as part of Ahidjo's preparations for his departure. Be that as it may, Biya initially appeared content to work with the cabinet and the other leadership cadre he inherited. His only major (first) appointment was Bouba Bello Maigari, a young (36 year old) career bureaucrat, then minister of economy, to the vacant post of prime minister. Samuel Eboua, who had been secretary-general in the presidency since 1975, was moved to the ministry of agriculture, and Sadou Daoudou, Ahidjo's long-time armed forces minister (1961–1981) and close friend, moved from his position as deputy secretary-general in the presidency into the post vacated by Eboua. Then followed the momentous events of 1983–1984, and, after the dust had settled, Biya had almost completely changed the composition and character of the country's national leadership core. The scope and tenor of that change can be usefully described by considering some of the details of the 1982–1984 personnel turnover in three of the several leadership sectors and subsectors discussed earlier in this essay: the government, the party Central Committee, and what Ngayap (1983) called "*Les hauts fonctionnaires*" (the top bureaucrats). Moreover, given the role of the military during the period in question, changes in army and gendarmerie commands must also be mentioned, as must those that took place within the ranks of the heads of parastatal enterprises. (Except for the affair of the "gang of four," the composition and character of the National Assembly was little affected by the larger events of 1982–1984, though not, if Joseph Owona is to be believed, for want of trying by Ahidjo and his partisans.[8] For that reason, it can be left outside this analysis [Owona 1983, pp. 78–84].)

The Government

Ngayap's "lead squad" (*peloton de tete*) in the government is the group of top ten ministerial official ranking immediately below the president himself. It comprises the prime minister (before that office was abolished again), the ministers of state, and others so ranked because of the importance of their ministries, their seniority, or simply, their personal standing with the president (Ngayap 1983, pp. 25–26). Ngayap apparently chose ten as the number for this group because its members were almost invariably those individuals who most clearly combined seniority and long association with former President Ahidjo. That they would also be entrusted with the most important portfolios was virtually a foregone conclusion. Figure 2.1 describes the changing composition of the government beginning with Ahidjo's last (Janury 7, 1982) reshuffle through Biya's changes up to the latter's July 7, 1984, reconstitution, by which date (apparently) most of Biya's changes had been accomplished. The *pelotons de tete* are highlighted; in several instances Ngayap's ten was expanded to include individuals who, in my opinion, should be in that group, and a few names were revised to conform to conventional usage (e.g., Youssoufa to *Youssoufa Daouda,* Andze to *Andze Tsoungui,* Kome to *Ngome Kome*).

The point of the exercise emerges from the data in Figure 2.1: with his July 7, 1984, reshuffle, Biya had reconstituted the government (especially the *peloton de tete*) to make it his own. In the process, Ahidjo's old ministerial "barons" were removed (Eboua, S. Daoudou, Ayissi Mvodo, Hamadou, Eteme Oloa, Bwele), as were those of questionable loyalty (Bouba Bello Maigari, A. Maikano) or whose politics, dubious credentials, or past associations made them dispensable (Dontsop, Ntag, Engo, Nkoulou, Egbe Tabi, Bongwa, Yang, Oumarou, D. Tsanga, Ngome Kome, and Hele). As if to demonstrate that the dismissals were not all politically motivated, those displaced included Tonye Bog, one of Biya's oldest friends (and in the government since 1972), and two whom Biya had himself appointed (Tori Limangana and Fouman Akame). (It might be added that Victor Ayissi Mvodo, one of the Ahidjo "barons" dismissed on June 18, 1983, had also been a schoolmate of Biya's—at the Seminary of St. Joseph d'Akono—but the two men were hardly close after 1982.)[9] Biya's new *peleton de tete,* in particular, reflected not only the new regional shift of power, but also Biya's insistence on appointing people who combined personal loyalty to him with technical competence. In the July 7 *peloton* half were either Biya's coethnics or ethnic cousins from the country's Center South region: Tsoungui, Zambo, Ntsama, Ongolo, and Ngango. Only one, Youssoufa Daouda (a technocrat of proven ability and low political profile) was a northerner, and the rest hailed from the western areas (Sengat Kuo, Ouandji, and Mengueme), the coast (Eteki, a Douala), or the east (Doumba). Doumba, who has long been close to Biya, was removed from

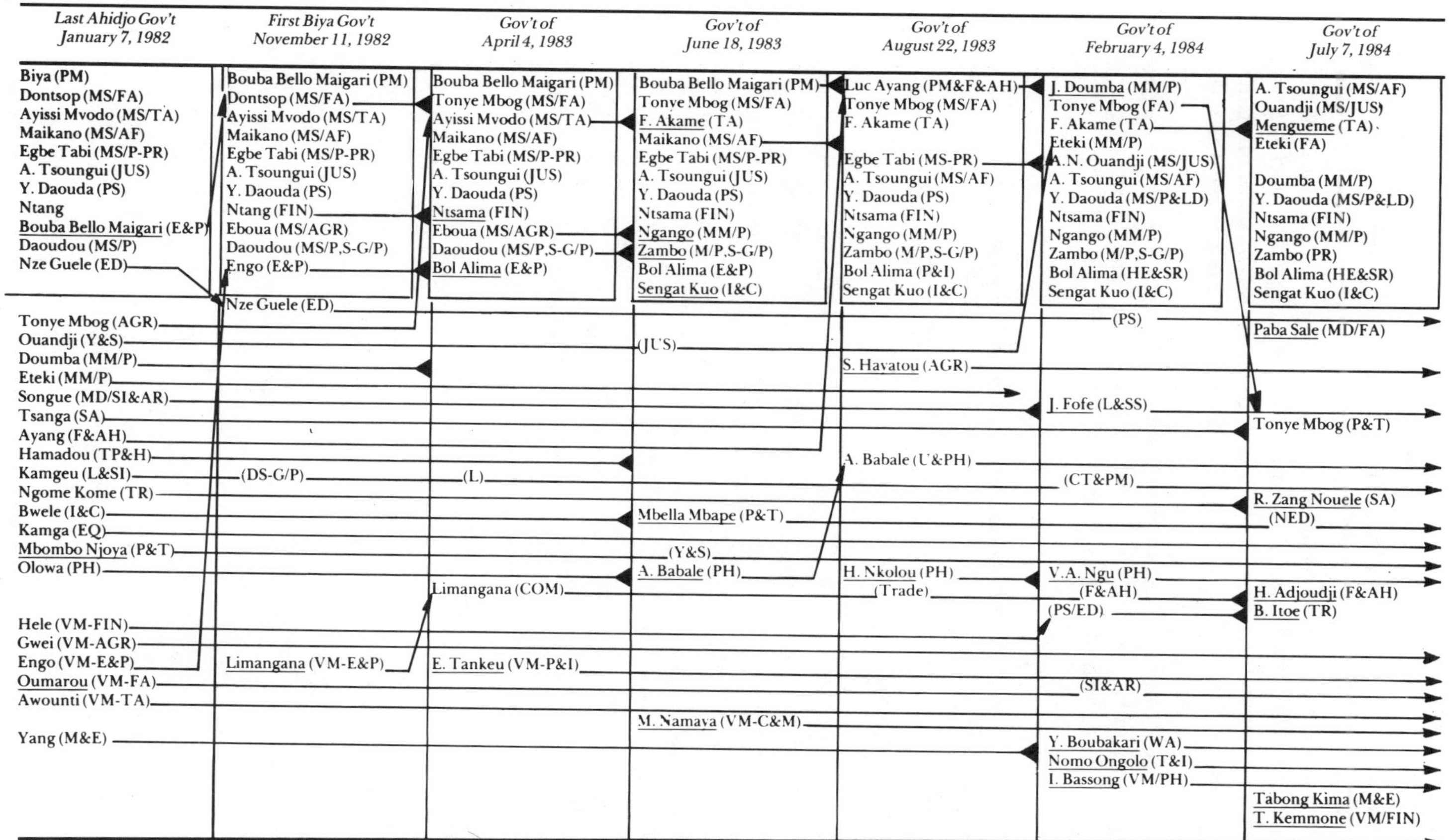

Sources: Ngayap 1983; *Cameroon Tribune, Cameroon Gazette, Africa Research Bulletin, Cameroon National Yearbook 1981, Le Mois en Afrique.*

Keys: [box] : *Peletons de tete*; Underlined name: new minister; ——◀ : Dropped from gov't; ——▶ : Continues in gov't; ——⁄▶ : Shift in position or rank

MINISTERIAL ABBREVIATIONS: *POSITIONS & RANKS:* PM: Prime Minister; MS: Minister of State; MD: Minister Delegate; VM: Vice or Deputy Minister; MM/: Minister for (special) Missions at Presidency; M/P: Minister at Presidency; ( ): Where no special rank is given, rank is Minister. *FUNCTIONAL TITLES:* AF: Armed Forces; AGR: Agriculture; COM: Commerce; CT&PM: Computer Techn. & Publ. Markets; ED: Education; E&P: Economy & Planning; EQ: Equipment; F&AH: (Livestock), Fishing & Animal Husbandry; FA: Foreign Affairs; FIN: Finance; HE&SR: Higher Educ. & Sci. Research; I&C: Info. & Culture.; JUS: Justice; L: Labor; L&SI: Labor & Social Insurance; L&SS: Labor & Social Security; M&E: Mines & Energy; M&P: Mines & Power; NED: Nati'l Education; PH: Public Health; P&I: Planning & Industries; PR: Parliamentary Relations; P&LD: Planning & Land Dev't; PS: Public Service; P&T: Posts & Telecomm'ns; PS/ED: Primary & Sec'dry Ed.; SI&AR: State Inspectorate & Admin. Reform; T&I: Trade & Industry; TP&H: Town Planning & Housing; U&PH: Urb'zation & Pub. Hous'g; WA: Women's Affairs; Y&S: Youth & Sports.

his job as minister at the presidency in April 1983 but returned in 1984 after he had reestablished his credentials with the president. To be sure, Biya's new peloton de tete included two men, Andze Tsoungui and Youssoufa Daouda, who had been appointed by Ahidjo, and two others, Doumba and Eteki, who, because of their proximity to Ahidjo as ministers at the presidency, might also have had their loyalty to Biya questioned. All four, however, managed to remain in place (I suspect) because they shared with the others proven technocratic skills and, critically, a record of political reticence, that is, the fortunate fact that they never became part of Ahidjo's group of "barons" and cronies.

Table 2.3. Key Post-1982 Personnel Turnover: The Party and Other Institutions

1. CNU POLITICAL BUREAU

Composition, May 24, 1984 (12 Members)	Out
Paul Biya (President)	F. Sabal Lecco
*F. Sengat Kuo**	V. Ayissi Mvodo†
*S. Hayatou**	A. Hayatou†
S. Tandeng Muna	S. Daoudou†
E. Egbe Tabi†	S. Kame
Luc Ayang*†	G. Bwele†
E. Basile	Y.N. Nchouwat
*J.-C. Doumba**	Bouba Bello Maigari†
*Mbombo Njoya**	
Bouba Bello	
J. Nkuete*	
*J.-M. Mengueme**	
N.P. Nsakwa	

2. CNU CENTRAL COMMITTEE

56 Members, May 24, 1984	Out
Paul Biya (President)	F. Sabal Lecco
*F. Sengat Kuo**	V. Ayissi Mvodo†
*J.-C. Doumba**	A. Hayatou†
*S. Hayatou**	S. Kame
*Mbombo Njoya**	G. Bwele†
J. Nkuete*	Bouba Bello Maigari†
*J.-M. Mengueme**	Moussa Yaya (1983)
V. Mukete*	
Ndongo Essamba*	

(Other notable members)

J.N. Foncha
S. Daoudou†
S.-P. Tchoungui†
E. Kwayeb†
A. Oumarou
H. Balla
C. Assale†
D. Tsanga
S.T. Muna
E. Eteme Oloa†
V. Ngu
H. Mayi-Matip
S.N. Mbile
J. Keutcha†
T. Ebongalame†
G. Bol Alima†
M. Yondo†
J. Ekwabi†
E. Basile
Bouba Bello
N.P. Nsakwa
E. Egbe Tabi†
Y.N. Tchouwat
E.M.L. Endeley†
B. Fonlon†
L. Ayang†

3. MILITARY AND SECURITY INSTITUTIONS

A. The Military & Gendarmerie

In	Out
Andze Tsongui, Minister Armed Forces, August 22, 1983	A. Maikano, August 22, 1983
P. Semengue, Chief of Staff, General	Col. Ousmanou Daouda, Chief of Staff to President, April 12, 1984
General Oumaroudjam Yaya Gendarmerie	Col. Ngoura Belladji, Commandant 1st Military Sector and Yaounde, April 12, 1984
General Nganso Sanji, Air Force	Commandant O. Ibrahima and Capt. A. Salatou, aides to Ahidjo, August 22, 1983
General James Tataw, Land Forces	

B. The Security Apparatus

In	Out
S. Missomba, Director, CND, Director, Public Security August 4, 1984	Jean Fochive
M. Mouiche, Deputy Director Public Security, August 4, 1984	
D. Ekani, General Delegate, Surete, August 4, 1984	M. Mbarga R. Nguele (Deputy)
P. Minlo'o, Director, Presidential Security, August 4, 1984	Col. C. Meka, April 21, 1984

Lt. Col. D. Massango, E. Legion, Gendarmes	Col. Sale Ibrahim, Commandant Presidential Guard, April 7, 1984

4. MINISTERIAL SECRETARIATS

New Appointments July 7, 1984

Secretary-General (S-G), Presidency	D.A.A. Tchoyi
Deputy S-G, Presidency	C. Nsalai
S-G, Commerce & Industry	Sone Ebongue
S-G, Planning	Zoa Oloa
S-G, Health	Mbondjo Edjangue
S-G, Finance	D. Nan Kam
S-G, Social Affairs	H. Malloum
S-G, Agriculture	Ndiawana Moushili

5. PARASTATAL DIRECTORS-GENERAL as of May 15, 1984

In	Organization	Out
J.P. Boupda	SONEL	M. Njipenji Niat
A. Kodock	CAMAIR	A. Bello
R. Melingui	ONCPB	B. Hama Toukour
J. Godwe	SOTUC	Diakole Diasalla
H.B. Maimo	FONADER	Issa Adoum
A. Vamoulke	Imprimerie Nationale	M. Rodo
J. Assoumou	SNH	S. Libock
Mohammed Iya	SODECOTON	A. Bossourou
Siyam Siwe	LABOGENIE	?
P.-D. Engo	National Insurance Fund	D. Potounjou Taponzie

* New Members
† Former government ministers
italics: Government members, July 7, 1984

Table 2.3 records key personnel changes in some of the other critical political and governmental decision-making arenas: the CNU's Central Committee (particularly, its Political Bureau), the ministerial secretariats, the security apparatus and the military, and the public and parastatal corporations. Most interesting here, of course, is the Central Committee, the Cameroon Nation Union's permanent governing body, of which the Political Bureau (Committee) is the inner circle. As was noted earlier, when Ahidjo gave up the state presidency, he retained the national presidency of the CNU and, thereby, the chairmanship of both the Central and

Political Committees. Initially, Biya accepted the post of national first vice-president, ostensibly in charge of the day-to-day operations of the party's central organs. However, once Ahidjo's attempt to give the party real instead of nominal power over the government had failed Biya himself took over the CNU national presidency and, in order to put the party back in its place, proceeded to reorganize both the Central and Political Committees.

Biya made his point in four ways: first, he expanded the Central Committee by 8 to 56 members, in the process removing Felix Sabal Lecco (ex-president of the Social and Economic Council), Victor Ayissi Mvodo, Ahmadou Hayatou, Samuel Kame (once the CNU's main ideologist), Guillaume Bwele, and Bouba Bello Maigari, the former prime minister. (Moussa Yaya had been expelled earlier in 1983 in the wake of the "gang of four" incident.) Of this group, only Sabal Lecco, an old friend of Biya's, was given another job, that of ambassador to the Vatican. Second, Biya completely overhauled the Political Committee, dropping 8 of its 12 members, and replacing them with trusted old and rehabilitated partisans (Francois Sengat Kuo, Sadou Hayatou, Luc Ayang, Joseph-Charles Doumba, Mbombo Njoya, Jean Nkuete, and Jean-Marcel Mengueme). Third, and perhaps most importantly, he conferred the critical post of party political secretary on Francois Sengat Kuo, a veteran political operative, bureaucrat, and once Ahidjo's chief speech writer. With this appointment, Sengat Kuo, an intellectual of the first order but in forced retirement since 1979, reemerged to become principal party propagandist and expositor of the president's new doctrines of "rigor" and "moralization" and (according to one observer) "possibly the most powerful politician in Cameroon after Biya" (*West Africa,* July 9, 1984, p. 1399).

Finally, with his people firmly in place and Ahidjo's loyalists ousted or neutralized, Biya could also play the pragmatic politician by keeping several influential northerners near the top (Sadou Hayatou, son of the Lamido of Garoua and brother of the ousted Ahmadou Hayatou, Bello Bouba, a prominent Garoua businessman and politician; and Sadou Daoudou, now one of the four CNU vice-presidents and apparently a willing candidate for rehabilitation). Ahidjo, throughout his long career as Cameroon's president, usually preferred (if possible) to coopt his opponents instead of punishing them. Biya may well have learned the wisdom of this policy: thus the Central Committee, even after the April 1984 attempted coup, still contained several individuals (besides Sadou Daoudou) whom he had previously sacked from the government (e.g., Delphine Tsanga, Eteme Oloa, Thomas Ebongalame, A. Oumarou).

The other key personnel changes need little additional comment. After the April 1984 coup attempt, it obviously became necessary to replace military and gendarme commanders implicated in the revolt, remove or shift others who had failed to perform up to expectations, and reward those who had led the loyalist troops against the rebels. Perhaps even more important to the outcome of the April revolt was the promotion, some ten months earlier, of three new generals: Oumaroudjam Yaya (a northerner) of the gendarmerie, Nganso Sunji (a Bamileke) at the air force, and James Tataw (from the South-West regions) at land forces. It was this disparate group of officers headed by General Pierre Semengue (an old friend and a classmate of Biya at the Lycee Leclerc) who rallied to "legality" and ultimately saved both Biya's skin and job.

The April 6 revolt also resulted, perhaps inevitably, in the wholesale replacement of the heads of the security apparatus, some of whom had been implicated in the attempted coup and others of whom had been blamed (rightly or wrongly) for not ferreting out the plot in advance or failing to take the proper measures to prevent it. The most prominent of those removed was Jean Fochive, head of the secret police (in its most recent guise known as the CND, or National Documentation Center) since 1961. Fochive was also the director of presidential security, and hence it was to him that the officers of the Legion of the Republican Guard and the Presidential Palace Command reported. These two units, it will be recalled, led the April 7 attempted coup.[10]

The director-general of the parastatal National Fund for Rural Development (FONADER), Issa Adoum, was apparently one of the "brains" behind the April 6 revolt, and Augustin Kodock, director-general of Cameroon Airlines, was also allegedly involved in the conspiracy. Issa Adoum was reported executed on May 2, 1984. Issa's and Kodock's disloyalty permitted Biya to replace 11 heads of the more than 20 parastatal corporations and institutions. Table 2.3 also takes note of these changes.

Several other interesting observations can be drawn from both the personnel changes that took place between November 6, 1982, and mid-1984 (summarized partially in Figure 2.1 and Table 2.3) and the larger political events to which they are related. First and foremost is the fact that while Biya's political housecleaning was thorough and—compared to past experience—wholesale, it was still extremely selective. If one accepts Ngayap's 950-person *classe dirigeante* as a reasonable approximation of the size of Cameroon's governing elite, then Biya's replacements, displacements, shuffles, and purges probably affected no more than about 13 or 14 percent of the total. The data available suggest that somewhere around 125 top leaders were purged or lost their jobs during this period, some of whom, to be sure, were shifted to less important or less sensitive positions. In the government (see Figure 2.1 for details), some 25 new ministers entered and 22 were dropped altogether; the turnover in the Party Central and Political Committees affected another 16; in the military and security apparatuses, perhaps 25 command positions were affected; and in the parastatals, the top government bureaucracy, and the diplomatic corps, taken together, perhaps another 60 were removed or displaced, all of which adds up to about 125.

The events of 1983 and particularly of 1984 undeniably gave Biya the opportunity to replace many more in the top cadres had he so wished to do. The fact is that he did not, be it out of timidity or indecisiveness (as some have suggested), or because he recognized and deferred to the power and influence of some of the older politicians, or simply because he felt he could gain the willing cooperation (if not the affection) of the remaining leaders by coopting them into his regime. Though Biya may have been somewhat indecisive during the initial phases of his conflict with Ahidjo, he was certainly neither indecisive nor timid in playing that confrontation to a showdown. The latter two reasons seem more credible, given the facts, because they speak to a political pragmatism that Biya may well have learned from his predecessor and mentor.

Second, in all of the personnel changes in the government, the party, and elsewhere, Biya appeared generally to have continued to honor the principle of "regional" (that is, ethnic) balance. For example, I count at least six northerners (one of whom, Youssoufa Daouda, remains in the *peloton de tete*), five Anglophone westerners, three easterners, three coastals, ten Francophone westerners, and nine from the Center-South in Biya's July 7, 1984 government. On the other hand, just as some of Ahidjo's closest advisors were *fideles* from the North, so is it hardly surprising that Biya would rely heavily on the advice of old friends and/or coethnics such as Georges Ngango, Joseph Zambo, Andze Tsoungui, Eduard Nomo Ongolo, Etienne Ntsama, and Laurent Esso. Yet it was to William Eteki Mboumoua and Francois Sengat Kuo, both Dualas, that Biya confided the critical portfolios of foreign affairs and information and culture, respectively, and it was Sengat who, for all intents and purposes, became the second most powerful member of the Party Central Committee after Biya himself.

Finally, to turn the coin, it is apparent that Biya sought as much continuity within the elite as was possible under the circumstances. Himself a technocrat, Biya seems to have tried to retain most of the older technocrats who were not too closely identified with Ahidjo or who had remained neutral (or at least, passive) during the plot of 1983 and the revolt of 1984. Thirteen of the ministers who were in Ahidjo's last government (of January 7, 1982) were still in Biya's government of July 7, 1984, that is, slightly more than a third of the 36 in the latter group. And even more significant, 5 of the 11 in the latter peloton de tete were also holdovers from January 1982.

Granted, the events of 1983 and 1984 did shake the Cameroonian system to its roots, but if the evidence and analysis presented above is at all reasonable, thanks to Biya's pragmatic politics its governing elite emerged somewhat scarred but eminently able to carry on the tasks set for it by the new president.

A PERSONAL POSTSCRIPT

The abortive military *putsch* of April 6–7, 1984 reminds us of a constant danger facing those of us foolish enough to commit to paper commentary about contemporary events in Africa: we can be overtaken by events at any moment and our "expertise" confounded, if not completely undermined. Had things turned out differently in Cameroon, this essay might at worst have become largely irrelevant or at best have had to be drastically revised to make the author look extraordinarily prescient and insightful. I wish I could claim to have had the foresight to recognize that the events of 1983 made military intervention more likely in Cameroon, but I did not. At most I can say that I have always maintained that a military coup was remotely possible but hardly probable and that I was surprised but not terribly shocked when I learned what was happening in Yaounde.

Now that matters in Cameroon have apparently resolved themselves in favor of President Biya, some preliminary reflections are safely in order. First, it is fair to assume that if Ahidjo had continued to play the role he had initially set out for himself when he turned power over to Biya—of acting as guarantor of the transition—the events of April 6–7 probably would not have happened. Though Ahidjo denied having had a hand in the uprising, he must still bear some responsibility for it because he permitted the military Pandora's box to be opened during the June 1983 plot. It now appears that Biya could not have closed it, short (perhaps) of shooting all the military plotters and purging official ranks of all Ahidjo sympathizers. Obviously, neither course was possible under the circumstances, and in any case Biya may have thought he could defuse continued northern resentment by granting executive clemency to Ahidjo, Major Oumarou, and Captain Salatou, all three of whom had been condemned to death by a military court on February 24, 1984.

Second, there is some irony in the April events: if Ahidjo bears indirect responsibility for the *coup manque* of April 6–7, he probably also deserves to be thanked for its failure. If he had not done such a good job of restraining the military all the years he was in power, of continually reminding it of its civic responsibilities, and (most crucially) of so organizing its command system and deployment so that no one local unit could mount independent action against him, the April 6–7 attempt might well have succeeded. A further irony is that the new presidential palace, much criticized for its cost and extravagant style, safely shielded President Biya in its concrete and steel bunkers during the very hours when the mutineers occupied its above-ground structures.

The future remains clouded. According to Amnesty International, some 120 people had already been executed by the end of September 1984, including the principal civilian and military conspirators of the

April putsch. Biya probably had little choice in the matter; he had to punish those who rose against him, or lose credibility in the government and the country. Ahidjo would have done no less and perhaps much more. There is also little question that the political air has been further poisoned by the April events and that the draconian scope of the new regime's punishments of the April conspirators will leave that air heavy with bitter memories for a long time to come. Here, without doubt, is the first critical test of Biya's leadership: he must continue to be firm, even just, and in any case must act not only to discourage further attempts on his regime, but be *seen* to be in full control of the situation. Unfortunately, perhaps, the country has no other model than Ahidjo by which to judge Biya's response, and he (Biya) will be expected at least to behave with Ahidjo's customary decisiveness and aplomb. At the same time, Biya must also act so as not to dash the hopes of those who saw in his presidency the possibility of a more liberal and enlightened exercise of power. Finally, Biya must cope with the uncertainties generated by the events of 1983 and 1984, not the least of which is the incalculable debt he incurred to his loyal military officers. It remains to be seen if they will be content to remain in their barracks or if they will now—or later—demand an active role in the government of the country. In the wake of April 6–7, Biya bestowed praise, medals, and promotions on his officers; he can only pray that that will satisfy them for now.

NOTES

1. My 1983 piece on Cameroon's presidential succession (Le Vine 1983) argued that the available evidence allowed the conclusion that Ahidjo had been carefully preparing for his departure for several years. Nothing that I have seen or heard since has persuaded me otherwise, including the argument that Ahidjo resigned primarily because of dire medical warnings about his health. That may have been sufficient reason, but it is certainly not the entire story. If Ahidjo blamed his doctors for "misleading" him, the charge sounds disingenuous at best; it is hardly surprising that he would feel better after stepping down, given the psychological release he must have experienced after relinquishing the extraordinary burdens of his office. Besides, he did smoke to excees, drank too much, exercised little, and was quite overweight. The combination of over 20 wearing years in power plus the visible evidence of his deteriorating physical condition was undoubtedly enough to persuade him of the wisdom of stepping down. The partial evidence that became available since suggests not only better health, but massive persuasion and pressure from his loyalists and northern friends, as well Biya's unexpectedly rapid mastery of the levers of power, as the main reasons for Ahidjo's attempt to reclaim his former job. It is possible, as some observers have argued, the Ahidjo intended all along to remain as Biya's *eminence grise,* manipulating the levers of power from his (Ahidjo's) position as the CNU's president. If so, Biya apparently refused to play along, leading Ahidjo to attempt to regain power by amending the Con-

stitution to make the party the supreme national decision maker. This theory becomes plausible, however, only if one assumes that (1) Biya initially agreed to the arrangement, (2) Ahidjo really had no intention of giving up power, and (3) Ahidjo was perfectly willing to undermine (fatally) the constitution and laws he had so carefully crafted during his long years in power. I find it all difficult to believe, if only because Ahidjo could easily have remained president, with all his authority intact, had he so chosen.

2. The rest of their definition of "regime" is as follows:

> This arrangement may be constitutional or it may be informal, as it is in personal systems. If informal, it is likely to change when rulers change in response to a new ruler's desires and aversions, interests and indifferences, strengths and weaknesses, and political formula—i.e., his ideas, procedures, and manner of ruling (p. 21).

Ahidjo's regime had obvious informal, that is, personalist, aspects, and if Jackson and Rosberg's definition is accepted, the Ahidjo–Biya transition was not only a leadership change, but one of regime as well.

3. The creation of Cameroon's first Council of Government in 1957 represents an important exception, as does the replacement of Prime Minister Jean-Marie Mbida by Ahidjo in 1958, the latter being the only instance before 1982 when an effective change in government was not also accompanied by important constitutional/institutional changes. Arguably, the Ahidjo–Mbida transition was also not a regime change; in all the other cases personnel changes occurred as an integral part of constitutional/institutional change or as a direct consequence thereof. To be sure, later in 1958, Cameroon received a revised *statut* from Paris, which changed it from a "state under trusteeship" (under the 1957 *statut*) to the autonomous "State of Cameroon"; this was specifically designated as an interim constitutional arrangement in view of an imminent grant of independence, which took place on January 1, 1960. None of the key political structures (e.g., the role of the high commissioner, prime minister, etc.) described in the 1958 law were changed from the 1957 *statut,* however.

4. One has only to read the relevant texts themselves to see the broad latitude given the high commissioners. Specifically, see *Decret du 4 mai 1945 Determinant les pouvoirs particuliers et temporaires des Hauts-commissaires de la Republique (J.O.C. 1946, p. 707); . . . Decret du 25 Octobre 1946 Portant creation d'une Assemblee representative au Cameroun (J.O.C. 1946, p. 1302); . . . Accord de Tutelle pour le Territoire du 6 fevrier 1952 (complete par la loi du 17 avril 1952) Relative a la formation des assemblees de groupe (J.O.C. 1956, pp. 188 and 937) . . .*

5. I have no intention here of elaborating on Mosca's theories. For a good discussion of the subject, see James H. Meisel, *The Myth of the Ruling Class: Gaetano Mosca and the "Elite."* (Ann Arbor, Michigan: University of Michigan Press, 1958).

6. The 1952–1957 Territorial Assembly officially had 18 members in its first (French national) college and 32 in its second (African) college. However,

three Frenchmen—Aujoulat, Martin, and Ninine—were elected to second college seats. Thus, the assembly in fact contained 29 Cameroonians and 21 Frenchmen.

7. I do not think I am being overly harsh on Cameroon's legislators. While it is true that the National Assembly can and does often amend the government's *projets de loi* and has even several times sent a proposed bill back to its ministerial drafters, I could not discover an instance in which it eventually failed to pass or substantially modified a law the government wished to have enacted. In 1981 I was informed by officials of the National Assembly that Ahidjo sometimes used it to test the mettle of his ministers, and at least on two occasions ministers who performed poorly during an assembly interpellation (which they cannot refuse) were dismissed shortly thereafter.

8. According to the rules, the party—through its Political Bureau—formally invests candidates to the National Assembly. Owona argues that because Ahidjo was still party president when the list for the May 29 elections was confirmed and as a consequence had a major hand in its selection, he could expect the new parliament to agree to a constitutional amendment that enshrined the supremacy of the party over the government. On May 9, 1983, the Political Bureau confirmed a list of 120 candidates, despite attempts by Biya to introduce multiple candidacies for each seat and to bring the number of deputies to 150 (for which ideas, apparently, Ahidjo took credit). The elections of May 29 returned 78 deputies to their old seats; 42 were new, and there were now 17 women, most of whom were also newly elected. During the new National Assembly's first sessions in June, Ahidjo apparently tried to get the parliament to accept his constitutional amendment on party supremacy but failed in the attempt (Owona 1983, pp. 82–84; *Afrique-Asie* 1983).

9. A semiofficial biography of Biya, published shortly after he became president (*Paul Biya ou l'incarnation de la rigueur*), identifies a number of his old friends, associates, and schoolmates who later rose to political prominence. The group includes Ayissi Mvodo (former minister of state for territorial administration), Tonye Mbog (former minister of agriculture, then labor), and Jean Mfulu (or Mfoulou, one of the authors of the biography and a professor at the University of Yaounde), all Biya's schoolmates at the seminaries of Akono and Edea; Pierre Semengue (Cameroon's armed forces chief of staff), who graduated with Biya in 1956 from Yaounde's Lycee Leclerc; and four who were his classmates in Paris at the Institute for Higher Overseas Studies (Institut des Hautes Etudes d'Outre-Mer), that is, Felix Sabal Lecco (ex-president of the Social and Economic Council and after July 7, 1984, ambassador to the Vatican), Joseph Zambo (Biya's second secretary-general at the presidency and later minister at the presidency for parliamentary liaison), Emile Mbarga (ex-secretary-general of the Economic and Social Council) and Happi Daniel Kemayou (a member of the powerful Bamileke Kemayou clan and former high court judge). Mention should also be made of Father Thomas Melone, who has known Biya since 1948 when the two were classmates at the Little Seminary of Edea and who also numbers among the president's closest friends. In 1983 Melone was a professor of comparative literature at the University of Paris Val de Marne (XII) and, at one time, an outspoken critic of the Ahidjo regime. It is not improbable, given the change in regime, that he might return to Cameroon and some role in Biya's leadership group.

10. General Oumaroudjam Yaya perhaps had yet another reason to be both grateful and loyal to Biya: before his poromotion to general, he had been Deputy Director of the secret police (CND) under Jean Fochive. I assume General Oumaroudjam's promotion took him beyond the reach of conspiratorial temptations and, fortunately, clear of the secret police before Fochive was himself compromised by the April 6 attempted coup.

3

ETHNICITY, REGIONALISM, AND POLITICAL POWER: A POST-MORTEM OF AHIDJO'S CAMEROON

Ndiva Kofele-Kale

Few African states have succeeded to the degree that Cameroon has in maintaining the stability and continuity of its polity for a protracted period after constitutional independence was granted. Fewer still have been successful in experimenting with various forms of political arrangements without upsetting the delicate patchwork of national unity. Yet Cameroon has in the last 23 years gone from a federal system (1961–1972) to a unitary form of government (post 1972) and from multiparty politics (1960–1966) to one-party dictatorship (1966). And these major changes to the basic structures of the system were effected, as Le Vine reminds us, without the polity getting scarred "by the all too common traumas afflicting its neighbors—civil war, coups d'etat, military dictatorship, brutal tyranny" (Le Vine 1980, p. 1).

Indeed, the words "peace" and "stability" have now become the central pillars of a state ideology in Cameroon. This was attested to in an interview with the government-owned *Cameroon Tribune* (February 23, 1980, p. 32) by S.T. Muna, speaker of the National Assembly who, when asked to comment on the country's greatest achievement since reunification, responded this way: "I would say right off—the formation of the C.N.U. [Cameroon National Union] party in September 1966 . . . Because

---

The paper is an abridged version of a much longer study: "Class, Status, and Power in Post-Reunification Cameroon: The Rise of an Anglophone Bourgeoisie, 1961–1980," prepared under the auspices of a National Endowment for the Humanities (NEH) faculty fellowship and soon to appear in *Studies in Power and Class in Africa,* Irving Leonard Markovitz, ed. I would like to express special thanks to Professor Martin Z. Njeuma of the University of Yaounde who read and commented on an earlier draft of this paper and to countless Cameroonians here and at home for their many helpful comments and suggestions.

the CNU has enabled us to build our country in unity, peace and political stability" (my emphasis). This same theme was articulated by the former president of the CNU, Ahmadou Ahidjo, in a general policy speech to the CNU at the Third Ordinary Congress in Bafoussam in 1980: "Judging from our achievement whose stock we will take, our progress as a whole speaks for itself. It is also indicative of encouraging perspectives and reflects the image we want to present to Africa and the World; *an image of a young nation assured of security and stability* . . ." (my emphasis).

To a certain extent the regime has been successful in promoting its version of Cameroonian reality both at home and abroad. (See *West Africa,* April 14, 1980, pp. 665–666; *West Africa,* May 5, 1980, pp. 786–787.)[1] Yet this rosy picture of uninterrupted postcolonial history characterized by political stability and peaceful change tends to conceal significant discontinuities and contradictions within the Cameroonian polity and to gloss over tensions of a potentially disruptive nature. More importantly, this obsession with "peace" and "stability" leaves unanswered the all important questions: stability for whom, at what price, and for whose benefit (cf. Markovitz 1977)? A major objective of this inquiry is to identify the major contradictions in postreunification Cameroon and to show how these contradictions have influenced the distribution of wealth, status, and power in the society. The focus is on Cameroon under Ahidjo's leadership, 1961–1980.

Current orthodoxy attempts to explain disparities in wealth, status, and power as rooted in primordial factors. Out of this thesis has emerged three images of Cameroonian society. One image shows a society cleaved along *ethnic/regional lines* the most prominent manifestation of which is the dichotomy between the North of Cameroon and the South (Azarya 1976; Beti 1977; Nelson et al. 1974; Prouzet 1974). A second image is that of a society divided along *religious lines* with a predominantly Muslim North opposed by a heavily dominated Christian South (Azarya 1976; Nelson et al. 1974; Prouzet 1974). In both of these images, the Muslim North, although fearful of the Christian South, is able to dominate the latter through the advantage it enjoys in numbers and its monopoly of the levers of power. The third image of Cameroonian reality is set against the backdrop of the *different colonial experiences* sectors of Cameroon underwent; the result, a Francophone–Anglophone contradiction, so explosive that it threatens to destroy 20 years of national unity (Benjamin 1972; Buo 1976; Kofele-Kale 1983; Nelson et al. 1974).[2] In fact, for some writers, the postreunification marriage between ex-British Cameroons and the former Cameroon Republic was a union of unequals with the seeds of its own eventual destruction imbedded into it from the moment of its birth (Benjamin 1972; Stark 1980). At issue is the widespread perception by Anglophones that the more dominant French-speaking sector wants to erase all remaining vestiges of the English-speaking "personality." Anglophones resent the hubris implied in the "frenchification" of Cameroon and are rankled by Francophone domination in every sphere of Cameroonian life. These cleavages are examined in greater detail in the pages that follow.

CLEAVAGES IN CAMEROONIAN SOCIETY

The North–South Split

Many students of contemporary Cameroon have fallen into the habit of bifurcating the country into two hostile geographical camps: a North fearful of southern infiltration and domination, and a South resentful of northern privileges and political hegemony (Azarya 1976; Bayart 1978b, p. 51; Nelson et al. 1974; Prouzet, 1974). According to one group of authors, this feeling of mutual distrust and antagonism between the North and South is deep seated: "Traditionally the Fulani have been almost universally resented by the southern groups, except perhaps for the Bamoun. The reasons for this animosity include a history of conflicts as well as religious and cultural differences. In recent years a major factor has been the belief among the southerners that Fulani leaders, by their control over their society, can produce monolithic support for political objectives" (Nelson et al. 1974, p. 159; see also Azarya 1976, pp. 40–44, 64–65). Following Nelson and Azarya, it is possible to identify three possible factors that have helped to reinforce the prevalent view of a North–South cleavage in Cameroon. These are the view of the North as (1) an ethnic/cultural and religious monolith, (2) the dominant political group, and (3) the group with privileged access to and control over a disproportionate share of the economic and political spoils.

Cameroon is noted for its bewildering cultural and ethnic heterogeneity. However, the North presents a contrasting view to this general pattern of ethnic diversity. Unlike the South where ethnic multiplicity is at its highest, the North appears, on the surface at least, to be an unusually homogeneous society united under one dominant ethnic congeries, the Fulbe. The truth of the matter is that the majority of northern peoples are *not* Fulbe, but the so-called pagan groups such as the Kirdi who make up roughly 75 percent of the total population of North Cameroon. This notwithstanding, the fact that these groups have been under Fulbe subjugation for over a century has led some writers to suggest that these dominated groups usually go along with their Fulbe overlords in their opposition to and fear of southern groups (Nelson et al. 1974, p. 159; Azarya 1976, pp. 64–65). In this respect the North is treated as one huge undifferentiated ethnic leviathan held together by collective distrust of the South.

But the North is far from being a homogeneous society. Its population is cleaved into a dominant Islamized Fulbe who number less than one third of the total population and the dominated "Kirdi" peoples, by far the majority in this region. This is a most significant division despite the tendency among some observers to underplay it. However, Willard Johnson, a keen observer of Cameroon politics, succeeds in driving home this point: "The cleavage in the northern society most threatening to the political stability of the state and most difficult to overcome is that which distinguishes the immigrant Fulbe and the mostly pagan (called 'Kirdi' by the Fulbe) communities which originally occupied the northern plains" (Johnson 1970a, p. 65). This cleavage aside, we also find that even among the Kirdi peoples great diversity exists—Mundang, Tupuri, Guisiga, Massa, Mbum, Duru, etc.—which belies the popular view of an ethnically homogeneous north.

The North accounts for approximately 30 percent of the Cameroon population and covers roughly one-third of the land space. It therefore enjoys an advantage in size that could easily be mistaken for political hegemony. But the case for northern political control goes beyond the issue of population size and area. Cameroon achieved independence in 1960 (and reunification in 1961) under the leadership of a northerner, Ahmadou Ahidjo, and a northern-based party, the Union Camerounaise (UC). Of equal significance in coming to grips with this issue of northern hegemony, is the fact that (1) the man Ahidjo replaced as prime minister on the eve of independence, Andre-Marie Mbida, was a southerner, and (2) the radical nationalist party—the Union des Populations du Cameroun (UPC)—which led the struggle for freedom and reunification and which was subsequently destroyed under Ahidjo's early rule, was predominantly a southern movement (Chaffard 1965, pp. 397–410). The UPC's top leadership—Um Nyobe, Moumie, Ouandie, Mayi Matip, Osende Afana—was in the main southern; and the party drew its strongest support from the southern region (Joseph 1977).

Although Ahidjo's UC was later to broaden its regional base and become the a nucleus for the national party, the Cameroon National Union (CNU), the view has continued to persist that the Cameroon government during the Ahidjo years was dominated by a northern/Fulbe-based political party. Azarya (1976, p. 50) observes that:

> When the UC became a national party, the Northern monopoly over top party positions was broken and some southerners were given important positions in the party and government. However, the real influence of southerners on central decision-making did not match their high official position. *The inner clique around Ahidjo, where the real political power was located, remained exclusively composed of oldtime friends of Ahidjo*

> *and founders of the UC in the North. These people were Muslim and most of them were Fulbe* (my emphasis).

Writing in a similar vein, Le Vine talks of a small inner circle of such northern Muslim Fulani party leaders as Moussa Yaya, Mohammane Lamine, Sanda Oumarou, and Sadou Daoudou who ran the country. In Le Vine's view, they were all "Ahidjo's men, they owed their positions to him and were schooled under his auspices in politics and in the uses of power. Of the group, probably the most important until recently was Moussa Yaya, whose rise in the party suggested to some observers that he was being groomed for one of the top government positions" (Le Vine 1971, p. 118).

The problem with this notion of an "inner circle" of northerners that ran the country is the failure to delimit the boundaries of this clique. Was it made up, for instance, of the members of the party's Central Committee or the Political Bureau? Did it include the senior government ministers (*ministres d'etat*)? What about the longest surviving members of Ahidjo's cabinet, were they also included? The lack of consensus as to the criteria for inclusion into the inner circle means that determination of its composition will vary with the observer. Frequently mentioned as members of this inner circle are cabinet ministers who had served in one position or another without interruption since the early 1960s; those occupants of such strategic ministries as the armed forces, territorial administration, education, and foreign affairs; the senior ministers (*ministres d'etat*); and the top leaders of the national party. But can be identifiable *northern* clique emerge from these various levels of decision making? Not quite. In what amounts to a major reversal of his earlier position, Le Vine recently pointed out that Ahidjo "may in fact [have controlled] the system through some sort of 'northern mafia'; *but the composition of his governments and party central committees belied that charge*" (Le Vine 1980, p. 3, my emphasis). The evidence to back up Le Vine's position is quite convincing. I have examined the composition of President Ahidjo's cabinet on the eve of the unitary state and the one appointed shortly after May 1972. Of the 19-member preunitary cabinet only 3 were northerners and in the immediate postunitary cabinet of 29 ministers and vice-ministers, 6 or 20 percent of the cabinet positions were held by people from the North. Northerners were by far a minority in the preunitary federal cabinet, outnumbered by the South Central region with seven cabinet positions and the West with four. Only the Littoral with two posts and the East with no representative held fewer if any cabinet positions in 1969 than the North. The same pattern of distribution was carried over into the 1973 cabinet: North and West each held six portfolios, the East one, the Littoral one, while Anglophone Cameroon claimed seven and the South-Central region eight positions; the last two regions accounting for almost one-half the entire cabinet.

An examination of the regional origin of the 31-member cabinet appointed in 1975 showed that, of the nine ministers who had been in the cabinet eight or more years, only one was from the North (Sadou Daoudou) while five came from the South (Biya, Ayissi Mvodo, Tsanga, Kamga, and Onana Awana). Of the five who had been cabinet ministers 16 years or more, again only one was a northerner. It is true that the key ministry of Armed Forces, which had always been held by a northerner (Sadou Daoudou, 1960–1979, and Maikano Abdoulaye, 1979–1983), did not change hands, but the equally important portfolio of Territorial Administration has remained in southern hands since 1960 (first Enoch Kwayeb, then Ayissi Mvodo, and now Fouman Akame). The four *senior* ministers in the 1978 cabinet, all of whom had held office for at least a decade, included one northerner. Turning attention to the key decision-making organs of the Cameroon National Union, that is, the Central Committee and the National Political Bureau, their composition belied the charge of northern dominance. Of the 42 elected members (1973–1980) only 10 (24 percent) were from the North. If representation was based on proportion of population, then the North would have been entitled to 12 members in the Central Committee. In the National Political Bureau the combined southern representation was 75 percent of the total membership. In addition, the second most influential leadership position after the national president (Ahidjo)—the political secretary—was held by a southerner (Ayissi Mvodo and subsequently Sabal Lecco); so too were the four vice-presidents (in 1980 Foncha, Biya, Tsoungui and Kwayeb).

It is obvious from the preceding discussion that the charge against a northern mafia/clique that dominated the political life of Cameroon during the first republic has been slightly overdrawn. Southerners as much as northerners were intimately involved in the running of the system.

Other factors that have reinforced the North–South cleavage are widespread perceptions held by southerners that northerners are unfairly favored in terms of access to positions of prestige and power. Usually cited are the advantages northerners enjoy in terms of recruitment into the senior cadres of the civil service, the granting of scholarships for secondary and university studies, and access to bank loans on very liberal credit terms (Schissel 1983). For example, decree number 66-436 of December 20, 1966, which outlines the criteria for recruitment into the public service, differentiates two lists of candidates who are successful in the examinations for entry into civil service categories B, C, and D. Candidates from list A are those from educationally backward regions—"*originaires des regions insuffisamment scolarisees*"—while list B is comprised of candidates from the rest of the country. In practice this distinction, as Prouzet points out, tends to favor candidates from the North who are recruited under less stringent conditions and criteria in contrast to their colleagues from the South (Prouzet 1974, p. 120). A similar policy obtains with the granting of scholarships for study at the University of Yaounde and recruitment into the Joint Forces Military Academy (EMIAC) and into the National School of Administration and Magistracy (ENAM), training ground for the nation's bureaucratic bourgeoisie and popularly referred to as *l'ecole du Nord* to indicate northern domination:

> In the first place, a special preparatory cycle for the entrance examination is set up only for candidates "coming from insufficiently educated regions." In addition, although a secondary school degree [*baccalaureat*] is required in principle for admission to this school, candidates from these regions can enter on the basis of [lower degrees]: the BEPC, the elementary school certificate, or the *capacite en droit,* according to their geographic origins. Policies governing the distribution of fellowships are also based on the same considerations. In the educated regions of the country, a student will receive a full scholarship only if the secondary school degree was received before age 18, whereas students from under-educated regions have till age 23 to pass the *baccalaureat* in order to obtain the same financial aid (Prouzet 1974, pp. 120–121, editors' translation).

The admirable objective behind this policy of affirmative action, which was to close the chasm separating North and South in terms of socioeconomic development, should be noted. However, this factor does not appear to have struck a sympathetic chord among the equally deprived southern masses who are just as in need of these opportunities as their northern compatriots.

The fact of the matter is that the northern population has always lagged behind the South in the acquisition of education and professional skills. In 1970, for instance, school enrollments averaged 64 percent nationwide, 94 percent for the South-Central, 83 percent for the Littoral, 80 percent for the West, and only 22 percent for the North (Clignet 1976, p. 31). Six years later, the relative position of the North in the area of school enrollment had hardly changed. The 1976 census reports a 9 percent increase in school enrollment for 6 to 14 year olds in the North, up from 22 to 30.9 percent. And although the North comprises 29 percent of the population, only 4 percent of all secondary school pupils were from this region (Azarya 1976, p. 52). The gross disparities in educational benefits between the North and South aside, the North has also trailed the South in terms of representation among the higher and middle ranking administrative personnel where recruitment has always depended on the possession of superior educational or technical and professional skills.

These positions were usually monopolized by the better educated southerners. In 1961 only 3 percent of these positions were occupied by nationals from the North (Binet 1961, p. 23; Azarya 1976, p. 51). Azarya found not a single judge nor a secondary school principal of northern origin in 1971 (p. 51). Not much has changed since then. Of the nine titular and substitute judges of the Supreme Court in 1978, not one was from the North. And of the entire phalanx of top judicial officers in the country (titular and substitute judges of the supreme court, high court judges, chief magistrates, and the various *procureurs generaux* and their deputies) only two were of northern origin (EDIAFRIC 1977b, pp. xxiii–xxvii). To bridge the gap between the North and South, the former was "systematically advantaged in the allocation of financial resources by the government; *this was openly admitted and justified as giving priority to the development of the least developed parts of the country*" (Azarya 1976, p. 51, emphasis added).

The Christian–Muslim Division

Another variant of the North–South contradiction is expressed in the form of a so-called religious division between a predominantly Christian South and an Islamized North. One writer claims that: "A certain amount of unease existed in the early 1970s between the Muslim President and the Roman Catholic Church, in part because of different concepts of the duty and powers of the state over the individual but *primarily because of the coincidental association of Christianity with the Southern peoples. Southern Roman Catholics were particularly strong among the ethnic groups most hostile to northerners*" (Nelson et al. 1974, p. 164, emphasis added). Much has been made of the fact that it was a Muslim leader and a northern-based party that replaced Mbida (who was a staunch Catholic and an ex-seminarian) in 1959, and that this same leadership was responsible for the brutal suppression of the radical nationalist movement whose preeminent leader, Um Nyobe, was a southerner and a Christian to boot (Prouzet 1974, p. 109; Bayart 1978b, pp. 54–55). Additional evidence to support the Christian–Muslim division thesis consists of an ad nauseum recitation of instances where the Christian Church has clashed with the State, for example, the deportation in 1962 of the editor of the Catholic newspaper *La Semaine Camerounaise* for publishing a story that the government found particularly offensive (Prouzet 1974, pp. 107–108; Bayart 1978b, p. 63; Le Vine 1971, pp. 129–130) and the Ndongmo affair (Le Vine 1971, pp. 130–132; Beti 1977) where the Catholic Bishop of Nkongsamba was tried and sentenced to life imprisonment (later commuted) for subversive activities.

Historically Christian missionary penetration was confined to the southern regions of Cameroon while Muslim influences swept most of the north (Horner 1956). This in part explains why, numerically, more Christians are found in the south and conversely more Muslims are in the North. But despite the fact that both Islamic and Christian proselytization has been going on for over a century, the Cameroonian population is still overwhelmingly animist. Most estimates put the number of Christians at around 2 million and Muslims anywhere from 700,000 to 1 million[3] in a total population of over 7 million. When appropriate allowance is made for nominal as opposed to practicing converts, the number of Christians and Muslims is likely to drop appreciably. Give the fact that about 65 percent of the population propitiates their deity outside the framework of the main religious denominations, it would seem that the Christian–Muslim division is overdrawn, to say the least.

What we find instead is that Cameroon is neither a religiously homogeneous society nor a highly fragmented one. Of the several religions practiced, no one appears to dominate. Furthermore, the membership of the major foreign religions cuts across several ethnic lines. Thus, it is safe to conclude that religion in Cameroon is not in Crawford Young's (1976, p. 21) words a "primary basis of politically relevant collective identity." Religion has yet to produce the phenomenon of Islamic brotherhoods that one finds in Senegal (Behrman 1970; Cruise O'Brien 1971) and Nigeria (Paden 1973). Nor has it provoked the kind of intense political rivalry among political groups that one finds in, say, India (Young 1976) or Lebanon (Hudson 1968; Binder 1966) or Uganda (Lockard 1980; Young 1976).

An examination of the religious affiliation of key members of the party and government will indicate a reasonable balance between Christians and Muslims. Ahidjo is a Muslim while his prime minister, Biya, who succeeded him as president in 1982, is a Catholic. Roughly 75 percent of the members of the CNU Political Bureau are Christians and only 25 percent of the Central Committee members are Muslims. All the party vice-presidents are Christians. As Prouzet points out:

> certain politicians never hid their Christian origins. A case in point is Andre Fouda, mayor of Yaounde, former minister, and member of the UNC Political Bureau, who is a practicing Catholic. Another case is Eteki Mboumoua, National Education Minister from 1961 to 1968, [former] Secretary General of the OAU, considered to have been too favorable toward religious schools; another is Public Health Minister Bernard Fonlon, also criticized for taking too lenient positions toward health institutions of the churches (Prouzet 1974, p. 106, editors' translation).

Not only was the government and party heavily saturated with Christians but of the type who made no pretense about their faith. Yet they were able to interact and work closely with their Muslim colleagues without any overt signs of hostility.

It is true that the church establishment, especially the very powerful Catholic hierarchy and the central government, has had a number of clashes over the years, provoked in part by the regime's view of the church establishment as a potential opposition capable of attracting a sizeable following. In a country where the one party dominates, such opposition can hardly be looked on too kindly by party leaders, be they Muslims or Christians. Again, tensions between the Church and State have erupted over differing interpretations of the central government's role in the promotion and protection of the fundamental human rights of the Cameroonian citizens guaranteed in the Constitution. The Ahidjo regime was notorious for its disregard of these basic rights (Prouzet 1974, pp. 142–146, 260–262, 270–271, and 278–299; U.S. State Department 1981, pp. 36–41; Derrick 1983, pp. 2273–2274; Bayart 1978b, p. 63). These institutional conflicts have, however, not risen to the level of violent and protracted church–state confrontations such as we have witnessed in Poland and Iran under the Shah.

The Francophone–Anglophone Contradiction

Cameroon entered its postcolonial phase with the distinction of being a rare African state (after Morocco and Somalia) to have included within its borders two territories that had undergone different colonial experiences. But what was to become the country's best known characteristic turned out, some would argue, to be its most enduring contradiction. I am referring here to the post-World War I partition of the German colony of Kamerun into British and French mandates under the League of Nations, and then after World War II as part of the UN trusteeship system. The legacy of this split is found contemporaneously in the persistence of French language in one sector of Cameroon and English in another. History aside, the Anglophone–Francophone dichotomy has been reinforced by several other factors. The first is size. A quick glance at a map will reveal that the two sectors are unevenly balanced. The Anglophone sector covers only 9 percent of the total area and supports about 21 percent of the total population (see Table 3.1). By way of contrast, Francophone Cameroon enjoys a 4 to 1 population advantage and a 10 to 1 advantage in size over the Anglophone sector. The differences in size offer only partial explanation for the Francophone–Anglophone dichotomy and the popular view of Francophone hegemony.

The origins of this perception go back to the very nature of reunification itself, that is, the negotiations leading to it and the eventual outcome. To begin with, when the two Cameroons reunited in October 1961, one of

Table 3.1. Population Breakdown by Region

Region	*Population*	*Percentage*	*Area (km²)*	*Percentage*
West Cameroon	1,495,272	21	42,210	9
North	2,089,791	29	164,050	35
South Central	1,393,608	20	115,940	25
West	968,856	13.5	13,890	3
Littoral	841,456	12	20,220	4
East	342,850	5	108,900	23
TOTAL	7,131,833		465,210	

Source: Cameroon Ministry of Economic Affairs and Planning *1976 Census.*

the contracting parties, the Cameroon Republic, was already an independent sovereign state. On the other hand, the British Trust Territory of Southern Cameroons was, by the terms of the UN plebescite, to have achieved its independence by *joining* the sovereign Cameroon Republic. The following statement by the leader of the Francophone delegation, Mr. Ahidjo, is quite revealing: "The Cameroon Republic and the territory previously under British trusteeship constituted a single historic unit. . . . But on the other hand, they were two distinct political entities: on one side, an *independent sovereign state possessing an international legal personality*; on the other, a territory *without a political international status*" (Ahidjo 1964, p. 23, my emphasis). In the negotiations for union, the representatives of the Cameroon Republic were to capitalize on this technicality, insisting all along that due recognition be given to their status as senior partners (Stark 1980). They did succeed in forcing through this point with the result that the Francophones were able to dictate the terms for federation, which proved to be quite advantageous to them (Benjamin 1972). One of the consequences of the apparent inequality in bargaining power was the fact that the Francophone sector made fewer institutional adjustments in entering the federation. For instance, throughout the federalist phase, 1961–1972, a low degree of differentiation was evident between the federal and east (Francophone) state organs. The federal and eastern capital was one and the same—Yaounde—and their respective institutions were essentially one "in origin as well as in function" (Ardener 1967, pp. 289–290). It was often difficult to tell in many instances where the eastern state jurisdiction left off and where that of the federal government began. The lines were quite blurred, and this only reinforced Anglophone perception of Francophone domination.

Reunification, for the Anglophone sector, has remained a dominant fact of life requiring greater adjustments (Ardener 1967, p. 290; Ndongko 1976, p. 98; *West Africa* 1966: 371). Edwin Ardener, who has monitored the political pulse of Anglophone Cameroon longer than most, has correctly observed that the story of the first few years of reunification was "one of various attempts to link West Cameroon in some effective way to its partner, and of the gradual discovery of new ways of doing this by the East" (Ardener 1967, p. 290). This was not a particularly smooth transition, and there were quite a few bumps on the way. Under the best of conditions the process of consolidating national boundaries and state power is frequently accompanied by tensions. In Cameroon where 40 years of different colonial experiences had to be taken into the calculus for change, these routine tensions that are a necessary part of nation-building were magnified several-fold. We can begin to trace the origins of the widespread perception of a postreunification Cameroon under Francophone hegemony to this period of adjustment and acquaintanceship. Writing in 1967, *West Africa's* itinerant correspondent for Francophone Africa made the following observations about Anglophone attitudes toward the federation. Said he:

> Though in the long run the advantages could well outweigh the disadvantages, right now West Cameroonians tend to feel they are getting a raw deal. The influence of the French-speaking East is now, for the first time, really being felt: not only are Yaounde's powers considerable, but prices have risen considerably; French and Common Market goods are replacing the familiar British or Nigerian goods; the power of East Cameroon is being felt. Good or bad, *if West Cameroonians were today given the choice, they might well choose independence—from Nigeria and the French-speaking east*" (*West Africa,* July 8, 1967, p. 880 in Le Vine 1971, p. 102, emphasis added).

What could have caused Anglophones, who so enthusiastically and overwhelmingly elected to rejoin their Francophone kith and kin, to begin to entertain grave doubts about the federation barely six years after it was consummated?

Anglophone complaints about the federation as well as other postreunification arrangements can be broken down into three areas. The first is *economic.* Anglophones point to the economic underdevelopment of their region and argue that it has become relatively more backward than when it first joined the federation in 1961. This view is properly captured in the following statement made in 1976 by an Anglophone Cameroonian. According to him, the region is

> . . . worse today than it was before reunification in 1961 or even during the federal period. Economic and political programs have been transfer-

> red from the regions to Yaounde, the political capital, and Douala, the economic capital . . . [the] once bustling and prosperous Anglophone cities such as Tiko, Victoria, Buea, and Kumba have virtually become ghost towns, while the Francophone areas such as Douala, Yaounde, and the Northern region, particularly the President's hometown of Garoua, are booming (Buo 1976, p. 18).

Eight years later a nonpartisan observer would echo this same refrain. Writing recently for the London publication *West Africa,* which enjoys a wide readership in Cameroon, Joseph Komla Naweri observed that:

> Whilst it is conceded that the last 25 years have seen some noteworthy development projects in Cameroon, it is altogether another question as to whether such development as has taken place is balanced in any sense. Everyone knows, for example, that certain areas of North Cameroon have excellent roads but without the motor vehicle traffic that would justify those roads, whereas certain areas of South Cameroon with very dense motor vehicle traffic have had to make do with very bad roads. Ironically, certain areas are actually less developed today, 25 years after independence, than they were at the close of the colonial period. Nowhere is this more glaring than in the anglophone South-West Province; in 1960 for example, certain stretches of roads in and around the main towns of Victoria, Buea, Tiko, Kumba and Mamfe were tarred, all of these towns had credible water supply systems, Buea with a sparkling golf course and Victoria with impeccable Botanical Gardens (1983, p. 2558).

Indeed, the relative underdevelopment of Anglophone Cameroon is a reality few people have bothered to contest. It is worth noting, however, and as the Cameroonian economist, Ndongko (1980), has ably demonstrated, that the problem of economic deprivation is not unique to this region. It is one shared by several other regions in the country. Table 3.2, which summarizes the most pertinent economic data for the former six regions of the Republic, shows that two regions, North and East, join Anglophone Cameroon in forming a triad of the most economically underdeveloped regions in the country. Having said this, it is again worth pointing out that in comparison to the North, the Anglophone region comes out considerably more advanced economically. This is not to suggest that Anglophone complaints about the relative backwardness of their region should be brushed aside especially when we take into account the fact that this region is the nation's breadbasket and the source of its considerable oil wealth. I only wish to signal the fact that this problem cannot be explained in isolation but can be better understood when viewed within the context

Table 3.2. The Regional Structure of Cameroon, 1970

	East	*West*	*North*	*Littoral*	*South Central*	*Former West Cameroon*
Area (km^2)	109,000	14,000	153,589	21,000	118,000	42,400
Population (1969)	288,000	800,000	1,400,000	680,000	1,170,000	1,250,000
Rural population (%)	90	80	92	32	70	90
Population growth rate (%)	2.0	1.5	1.3	4.5	2.0	2.3
Population density (km^2)	2.6	56.0	9.7	30.0	23.0	28.0
Education						
Primary school attendance (%)	63	80	27	81.2	88.8	57
% of population in school (%)	n.a.	45	20	n.a.	n.a.	14
The labor force	n.a.	310,000	n.a.	300,000	632,000	600,000
Number of wage earners	n.a.	16,000	n.a.	60,000	73,000	33,000
Health						
Number of persons per doctor	28,000	29,000	83,000	n.a.	14,500	40,000
Main products						
Coffee (tons)	6,297	32,600	260	27,380	5,406	11,430
Cocoa (tons)	7,500	n.a.	n.a.	3,368	94,200	8,000
Cotton (tons)	—	—	68,000	—	—	—
Bananas (tons)	—	—	—	28,000	350	61,036
Groundnuts (tons)	7,200	16,000	53,000	—	19,988	—
Maize (tons)	18,000	112,000	26,000	—	28,000	—
Plantains (tons)	153,000	73,000	—	200,000	273,000	n.a.
Manioc (tons)	111,700	—	119,000	92,000	180,390	—
Yams (tons)	—	18,000	—	26,000	12,000	n.a.
Sweet potatoes (tons)	560	47,000	35,000	—	5,000	20,000
Palm oil (tons)	—	n.a.	—	9,700	10,000	17,215

Source: Data compiled from Cameroon, Ministry of Information and Tourism 1970; *Elaboration de IIIe Plan Quinquennal 1971–76, Regional Synthesis*, November, 1960; *Third Five Year Economic & Social Development Plan:* 1971/72–1975/76—*The Regions,* Yaounde, June, 1972; and Ndongko, 1980.

of inequalities *among* and *within* the six regions in the country;[4] not in manichean terms as a distinction between a developed Francophone and an underdeveloped Anglophone Cameroon.

The fear of "gallicizing" everything that has gone into the molding of a separate and distinct Anglophone persona constitutes the second set of complaints leveled by this group against an insensitive Francophone-dominated (so it is perceived) regime. Having agreed to join in a *bilingual* union in which inherited colonial differences in language and institutions were to be respected and creatively integrated into a new collective national experience, Anglophones instead found themselves buried under the weight of the dominant French way of life. To them the reality of two decades of reunification has been the marked preference for French-styled institutions—administration, police, army, university, etc.—over their British-styled equivalents. Such was the case under the federal system, and this has continued to be the case in the subsequent unitary phase of postreunification history (Chumbow 1980, p. 298). They have watched with consternation the decline of the use of English in a country where English and French are the *constitutionally* designated official languages. Yet, for many Anglophones this basic document only paid lip service to the concept of bilingualism. For instance, during the first decade of reunification, the Constitution contained a glaring contradiction; on the one hand, it prescribed French and English as the country's official languages (Article 1:4) only to allow, on the other hand, until the provision was eventually dropped, that the French text was the authentic one (Article 44 of the 1972 Constitution)!

This perceived deliberate reduction of the importance of English cut deeply into the collective Anglophone ego. For to them language loyalty, as Chumbow (1980, p. 299) points out, has taken on the same significance as nationalism does for nationality. That is, a state of mind, following Weinreich (1953, p. 99 in Chumbow 1980, p. 299) in "which the language (like nationality) assumes a high position in a scale of values, a position in need of being defended" (Chumbow 1980, p. 299). Although French and English *theoretically* enjoy equal status as official languages in Cameroon, Chumbow has persuasively argued that with only one-fourth of the country's population, the Anglophone sector entered the union "from the onset [with] the scale naturally tilted in favour of French ascendancy" (p. 298). As a result, the trend toward bilingualism has tended to be

> unidirectional in that, . . . by far more anglophone conceded efforts and effectively achieved a respectable degree of bilingualism than francophones. This obviously retrogressive ascendancy of French over English as a result of the population factor . . . and in part to the "frenchification" effect of the French colonial policy which presented the French

> language to all its colonies as the language of civilization "par excellence." Since French has a *de facto* popularity and superiority (despite a *de jure* equality with English), francophones have a less natural urge or stimulus towards acquiring English (Chumbow, p. 298).

Strong support for Chumbow's argument comes from one who can hardly be accused of antigovernment bias, Dr. Solomon Nfor Gwei, who had served briefly as secretary-general in the faculty of arts and letters of the University of Yaounde and who since 1978 has been the vice-minister of agriculture. His 1974 study, based on extensive personal interviews with administrators, faculty (mostly Cameroonians, some of whom were products of the University of Yaounde) and students who were then enrolled at the university, conclusively demonstrated the inherent asymmetry in Cameroon's bilingual policy with respect to the University of Yaounde (Gwei 1975, pp. 435–447). Gwei found that in this citadel of higher education, Anglophone students averaged a pitiful 6 percent of the total student population over a ten year period, that is, 1964–1974 (Gwei 1975, p. 444). Anglophone students were not only outnumbered by their Francophone cohorts in the university as a whole, but in some faculties and specialized institutes, that is, the *grandes ecoles,* there were hardly any Anglophone students matriculating (Gwei 1975, p. 446). The problem of Anglophone student underenrollment was paralleled in the teaching and administrative staff (Gwei 1975, p. 436). Anglophone faculty personnel were then and continue now to be grossly outnumbered by Francophones while the administrative support services (clerical and secretarial staff) have always been inadequate. Gwei's study points out that:

> Because the English-speaking students form a tiny minority, the language of instruction, the teaching methods, the educational programmes, the examination system and the social atmosphere at the University do not tend to favor them but rather the French-speaking majority. That they are often ignored is obvious from the fact that the University calendar, publications, notices, etc. hardly ever appear in English (Gwei 1975, p. 447).

And with prophetic vision, Gwei warned that "unless steps are taken to protect the interest of the minority, the tendency is often to ignore them and their own interests and aspirations. The reaction of members of the minority groups to problems which weigh heavily on them would be either one of submission or protest!" (Gwei 1975, pp. 446–447). Over the years Anglophone students at the University of Yaounde have steadfastly refused to submit to the status quo. They have instead dared to express their dissatisfaction with the monolingual trend in the country as a whole in several celebrated bloody skirmishes with government forces. One occurred in 1983 when Anglophone students took to the streets to protest the former minister of national education's ill-advised and poorly thought out move to force-feed them French. The *casus belli*—if one may so call it—was a series of recently instituted reforms in the Cameroon General Certificate of Education, one of which required French as a compulsory subject even though English was not required as a compulsory subject for the *baccalaureat* for Francophone students (*Cameroon Tribune,* English edition, November 16, 23, and 30, 1983). "The publication of this Order," according to one observer, "sparked off an anglophone students' boycott of classes and demonstrations repressed by police brutality at Yaounde University and throughout the anglophone provinces of Buea, Kumba and Bamenda. The situation did not calm down until 11 days later when President Biya issued a statement calling on the students to return to classes and announcing the setting up of a Commission of qualified and experienced persons of both anglophone and francophone backgrounds to go into the students' grievances" (*West Africa* 1984, p. 202; see also *Cameroon Tribune,* English edition, December 7, 1983, p. 3 and *Cameroon Post,* December 1, 1983, pp. 3–4).

The third set of complaints voiced by Anglophone Cameroonians is political in nature. This is usually presented in two forms: (1) the loss of regional autonomy and hence control over their own state followed by the relegation of Anglophone leaders to inferior roles in the national decision-making councils, and (2) their numerical underrepresentation in the two branches of government concerned with policymaking (the party and the executive) as well as in the higher echelons of the bureaucracy. Sammy Kum Buo put forward the case for Anglophone Cameroon quite forcefully: ". . . since reunification . . . Anglophones have never constituted more than one-fourth of the cabinet and no Anglophone has ever held the powerful portfolios of defense, finance, foreign affairs, territorial administration or education. And of the country's eighteen ambassadors serving abroad, only two, Ambassadors Epie and Kisob in Canada and Liberia, respectively, are English-speakers" (1976, p. 18; see also Kofele-Kale 1983, pp. 2871–2872). During the federalist phase, when the country was divided into six administrative regions each under a federal inspector of administration, at no time was any one of these proconsuls an Anglophone. Following the dismantling of the federal inspectorate system and the introduction of provinces headed by governors, only one of the two provinces in the Anglophone sector was headed by a governor native to the region. He was also the only governor out of a total of seven.[5] During the early years of reunification, all the secretaries-general (that is, permanent secretaries) in the ministries were Francophone. Only in the last eight years have Anglophones been appointed to these positions—

and the number has never been greater than 2 (less than 10 percent)—out of a total of 24 as of 1978.

To take another example, of the ten major financial institutions,[6] that is, six commercial banks and four development banks (in which the Cameroon government held shares as of 1980), only *one,* Cameroon Bank Ltd., was headed by an Anglophone; and of the country's 14 principal development organizations,[7] only the Cameroon Development Corporation (CDC), principally located in Anglophone Cameroon since 1948, is headed by an indigene. Clearly the case for Anglophone underrepresentation in the middle and higher ranking levels of the administration as well as in the important party and executive policy-making bodies is strong; that is, if we persist in treating the Francophone sector as a monolith. As we have already indicated, for the purposes of this analysis, the country will be viewed as consisting of six regions the boundaries of which coincide with those of the former federal inspectorates. This approach forces us to avoid the parochialism implicit in Anglophone insistence on seeing their region as special and their problems as unique. By adopting the comparative regional approach, we are able to situate the Anglophone predicament in its national context while allowing for comparisons to be made not between Anglophones and Francophones but among the six regions. The portrait that emerges from this exercise shows a significant number, relatively speaking, of Anglophone representatives in all levels of policy making and execution, that is, in positions of real power as well as those with high visibility and prestige but of little political consequence.

Deputies in the National Assembly

Deputies in the National Assembly are positions with more prestige than political power (Etonga 1980; Bayart 1980a; Le Vine 1980). Anglophone representation in the 120 member (enlarged to 150 in 1983) assembly has always been 24 or 20 percent, roughly the proportion of Anglophones in the total population (21 percent). As Table 3.3 shows, of the six regions only the Littoral was underrepresented relative to its share of the total population. Among the chairmanships of the five parliamentary committees where most work on legislation takes place, at no time was at least one committee not chaired by an Anglophone. Between 1973–1980 the Committee on Production, Urbanization, Construction and Rural Exchange was under the chairmanship of Dr. E.M.L. Endeley while two other Anglophones served as vice-chairpersons, respectively, of the Committee on Constitutional Laws (Foretia) and the Committee on Education and Social Affairs (Gwen Burnley). Other committees and their respective chairmen in 1980 were: Foreign Affairs, Andre Fouda (South-Central); Finance, Economic Affairs, Planning and Infrastructure,

Malouma Raymond (East); Education, Information, Cultural and Social Affairs, Naoue 1973–1978, Poufong 1978– (West); and Constitutional Laws, Justice, Legislation, Rules and Armed Forces, Moussa Yaya (North). And of course, Speaker of the House Solomon Tandeng Muna was and still is an Anglophone.

Table 3.3. Distribution of Deputies in the National Assembly by Region, 1973–1980

Region	*Number of Deputies*	*Percentage*	*As a Proportion of Total Population*
North	36	30	35
West Cameroon	24	20	25
South Central	23	19	24
West	21	17.5	16
Littoral	10	8.5	14
East	6	5	6
TOTAL	120	100.0	120

Policy-making Bodies of the National Party

The policy-making bodies of the national party are the Central Committee and the National Political Bureau. Cameroon being a one-party state, these party councils play a crucial role in the formulation of national policy (see *CNU Militants' Guide* 1976, pp. 17–23). Membership in either or both of these organs could be viewed as an index of the politically powerful personalities in the country. Anglophone representation in both the Central Committee and National Political Bureau remained quite strong under Ahidjo as Tables 3.4 and 3.5 indicate. In the former body, Anglophones held 8 of the 42 elected positions and were tied with the North in having the largest number of representatives—three each—in the 12 member National Political Bureau.

The Powerful and Prestigious Positions

The powerful and prestigious positions are in the executive branch of government where a good deal of policy making and execution take place. These positions include the national executives, the regional executives, and the judiciary.

Table 3.4. Distribution of Seats in the Central Committee of the CNU by Regions (Elected Members), 1973–1980

Region	*Number of Members*	*Percentage*
North	10	23.8
West Cameroon	8	19.0
South Central	10	23.8
West	8	19.0
Littoral	3	7.0
East	3	7.0
TOTAL	42	100.0

Table 3.5. Distribution of Members of the National Political Bureau of the CNU by Regions, 1973–1978

Region	*Number of Members*	*Percentage*
North	3	25
West Cameroon	3	25
South Central	2	16.5
West	2	16.5
Littoral	1	8.5
East	1	8.5
TOTAL	12	100.0

The national executives are the ministers and vice-ministers. The 1968 cabinet contained two Anglophone full ministers and one Anglophone vice-minister for a total representation of roughly 16 percent. The North had three representatives in this cabinet, the West four, the South-Central seven, the Littoral two, and the East had no representatives (note that Speaker of the Federal House Marigoh Mboua and Secretary-General Doumba were both from the East). In the enlarged 29-member cabinet appointed shortly after the unitary state was declared in 1972, Anglophone representation improved from a sixth to a quarter (from three to seven cabinet members) and the percentage of northern representation also increased to a fifth (six members). Although the

South-Central continued to enjoy a lead in absolute numbers (eight members), its proportion of cabinet posts dropped from a 1968 high of over a third to about a quarter. Such too was the case with the West, which increased its absolute share in numbers from four to six but held on to the same proportion of cabinet positions. The obvious loser was the Littoral whose share dropped from a tenth (two members) to a thirtieth (one member) between 1968 and 1972. The biggest improvement was in the East, which for the first time received one cabinet position. In the 1975–1980 cabinet, which was now headed by a prime minister, Anglophone representation was the *second* highest, outnumbered only by the share of portfolios held by representatives from the South-Central region (see Table 3.6). Of 31 ministers and vice-ministers, the Anglophones held seven or nearly a quarter of the total. Among the four senior ministers (*ministres d'etat*), one was an Anglophone—E.T. Egbe, minister of state for posts and telecommunications—who, until he was cashiered from the cabinet in 1984, had the distinction of being one of the very few ministers to have held on to a cabinet position without interruption for over 20 years! The same proportions held roughly in the cabinet of the Biya consolidation of 1984 after the attempted coup, except for some increases in the South-Central and Littoral representations (from a sixth to a fifth, and a twelfth to a tenth, respectively (see Table 3.7).

Table 3.6. Distribution of Ministers and Vice-Ministers by Region in the 1968, 1972, and 1975 Cabinets

	1968		*1972*		*1975*	
Region	*Number*	*Percentage*	*Number*	*Percentage*	*Number*	*Percentage*
North	3	15.8	6	20.7	6	19.5
West Cameroon	3	15.8	7	24.2	7	22.5
South Central	7	37.0	8	27.6	8	25.8
West	4	21.0	6	20.7	5	16.2
Littoral	2	10.5	1	3.4	3	9.6
East	0	0	1	3.4	2	6.4
TOTAL	19	100	29	100	31	100

Table 3.7. Distribution of Ministers and Vice-Ministers by Region in the 1984 Cabinet

Region	*Number*	*Percentage*
North[a]	7	18.0
West Cameroon[b]	8	20.5
South Central[c]	8	20.5
West	9	23.0
Littoral	4	10.3
East	3	7.7
TOTAL	39	100.0

Note: There have been six cabinet changes between November 6, 1982, and July 16, 1984. This table reflects the cabinet as of January 1985.

[a]The old North province has now been carved up into three separate provinces: Adamawa, North, and Far North.

[b]The two Anglophone provinces—Northwest and Southwest—each have four cabinet positions.

[c]The South Central province is now two provinces Center and South.

The regional executives are the provincial and divisional service heads (governors, prefects, and subprefects).[8] In the higher ranks (governors and prefects), Anglophone representation was 28 percent compared to 35 percent for the South-Central and 15 percent for the North, 9 percent each for the West and the Littoral, and only 4 percent for the East. When all ranks are combined (governors, prefects, and subprefects) the proportion of Anglophone, North, and East representation dropped to a sixth, a seventh, and a thirtieth, respectively. The South-Central still maintained its lead with a third followed by the West with a fifth of the politically powerful regional executive positions. The greatest gain in this combined category was posted by the West whose share of regional positions increased from 8.7 percent at the higher ranks (governors and prefects) to 20 percent of all ranks (see Tables 3.8 and 3.9).

The judiciary is the third branch of government. Among the top judicial officials in the nation (titular and substitute judges of the supreme court; high court judges and magistrates; and the *procureurs-generaux* and their deputies) Anglophone representation was roughly 17 percent compared to 3.8 percent for the North. In addition, *all* the top law officers serving in Anglophone Cameroon were native to this region.

Table 3.8. Distribution of Administrative Departments (Headed by Prefects) by Region, 1973–1978

Region	*Number of Departments*	*Percentage*	*Number of Prefects By Region of Origin*	*Percentage*
North	6	15	6	15.3
West Cameroon	9	23	12	30.7
South Central	9	23	14	35.9
West	6	15	3	7.7
Littoral	5	12.8	2	5
East	4	10.2	2	5
TOTAL	39	100	39	100

Table 3.9. Distribution of Administrative Subdistricts (Headed by Subprefects) by Region, 1973–1978

Region	*Number of Subdistricts*	*Percentage*	*Number of Subprefects By Region of Origin*	*Percentage*
North	20	15	18	13
West Cameroon	22	16	20	15
South Central	47	35	45	33.3
West	17	12.5	33	24.5
Littoral	18	13	14	10.5
East	11	8	5	3.7
TOTAL	135	100	135	100

The preceding analysis has attempted to establish the strong Anglophone presence in all branches of government and party: in the National Assembly where the positions are sought more for their prestige and status than power; in the principal policy-making organs of the national party; and within the national and regional executive branches, which confer both power and prestige to their members. By way of contrast, and for the sake of perspective, the analysis shows that the North with close to one-third of the total population was, relatively speaking, underrepresented in the Central Committee of the CNU and within *all* ranks of the national and regional executives. How then can one reconcile this apparent ubiquity of Anglophones in the higher councils of state against persistent claims that their region has been treated as the orphan of the republic?

A possible approach and the one favored by this author is to distinguish between the Anglophone masses and their privileged ruling class. The complaints legitimately speak to the deprivation of the masses, as it were, the group that has yet to enjoy the fruits of two decades of postreunification progress. In contrast, a tiny minority of Anglophones, which has had access to the national corridors of power, wealth, and prestige since reunification, has effectively exploited mass discontent in order to advance its own narrow corporate interests. This group, together with an equally privileged Francophone minority, constitutes the dominant class, the national bourgeoisie, that is, in postreunification Cameroon. The Anglophone bourgeoisie has in the last 20 years kept its narrow class interests at the forefront while paying no heed to those of the majority population. Its support for or opposition to the major political changes the country has experienced during this period was predicated on calculations of the advantages to be gained from these arrangements and not out of any deep ideological commitment to ease the plight of the Anglophone majority.[9]

CONCLUSION: ETHNICITY, REGIONALISM, AND POWER

We have attempted to demonstrate in this essay that, during his years as president, Ahidjo was quite sensitive to regional differences and sought to mute them in the appointments he made to the cabinet, the party machinery, the national assembly, and parastatal organizations. Although all the major regions in the country were represented in the various councils of state, not all of the country's ethnic groups enjoyed comparable representation. This is quite understandable given the over 200 ethnic groups in the country. So in practice, certain ethnic groups were consistently given prominence in the allocation of choice executive positions. Included in this list were the major as well as the minor ethnic congeries within Cameroon. These were: (1) Fulbe with representatives usually drawn from Diamare (Maroua), Benoue (Garoua), and Adamawa (Ngaoundere), (2) Kirdi (both Christians and Moslems) and the Shuwa-

Arabs (Longone-Birni and Margui-Wandala), (3) Bafia, (4) Bamoun, (5) Bamileke, (6) Bassa (representation came equally from the Edea and Es-seka groups thus avoiding taking sides in the historical rivalry between these two camps), (7) Bakweri, (8) Banyang, (9) Bertoua (Maka, Baya, and Kozime), (10) Duala (with representation coming from the *heartland* as well as *outer* Duala, which embraces Yabassi and Mungo up to Nkongsamba), (11) Bulu, (12) Ewondo, and (13) Bamenda (in this scattered group prominence was usually given to Bafreng, Nkambe, and Nsaw). A representative from each of these groups was included in every successive postreunification cabinet reshuffle. In *Tribesmen and Patriots* (Kofele-Kale 1981a, pp. 23–27), I pointed out some of the negative consequences of this policy of employing ethnicity as the basis for allocating political power, especially at the executive level, a theme I again pick up in this essay.

The ethnic arithmetic formula for distributing political power was in reality a sophisticated patronage system through which ethnic groups were transformed into pressure groups with the responsibility of articulating, aggregating, and resolving particularist interests and demands. At the head of this system was none other than Ahidjo, the *grand patron,* and below him several tiers of ethnic barons. More often than not the senior ethnic barons, that is, cabinet ministers and the leadership of the National Assembly, owed their positions to Ahidjo who handpicked them. All the ethnic barons were members of the Cameroon National Union though some did not become active in the party until they were appointed to the cabinet. While these barons served as ethnic brokers or spokesmen for their respective ethnic constituencies at the national level, their junior counterparts—such as the section or subsection party chieftains—performed a similar function at the local level. The ethnic barons were also required to maintain peace and order in their respective fiefdoms, and, whenever their "natives" got restless, it was the ethnic barons who were usually sent out to whip them back into line.

This system of reward through ethnic channels completely bypassed the national party structures and relied instead on ethnic brokers for resolution of group complaints and grievances against the government or for help in bringing a particular project into a community. The ethnic patrons were in turn expected to delivere these services. As a result, it was not unusual to find that ". . . entire ministries, departments within ministries, para-statal organizations, etc. . . . [became] prebendary structures to reward members of the minister's ethnic group. In each ministry, preferential treatment in hiring and promotion is usually given to members of the minister's ethnic group" (Kofele-Kale 1981a, p. 24). And the more powerful and dynamic ministers-cum-ethnic barons were able to get more projects located in their areas, leading to a form of development I have referred to elsewhere as "helter-skelter" (Kofele-Kale 1981a, p. 24).

Since the most direct link between the masses and their government was through a few senior politicians, it was absolutely essential that these regional/ethnic spokesmen and women held claim to some ethnic base or at the very least were able to convey the appearance that they enjoyed the support of their ethnic constituents. The scramble to secure, establish, and consolidate an ethnic power base has contributed to the politicization of ethnic loyalties at both the leadership and mass levels. To the extent that identification with an ethnic group was a necessary precondition for remaining in power, the need to rekindle banked ethnic feelings and to rediscover long forgotten ethnic roots became an all-consuming passion for the ethnic barons. So much so that, in some instances, a few of the handpicked ones even went as far as carving out personal fiefdoms for themselves by detaching their clans or fringe groups from larger ethnic configurations. This was the case when Nguti and Ndian were pulled away from Kumba (Balong) by Ekangaki and Nwalipenja, respectively, while the all-powerful Samuel Eboua, once an *eminence grise* in Ahidjo's presidency, is reputed to have detached Abo from Duala. In each of these instances the ethnic spokesmen lacked and therefore had to create a political base the boundaries of which were coterminous with a live ethnic group.

The politicization of ethnic loyalties has also had some impact on the conduct of politics at the mass level. Two consequences can be detected: first is the inevitable retreat into an ethnic sanctuary, since the individual peasant or worker now sees this structure as the only reliable avenue for upward mobility. For these people, politics now revolves around the ethnic group and its spokesmen and women, since it is they who ultimately can deliver essential services to their communities. Much of their energy is invested in the process of selecting these ethnic barons (in those instances where they are not appointed from Yaounde). Taking cue from their leaders, the masses, rather than gathering around the totem of the Cameroon nation, find it expedient to organize along ethnic lines. The risk that such parochialism could ultimately lead to mass allegiance being directed away from the national center and its institutions to the various ethnic communities is apparently ignored by a leadership bent on remaining in power indefinitely. While it is true that this has not yet occurred, as I tried to show for Anglophone Cameroon (Kofele-Kale 1981a), that it could happen is something that should alert all to the fragility of Cameroonian unity.

The second consequence flowing from the politicization of ethnicity has been the emergence of a new ethnic person who, for lack of a better term, will be referred to as an *ethnic transvestite*. This group is comprised in the main of English-speaking Cameroonians whose parents or grandparents originally came from former French Cameroons to settle in the British sector. The vast majority of these ethnic transvestites were born in the Northwest and Southwest provinces, received their education there (primary through secondary and, for some, university studies in Nigeria, Britain, or the United States), and stayed or returned (for those who studied abroad) to work in the region. Following reunification, some of these Cameroonians began the mental trip of crossing over to the Francophone sector by the simple act of reaffirming ties with their erstwhile ethnic groups (a number of these groups did straddle the Anglo–French colonial divide). The process of rediscovery has been encouraged by two factors: (1) the widespread perception in the country that Francophones are the most privileged group in society and, therefore, close identification with them is the surest and quickest way to advance in the system, and (2) a patronage system that channels its rewards through ethnic groups. Given these two factors the urge to engage in ethnic transvestism is quite understandable. But the transformation from a somewhat ethnically-neutral Anglophone to an instant Francophone is rarely ever complete. For though these ethnic transvestites wear fancy ethnic drags and surround themselves with the trappings of their rediscovered ethnic cultures (they listen to its music, force themselves to speak a language now but all forgotten, take brides from their ancestral villages), when it is to their political advantage, they are also able to revert to Anglophonism when nothing of consequence is at stake.

The ethnic transvestites should be distinguished from their forebears who were the vanguard of the reunification movement (Ardener 1960, pp. 196–197; Ardener 1967, pp. 296–298; Le Vine 1964, p. 196) and without whose persistence Cameroon would very likely have continued to remain a divided nation. Equally important is the positive contribution the ethnic transvestites have made toward national integration. As the embodiment of the dual Cameroon persona (Francophone by origin and Anglophone through socialization), this group was able to serve as cultural interpreters between Anglophones and Francophones during the initial stages of reunification. This period was the most critical in the new experiment, because the two groups were still virtual strangers to each other and the future hinged precariously on how quickly they could learn to trust each other. The ethnic transvestites helped expedite this process because they were in a very real sense the common link between the two groups, trusted by both sides—by the Anglophones because they had lived among them for a protracted period and by the Francophones because of the common ties of ethnicity. But with time these artful ethnic transvestites discovered a Machiavellian way to profit from their role as cultural interpreters. They found that they could also play up the lost heritage game in order to enjoy the best of both worlds.

NOTES

1. The pride which the national bourgeoisie attaches to its version of reality is only matched by the ferocious attacks it levels against those Cameroonians who seek to offer an alternative version of the truth. In the same policy speech, President Ahidjo bitterly attacked those "nationals both at home and abroad *who aid and abet those who thirst for domination with the hope of bringing about the collapse of the fine structure of unity, stability and progress which we are patiently endeavoring to build.* We are aware of the subversive activities and the false and coarse propaganda of dreamers and ambitious persons who from their voluntary exile itch with envious nostalgia. . . . These subversive activities assume dangerous proportions when they are allowed to undermine the foundations of the solid and organized nation which we are proud to build in toil and perseverance." (emphasis added). It is clear that the national bourgeoisie has been engaging in a campaign of cynicism aimed at discrediting the bona fides of any Cameroonian who dares to stray from the official party line. Inherent in this cynical propaganda is the doctrine that only those inside Cameroon enjoy special perspectives and insights about that society to qualify them as its authentic "interpreters." These "insiders" claim that, as a matter of epistemological principle, only they—not the "outsiders," that is, those on "voluntary exile" abroad—have *privileged,* if not *monopolistic,* access to Cameroonian knowledge.

This peculiar strain of Cameroonian solipsism, as are all other strains of solipsism, is intellectually unsound because it simply negates the most elementary processes of logical reasoning. It suggests that one cannot understand situations and conditions external to one's own immediate experience and objective location in space and time. It threatens to extend the single dimension of experience to a total equation of *experience equals understanding*; it makes the whole intellectually incomprehensible except through the atomised element of *being.* Carried to its logical extreme, and as Robert Merton suggests, the catalogue of claims to privileged or monopolistic access of knowledge becomes indefinitely expansible to all manner of social formations (Merton 1973, pp. 99–136). An example of this would be a claim that only black South Africans living in South Africa are capable of *understanding* and *discussing* apartheid; mind you, not the Dennis Brutuses, Bloke Modisanes, Lewis Nkosis, Miriam Makebas, and Hugh Masakelas in exile abroad. At its most absurd, it allows for the argument that one must first live among swines before one can fundamentally understand and discuss that distinctive aroma that pig pens exude! Affirming this is tantamount to abdicating all claims to clear thinking. But this facile proposition that only those Cameroonians domiciled in the country have exclusive claims to the understanding and interpretation of Cameroonian reality has received the blessing of the ruling class. I, however, find it not only disingenuous but intellectually unsupportable.

Claiming lineal descent from this doctrine of exclusivity is a related one which consists of labeling anyone who publicly disagrees with government policies as subversive; of dismissing as revolutionary cant any form of criticism of the regime; and of treating the great helmsman as an infallible deity criticism of whom amounts to an unpardonable act of *les majeste.* Lost in all of this war of words is the fact that Cameroon transcends particular individuals and groups and is the collective patrimony of all living Cameroonians, as well as the millions that have gone before and the many yet unborn. No one person can appropriate this heritage for himself. It is the special obligation of every living Cameroonian to question and criticize the direction Cameroon is heading when such criticism is deserved.

2. This position has been most forcefully presented in a series of communiques put out since 1979 by the Cameroon Action Movement, a clandestine organization made up of Anglophone Cameroonians (see *West Africa,* January 28, 1980, p. 143).

3. The range represents the variation in figures given by different authors. Le Vine (1971, p. 11) puts the number of Muslims in Cameroon at 600,000 and for the other religions he lists 27 percent of the Anglophone population and 35 percent of the Francophone as Christians, and 65 percent and 45 percent, respectively, as animists. Prouzet (1974, p. 103) estimates the Christian population in Cameroon to be 2 million and the Muslim 1 million. Azarya (1976, p. 55) points out that only 43 percent of the total northern population is Islamized; and Joseph (1977, p. 17) gives a numerical estimate of Muslims in Cameroon as 395,000.

4. Under the federal system, the country was divided into six administrative regions, each headed by a federal inspector of administration. West Cameroon was one of the six regions. The other five were in East Cameroon: North, East, South-Central, Littoral, and West. I shall retain this regional division as a framework for analysis.

5. Of the ten provincial governors under the present Biya administration, two are Anglophones (Yakum Ntaw in the North and Ngomba Mutanga in the Northwest).

6. Banque des Etats de l'Afrique Centrale (BEAC), Banque Internationale pour l'Afrique Occidentale-Cameroun (BIAO), Banque Internationale pour le Commerce et l'Industrie du Cameroun (BICIC), Cameroon Bank Ltd. (Cambank), Societe Camerounaise de Banque (SCB), and Societe Generale de Banques au Cameroun, commercial banks; and Banque Camerounaise de Developpement (BCD), Fonds National de Developpement Rural (FONADER), Societe Financiere pour le Developpement du Cameroun, and Societe Nationale d'Investissement du Cameroun, development banks.

7. Cameroon Development Corporation, Mission de Developpement des Cultures Vivrieres, Maraicheres et Fruitieres (MIDEVIV), Mission de Developpement d'Ombessa, Societe Camerounaise des Tabacs (SCT), Societe de Developpement et la Transformation du Ble (SODEBLE), Societe de Developpement du Cacao (SODECAO), Societe de Developpement du Coton (SODECOTON), Societe de Developpement et d'Exploitation des Produits Animaux (SODEPA), Societe de Developpement du Haut-Nkam (SODENKAM), Societe de Developpement de la Riziculture de la plaine des Mbos (SODERIM), Societe d'Etudes des Bauxites de Cameroun (SEBECAM), Societe d'Expansion et de Modernisation de la Riziculture de Yagoua (SEMRY), Societe Regionale des Zones d'Actions Prioritaires Integrees du Centre-Sud (ZAPI du Centre Sud) and Societe Regionale des Zones d'Actions Prioritaires Integrees de l'Est (ZAPI de l'EST).

8. A list of all the provincial and divisional service heads was compiled from the various National Year Books and *Les Elites Camerounaises.* I then had six different Cameroonian students knowledgeable in Cameroon ethnography match the names of these administrators against their province of origin. Of the 181 names, we initially had agreement on 163. The remaining 18 names were then

given to a former Cameroonian administrator who had worked in several of the provinces before leaving the service for further study abroad. He was able to match this last group of names. Because so few Cameroonians from the East province hold national office and because of the relative isolation of this region from the rest of the country, we had the most difficulty in identifying Eastern names. My approach then was to classify administrators as of Eastern origin if their names could not be positively matched against the other five regions. My figures therefore contain some margin of error; however, a more positive identification of *all* the names on the list would probably affect the distribution but *not* the general pattern as described in our analysis.

9. The reader is referred to my essay on "Class, Status, and Power in Post-Reunification Cameroon: The Rise of An Anglophone Bourgeoisie, 1961–1980" in *Studies in Power and Class in Africa,* Irving Leonard Markovitz, ed. (forthcoming).

4

THE POLITICAL ECONOMY OF DEVELOPMENT IN CAMEROON: RELATIONS BETWEEN THE STATE, INDIGENOUS BUSINESS, AND FOREIGN INVESTORS

Wilfred A. Ndongko

Cameroon today is among a handful of African countries that have in the past two decades followed an admirable and well-documented path of economic growth and development. Once acknowledged as having one of the poorest, least developed economies in Africa, it is currently regarded as a "middle income developing country" and as "one of the twenty safest countries in the world for foreign investment." Cameroon's impressive political stability has also created an image that "favours a particularly healthy business climate."[1] This optimistic diagnosis of the economy is in fact an appreciation of its economic, political, and social achievements and potential in the past 23 years, as well as a reaction to the disappointing performance of Africa's success stories—the bursting of the "Ivory Coast miracle" and the collapse of the Kenyan economy, two market-oriented economies in Africa once believed to possess the zeal for autonomous industrial growth.

As Cameroon approached its quarter-century, its economic picture was characterized by positive aspects. In 1983, the economy was growing at 6 percent in real terms, giving a rate after inflation of over 3 percent per capita GDP. Presently, production is relatively well diversified, and the country earns foreign exchange from a wide array of products, while at the same time it is marching concretely on the road to self-sufficiency in food. While its trade balance is in surplus apparently because of the cushion provided by oil exports, the country is able to maintain a high level of creditworthiness at a time when such other countries as Nigeria and Mexico, rich in black gold, can barely service their debts.

The views expressed in this paper are personal and do not reflect those of the Institute of Human Sciences of which I am the Director. I wish to thank Dr. Joseph Ngu of CRED/ISH for the immense research assistance that he gave me during the preparation of this paper.

Compared to other oil-rich countries, Cameroon has pursued a conservative public investment policy by basically avoiding "pork barrel" projects, except perhaps for the infamous presidential palace completed in 1982 as a finale of the Ahidjo era. It is important to note that the 1983 budget, balanced at 410 billion francs CFA, an increase of nearly 33 percent over the 1982 budget of 310 billion francs, was financed from Cameroonian resources alone without any foreign borrowing (*Africa Research Bulletin—Economic* 1982, p. 6611c). Cameroon's debt service is relatively low, below 12 percent of current exports and it is presently taking advantage of its bilingual heritage by selling its exports increasingly for hard currency outside the franc zone.

Because of its disciplined policy of economic liberalism, which is open to foreign investors and planned at the same time, it is being referred to increasingly as "a businessman's paradise." Foreign investors, which include mostly French, Americans, British, Germans, and Dutch, invested in 1980 297 billion francs CFA, about 50 percent more than in 1979 (*Africa Research Bulletin—Economic* 1982, p. 6491a). Cameroon's development policies have earned the country one of the best balance sheets in Africa, and this prompted President Paul Biya proudly to declare recently that "Cameroon is healthy."

This paper will, therefore, attempt to explain why and how Cameroon has attained such international respectability by examining the relations between the government, indigenous business, and foreign investors. In order to undertake this exercise and to have an understanding of Cameroon's economic miracle, we must review the principles behind its development policies and how they have influenced the evolution of indigenous and foreign enterprises. The context for this review must include a political sociology of the triangular relationship between the state, indigenous business, and foreign investors in the process of capital formation and accumulation.

THE STATE, INDIGENOUS BUSINESS, AND FOREIGN INVESTORS: A CONCEPTUAL FRAMEWORK

The study of underdevelopment of the third world has dominated development thinking over the last 20 years. It falls broadly into two economic camps. The first, developed by neoclassical economics and modernization theory, has provided most of the core concepts that guided development policy throughout the 1960s and into the 1970s. According to this theory, developing countries are where they are not because of any exogenous forces, but due to the existence of the universal economic problem of scarcity. This feature is found in all forms of socioeconomic formations—slave, feudal, capitalist, and socialist.

Specifically, the developing countries should be concerned with the efficient utilization of their resources, which can be supplemented by foreign aid, loans, grants, and foreign capital investments (Rosenstein Rodan 1943; Nurske 1958; Lewis 1955, 1963). Massive capital investments in industry and the application of modern technology and skill together with a spirit of competitiveness and enterprise (that is, the Protestant ethic) would result in high rates of economic growth. Although phrased in theoretical terms and in econometric models such as those of Harrod (1948) and Domar (1946), this analysis was based on the experience of the advanced western countries, which, as a result of industrialization, reached a level of unprecedented prosperity.

Modernization theory was developed in the 1960s partly as a response to the frustration of planners impatient with the disappointing record of the first development decade. The argument was that if neoclassical economic theory was valid, and the experience of the rich countries suggested that it was, then it is industrialization that will transform the traditionally poverty ridden societies into affluent modern ones (Nurske 1958, 1976; Rostow 1960, 1963; Schultz 1961). The problem of development was essentially one of "encadrement," the need to create a new framework and structures for the reorganization of people, materials, and mentalities necessary for the process of development (Goode 1963; Hagen 1962; McClelland 1964; and Lerner 1958).

Marxists and neo-Marxists provide the second and competing theoretical framework for understanding the problem of underdevelopment in the third world, which has inspired the articulation of dependency theory. The intellectual context for the emergence of dependency theory was created by Latin American economists, notably Prebisch and his colleagues at the United Nations Economic Commission for Latin America (ECLA) (Prebisch 1950), who argued that the region's reliance on the export of primary commodities was not, as was then believed, providing the stimulus for economic growth. The central ideas of the ECLA economists were soon reformulated by other Latin American political economists and developed into the now familiar theory of dependency (Furtado 1970; Sunkel 1969; Cardoso 1972; Frank 1969; and Dos Santos 1973).

Protagonists of the dependency school explain underdevelopment as a necessary outcome of the systematic exploitation and manipulation of the periphery by the center. Underdevelopment is the product of the unequal relationships between interdependent economies characterized by what Dos Santos (1973) described as "a conditioning situation in which the economies of one group of countries are conditioned by the development or expansion of others."

Preindustrialized societies are conditioned by their economic relationships with advanced industrial economies to occupy a subordinate and dependent role that obstructs development by expropriating investable surplus. The relations of production lie at the heart of the problem of inequality both within and between nations. Indigenous elites, firmly wedded to the international capitalist system and rewarded handsomely by it, have no motivation to become less dependent and possess the power to prevent other classes in society from doing so.

With the experience of Latin America, Sunkel and Fuenzalida (1974) have developed a more subtle concept of dependency through their transnationalization thesis.[2] Sunkel and Fuenzalida's concept of transnational capitalism and national distintegration (although not as starkly mechanistic as the following brief characterization would imply), suggests that:

- The economic growth of poor countries must be separated into two communities: the *international system* with nations as its most important component, and a *transnational system* with multinational corporations, international organizations, and individuals transcending national boundaries;
- The differential impact of dependency in a peripheral political economy and the differential response to it from groups in the periphery;
- Some parts and sections of the different classes in the periphery can be integrated in the transnational system while other parts and sections cannot;
- The integrated segments in the transnational system will be more stable while nonintegrated segments will experience deep and enduring marginalization.

Three agents—the state, indigenous capitalists, and foreign economic agents—are responsible for the economic growth/development in third world countries.[3] Whereas the neoclassical approach in its pure form would postulate that the role of the state would be marginal vis-a-vis economic development, etatism assigns an inordinate role to the state. In this approach, it is assumed that the state provides the broad umbrella under which indigenous capitalists and foreign economic agents interact; thus its role of mediation. It also intervenes in the economic processes.

This chapter posits that there is a kernel of truth to this argument. At the same time, a more penetrating analysis using the transnationalist's conceptual terms reveals that the state is not a unitary actor; it represents the interest of a socioeconomic class, the center of the periphery. Consequently, it is simplistic to see the state as mediator. The state-qua-class has a vested interest in the system of socioeconomic relations that prevails within its eminent domain. This ipso facto renders more complex the relationship that exists between the state (S), foreign economic agents (F), and indigenous capital (I) (see Shaw and Grieve 1977a, 1977b).

The relationship that exists between the state and economic agents is conditioned by the phase at which it occurs. When access agreements are being negotiated between S and F or between I and F, F—considering its monopoly in several realms—possesses a lot of bargaining power. Normally, the relationship between S and F can be characterized as cooperation and that of I and F as collaboration at this phase. Cooperation can ensue between S and F only when and where S acts as a unitary actor. However, dependencia theorists have argued that this ideal situation hardly obtains. Failing this, there is ample chance for collusion, where S represents the center *of* the periphery and F represents the center *in* the periphery.

Once access has been obtained, it would be spurious to argue that relations between S and F or between I and F would continue to be conditioned solely by the access agreement(s). Other variables often come into play to alter the calculus of the operational phase. The imposition of new business rules—guide lines on an export basis by S, following the signing of access agreement with F, is apt to cause conflict between them. In such circumstances, there is a probability that resolution by collusion may obtain. However, this is not to imply that conflict between S and F is the only alternative to collusion at the operational phase. Where S does not place a curb on the concession gained by F at entry stage, cooperation as well as collusion would continue to be the order of the day.

In the case of I and F, the critical variable is whether their interests are complementary or competitive. Complementarity of interests between I and F always serves as a spur for their collaboration, whereas a divergence of interests sparks competition, if not outright conflict. In the case of conflicts, I is likely to seek protection from S so as to redress the situation. If conflict and collaboration are the opposite ends of the continuum, cooperation is the midpoint. Cooptation occurs when I is unflaggingly determined to monopolize its control of any business, whatever the level of conflict or collaboration. Cooptation is often carried out in the favor of I, which is/are interested in both vertical and horizontal mergers. This is an act, if not a process, that is born of false consciousness.

If the relationships between S and F, and I and F, display a systematic tendency to undergo change, the relations between S and I are more or less stable. This is attributable to the convergence of interests, prima facie, that exists between these two agents. Thus they are apt to cooperate. However, instances crop up where there are divergences of interest between S and I. This normally is the case where S is not acting as S per se but S-qua-class.

It should be noted that relations between the actors in question are usually affected by interfering variables, inter alia, foreign states, international organizations, and nongovernmental organizations. The state may either be sensitive or vulnerable to these pressures. Its degree of sensitivity or vulnerability is a crucial variable in defining stability/instability in the triangular relationship between S, I, and F (see Keohane and Nye 1977).

FOREIGN AND INDIGENOUS BUSINESS IN CAMEROON

The colonial occupation of Cameroon by Germany formally began in July 1884.[4] During its 76 years under foreign domination, Cameroon evolved from being a classic example of a colonial economy, in which primitive capital accumulation along Marxist lines occurred with stark simplicity, to an independent state with a small modern sector dependent on foreign capital and skills. The early years of German rule were characterized by a mixture of brutal application of force and the development, albeit small, of a modern economy with an infrastructural network: roads, railways, ports, post offices, towns, hospitals, and plantations (Rudin 1938). In their territorial expansion in quest of commercial opportunities, German- and later French-chartered companies and concessionaires, in collaboration with their imperial mother-countries, fought bloody battles of subjugation, especially in their attempt to penetrate the interior to seek and extract free or cheap labor needed to develop the new coastal plantations.

The railway lines that were constructed from Douala, the coastal and economic hub of Cameroon, to the central, southern central and southwestern parts were primarily for strategic military and administrative reasons of the colonial authorities. Essentially, the basis on which the colonial government operated could be summarized by what Adam Smith aptly expressed some 200 years ago when he declared that:

> Little else is requisite to carry a state to the highest degree of opulence from the lowest barbarism but peace, easy taxes and a tolerable administration of justice, all the rest being brought about by the nature of things.[5]

To achieve peace, the Germans did not hestiate to use forced African labor on the plantations; in collecting and transporting cocoa, rubber, and bananas, and in building the railways. However, in their favor, colonial rule in Cameroon put an end to slavery and slave raiding. The roads and railways opened up the southern section of the country and gave enormous economies of scale not only to the German- and French-controlled plantation agriculture, but also to the emerging African commercial agriculture (Rudin 1938, p. 353).

Foreign Capital

Toward the end of World War II, the economic development of Cameroon was restricted to the coastal and southern parts of the country. The financing of development through development plans was introduced by the French in the former East Cameroon while in the former West Cameroon (formerly known as British Southern Cameroons) development financing was carried out through direct capital grants from the British government but actually allocated through the colonial governor of Nigeria.

Between 1947 and 1957, two development plans were elaborated for East Cameroon with capital projects amounting to 96 million CFA francs. These plans were developed by the French colonial authorities and supported mainly by the Investment Fund for Economic and Social Development (FIDES). Although the British colonial government did not develop a similar plan for the Southern Cameroons, largely because this part of the territory was administered as a district of Eastern Nigeria, a plan for the 1955 to 1960 period was initiated with investment projects estimated to £8.8 million (Cameroon Chamber of Commerce 1965, p. 38).

It should be noted that these early plans, in both the French and the British controlled territories, placed great emphasis on the development of an infrastructural network to permit the transportation of goods in and out of the country. In this regard then, a greater part of the funding (85 percent) in these plans was devoted to construction of roads, ports, railways, and telecommunication. Later plans, however, gave greater attention to the expansion of production through social and educational advancement as well as through agricultural improvements (see Table 4.1).

Table 4.1. East Cameroon: Development Financing, 1947–1959 (in Millions of CFA Francs)

Sector	*First Plan 1947–1953*	*Percentage*	*Second Plan 1954–1955*	*Percentage*	*Total*	*Percentage*
Production	733	4.0	7,129.6	39.3	7,862.6	21.0
Infrastructure	15,547	85.1	7,406.5	40.7	22,953.5	62.0
Social equipment	1,762	9.8	3,544.7	19.6	5,306.7	16.2
Studies research	197	1.1	76.0	0.4	273	0.8
TOTAL	18,239	100	18,156.8	100	36,395.8	100

Source: Ministere de la Cooperation 1962.

Since the economy was largely based on plantation agriculture, foreign public and private investments were concentrated in agriculture with the accent on producing primary goods for export rather than for local consumption. Such investments were characterized by static comparative advantage through the expansion of tropical agriculture by creating large plantations. There was a comparative advantage in geography or climate in growing certain crops on these plantations. Thus, as can be seen in Table 4.2, cocoa, coffee, bananas, rubber, palm oil, tobacco, and tea were established in both East and West Cameroon. These plantations were essentially the same type of capital for production as had been used before the Europeans came. They did achieve substantial economies of scale through reorganization; they employed large numbers of people cheaply; they shifted large areas of land from subsistence to market crops; they invited private foreign companies and concessionnaires (limited in British Cameroon to Elders and Files and the C.D.C.) to establish firms and trading houses; and they introduced modern methods of transporting crops to the coast and from there to France and Britain.

Table 4.2. East and West Cameroon Principal Agricultural Export Crops, 1960 (Volume in Metric Tons and Value in Millions CFA Francs)

	East	*Share (percent)*	*West*	*Share (percent)*	*Total*	*Values*
Main exports						
Cocoa	68,000	92	6,000	8	74,000	8,781
Coffee	40,000	95	2,200	5	42,200	5,018
Bananas	52,000	37	85,000	63	137,000	2,425
Rubber	3,600	55	2,900	45	6,500	1,179
Palm oil	1,100	20	4,200	80	5,300	2,581
Palm kernels	13,800	86	2,200	14	16,000	617
Tobacco	1,300	100	—	0	1,300	823
Tea	—	0	34	100	34	n.a.
Pepper	—	0	18	100	8	n.a.
Timber	298,000	62	125,000	38	333,000	2,107
Cotton	11,000	100	—	0	11,000	1,047
Groundnuts	10,000	100	—	0	10,000	35
Domestic consumption						
Foodstuff	2,616,000	98.4	508,000	1.6	3,124,000	n.a.

Source: Ministere de la Cooperation, 1962.

The French government's policy toward the private sector consisted of agreements with private firms. Some of the important ones included the French West African Company[6] and La Societe Agricole et Forestiere Africaine (SAFA). Most of the investments that were undertaken in East Cameroon were businesses or industries engaged in the exploitation and transformation of timber and wood products. One of the earliest firms established in Cameroon was in Douala in 1944. This firm, La Societe d'Exploitation Forestiere et Industrielle du Cameroun (SIFIC), located at Douala-Bassa, was created with a capital of 450.8 million CFA francs and largely funded (97 percent) by French private interests.[7] Two years later, Les Bois du Cameroun (LBC) was created in 1946 with a capital of 102 million CFA francs and jointly owned by Societe Nationale d'Investissement (SNI), a public investment company with about 8.8 percent ownership, while French private interest had a third (33 percent). By independence in 1960, three similar enterprises were created, all located in the Mungo-Douala area.[8]

Some of the agreements between the French government and private foreign firms (mostly French) included tariff and tax concessions that benefitted French investment and trade. This led to an increase of French private investment of 15 billion CFA francs during the period 1947 to 1954, as compared with public investment of 18 billion CFA francs during the same period (Ndongko 1979, p. 34).

In the former West Cameroon, British policy of financing development projects was far less interventionist than that of the French in the East. The Colonial Development Corporation (now known as the Cameroon Development Corporation, CDC) was created in 1947 with a capital of 4 billion CFA francs and since then has emerged as the leading producer of primary exports in all of Cameroon. The CDC came into being not as a direct result of any policy of ownership or economic planning but rather from the British confiscation of German plantations in 1939. Indeed, the CDC, which is now an autonomous body, has played an important development role in transforming the stagnant structure of the former West Cameroon economy.[9]

Although British public capital investments in West Cameroon increased, no attempt was made to encourage private investment in the territory from Britain. Between 1955 and 1960, grants made by the United Kingdom Colonial Development Welfare Fund (CDWF)[10] amounted to £2,283,000 roughly 6.2 percent of the funds invested by FIDES in the East during the periods 1947–1953 or 1954–1959. Consequently, no directly productive investments were undertaken to complement the physical infrastructure that was provided through grants made by CDWF. The result was that West Cameroon remained a producer of primary products for export, with little or no secondary and tertiary industries, while in the East the pace of formation of many enterprises kept up with the growth of primary exports (see Table 4.2).

In both East and West Cameroon, these investments brought about a large increase in the output and employed a great number of unskilled people. During the colonial period, the majority of salaried Cameroonians worked for private European-owned firms, which at various times competed with the colonial administration for unskilled labor.

Differences in the relative development of the regions in Cameroon are associated with the contrasts in the number, nature, and age of modern enterprises. As industrial activities in the country originally involved both exports and imports, and because of colonial investment policy in locating firms to take advantage of the infrastructural network, there was and still is a relatively high concentration of older enterprises in and around the Mungo area, firms engaged in primary activities or in the processing and transformation of raw materials for export.

According to Clignet's (1976) study, Douala, the earliest focus of industrial development in Cameroon, accommodates one-half of all the business organizations in the country, the majority of them belonging to the secondary sector of the economy. Yaounde and Edea are two additional areas that have seen the growth of new firms, although in the former two-thirds of all the enterprises were created after independence (see Table 4.3).

Table 4.3. Age and Location of Cameroonian Firms (Percentage Distribution)

	Date of Foundation				
Main Location	*Post-Independence (after 1960)*	*Post-World War II (1945–1958)*	*Pre-World War II (before 1945)*	*Total*	*Number*
Yaounde	60.0	32.8	7.2	100.0	101
Douala	49.0	36.4	14.6	100.0	255
Nkongsamba	47.0	28.4	23.6	99.0	17
Mungo	17.4	21.7	60.9	99.1	23
Edea	69.0	31.0	0.0	100.0	13
Sanaga	55.5	22.2	22.2	99.9	9
Others	32.0	36.0	32.0	100.0	23

Source: Clignet 1976, p. 39. Reprinted with permission.

In 1980, of 100 largest enterprises in Cameroon, foreign capital contributed 28.6 billion CFA francs or 48 percent of the total social capital of 59.6 billion CFA francs.[11] Although total plan investment has grown since 1960, the continuous reliance on foreign public and private capital is falling (57.5 percent at the end of 1976), and the government has emphasized its policy of increasingly diversifying the sources of financing investment projects in the country. In 1980, for example, 34.5 percent of total investment commitments were derived from French public and private capital compared to 45 percent of similar investment in 1976. National participation has steadily increased, from 42.5 percent in 1976 to 52 percent in 1980, and, of this, 44 percent of the capital came from the public compared to 39 percent at the end of 1976.

Foreign capital is dominant in the basic and final consumption industries: food (81 percent), drinks (69 percent), tobacco (75 percent), textiles (73 percent), timber and wood processing (80 percent), and metal processing (76 percent). It should also be noted that both private and public interests contributed more than half the investment capital in most sectors (see Table 4.4).

Table 4.4. Sectoral Investment Participation, 1980 (in Millions CFA Francs)

		National Interest			*Foreign Interest*	
Branch of Activity	*Social Capital*	*Total (%)*	*Public (%)*	*Private (%)*	*Total (%)*	*French (%)*
Agro industry	16,185	81	76	5	19	17
Food industries	2,388	19	10	9	81	72
Drinks	5,913	31	11	20	69	49
Tobacco	1,670	25	—	25	75	75
Textile industries	3,890	27	19	8	73	37.5
Leather products	2,370	77	59	18	23	—
Timber processing	5,055	20	19.8	0.2	80	39
Chemical industries	4,520	43	24	19	57	46
Construction materials	3,088	52	51	1	48	17
Metal processing	9,153	24	23	1	76	72
Paper and pulp processing	250	100	—	100	—	—
Gas, electricity, and water	5,074	99	99	—	1	1
TOTAL (estimated)	59,556	52	44	8	48	34.5

Source: L'industrie Camerounaise en 1980–1981, (1981).

So far we have concentrated our discussion on the growth of foreign capital in Cameroon and have already pointed out that plantation agriculture was characteristic of colonial economic life. The nature of this type of economic activity in itself prevented the development of large secondary and tertiary sectors. Any expansion that has occurred within these sectors has been a postindependence phenomenon.

However, since colonial policy limited to a certain extent the number of lower-skilled, lower-class white citizens in migrating from the metropolitan countries to the colonies, and because Cameroon lacked a "white-settler" population, as in Kenya or Zimbabwe for example, it became possible to develop a class of African-owned large and small scale enterprises as well as a class of African commercial and peasant farmers who were able to compete with the well established European-owned plantations and commercial houses. It is to this class of indigenous African accumulators that we now turn our attention.

Indigenous Capital

An examination of the financing of Cameroon's five-year development plans (there have been five between 1960 and 1986) suggests that overall available domestic savings in any planned period was far less than projected investments, thus implying that the state had to rely on private foreign capital investment and public foreign loans and grants to fill the gap.[12]

The interpretation of this is simple. Opportunities for local businessmen to accumulate capital and lead this country along the path of an independent industrialization are simply not present. While the reasons for this lack of opportunities are debatable, the cause often emphasized is that the structure of the economy in the postcolonial state continues the pattern of the colonial state in placing constraints on the development of an indigenous class of capitalists.

At independence in 1960, Cameroon had a small open economy with foreign trade accounting for more than 25 percent of the national product. The export trade was characterized by a heavy dependence on a few primary agricultural commodities—including cocoa, coffee, tea, palm oil, and cotton (see Table 4.2). As of 1980, the situation had hardly changed, as Table 4.5 shows.

Table 4.5. Principal Export Groups (Value in Millions CFA Francs)

	Agricultural Products		*Crude Mineral Products*		*Industrial Products*		*Other Products*		*Total Exports*	
Year	*Value*	*Percentage*	*Value*	*Percentage*	*Value*	*Percentage*	*Value*	*Percentage*	*Value*	*Percentage*
1974–1975	75,823	70.93	—	—	26,099	24.41	4,978	4.66	106,900	100
1975–1976	81,328	72.45	—	—	26,293	23.42	4,631	4.13	112,252	100
1976–1977	117,663	72.97	—	—	37,262	23.11	6,317	3.92	161,242	100
1977–1978	138,494	72.51	2,744	1.44	45,171	23.65	4,601	2.40	191,010	100
1978–1979	129,114	64.91	23,172	11.65	42,347	21.29	4,272	2.15	198,905	100
1979–1980	157,244	52.37	83,583	27.84	52,553	17.50	6,850	2.29	300,230	100

Source: Compiled from Direction Statistique 1982.

Thus, from 1974 to 1980, industrial goods accounted for 18 percent of total exports by volume and for 21.5 percent of the value of these exports.[13] There were few interindustry links since the overwhelming part of the processing of exportable agricultural surplus was carried out in western Europe, and most of what was traded was made of raw products or only minimally transformed. The repatriated earnings of foreign capital exceeded the inflow of new resources into the country. Thus Cameroonian business was unable to develop independently of foreign investors. Because of the lack of a sizeable class of indigenous businessmen, foreign firms were able to move in and fill the vacuum, preempting the most important markets in the local economy through their resources, experience, and technological advantages.

An appreciation of the overall industrial situation of Cameroon since it became independent is necessary at this point. The general observation is Cameroon's industrial development is characterized by a change in industrial strategy and separated by two distinct periods: 1960–1970 and 1971–1983, with 1971–1972 being the most decisive year.[14] The 1960–1971 period was marked by (1) an emphasis on attracting foreign capital and know-how, (2) import substitution industrialization, (3) a political and administrative climate conducive to "imported" industrial development, tarrif and nontariff protection of domestic markets, establishment of the 1962 and 1966 investment codes, and founding membership in the Central African Customs and Economic Union (UDEAC).

The 1971–1983 period is noted for its industrial pragmatism, initiated at the beginning of the third plan (1971–1976). The fourth plan (1976–1981) projected this slant in industrial policy, which was justified by (1) the initial impact of investments in industry, (2) the advent of a unitary state in 1972, (3) the encouraging progress made in research on and exploitation of large reserves of oils and minerals, (4) the difficulties encountered in substituting imports with local products, and (5) the increasing supply of Cameroonian skilled labor and executive staff. The result was positive with the rate at which industries were established annually maintained at 15 percent while the industrial sector itself contributed 20.2 percent to overall GDP.[15] In general, the contribution of this sector to total GDP is still low compared to that of the primary and tertiary sectors (see Table 4.6).

Who are Cameroonian businessmen? How much have they contributed to domestic capital formation and in what sectors are they concentrated? Answers to these questions will allow us to analyze (in the next section) how they relate to the state and foreign capital.

In the early years of statehood, there appeared to be two potential sources of an indigenous industrial class ready to cross over from circulation to production of goods and services. The first and more visible group is composed mainly of small holder commercial farmers, petty traders, retailers, and handicraft artisans, who, by the mid-1970s, were providing a fair amount of competition to foreign capital. Unfortunately this sector is still unstructured, and a systematic study of this group of capitalists is still to be done.

Table 4.6. Distribution of the Gross Domestic Product by Sector

Year	*Primary Sector (1)*	*Secondary Sector (2)*	*Tertiary Sector (3)*	*Total (4)*	*(2)/(4) (%)*
1960–1961	40.3	24.4	45.4	110.1	22
1965–1966	55.7	33.4	64.4	153.5	22
1969–1970	90.5	46.0	119.7	256.2	18
1974–1975	166.1	73.5	185.7	435.3	17
1977–1978	305.4	147.4	384.2	801.0	18
1980–1981	420.2	280.8	490.8	1,191.8	24

*Source:*Cameroon, Ministry of Economic Affairs and Planning 1981b.

The second source of indigenous industrialists covers those currently engaged in medium and large-scale capital accumulation, assisted by links with the state and/or foreign capital. Table 4.4 shows, for example, that Cameroon public interests have been increasing in many sectors: agro-industry, 76 percent in 1980 against 71 percent in 1976; drinks, 11 percent against 7.5 percent; food industries, 10 percent against 2.3 percent; leather products, 59 percent against 13 percent; timber processing, 19.8 percent against 14 percent; metal processing, 23 percent against 9 percent; gas, electricity, and water, 99 percent against 80.5 percent.[16] Public participation is completely absent in two industries: tobacco and the processing of paper. It has maintained a steady interest throughout the years in the construction materials industry, but it has retreated in two sectors: food industries (from 16.5 to 10 percent) and chemical industries (from 31 to 24 percent). Cameroon public participation has been largely in those sectors or industries for which private capital has been lacking (agro-industry, energy, etc.); those industries in a commanding position for which public investors would normally prevail over private investors because of the low rate of national savings; and public utilities and industries that are less profitable as commercial enterprises. Furthermore, such public participation is not only less selective in nature, but normally is carried out through an intermediary institution, the National Investment Company (SNI), which has been participating in almost all sectors of the economy.

From Table 4.4, we also note that total private investment in 1980 was 8 percent and that private participation was relatively strong in two sectors: drinks (20 percent) and tobacco (25 percent). Private participation completely dominated the paper and pulp industries contributing 100 percent of the investment capital. At this junction, we turn our attention to the instruments and incentives employed by the state not only to increase public and private indigenous capital accumulation as well as joint ventures, but also to make sure that they conform to its development policies.

CAMEROONIAN DEVELOPMENT PRINCIPLES

During the decade preceding independence in 1960, Cameroon faced acute economic problems. Production was stagnant and private investment—foreign and domestic—was minimal because of political instability.[17] In the subsequent quarter century, the government's efforts to reinforce political unity resulted in an impressive reversal of the situation, and the state embraced four relatively centrist and dirigistic political economic principles as the touchstones of its development. Through these principles—planned liberalism, self-reliance, balanced development, social justice—the country has sought to increase its international commerce, expand effective government participation in and control over economic development, and broaden the ownership as well as employment participation of Cameroonians in the directly productive sector.

Planned Liberalism

Planned liberalism as espoused by the Cameroon National Union (CNU) and implemented by the government has economic and political goals. On the one hand, it promotes and encourages private initiatives and on the other hand, assigns to the state the task of mobilizing, coordinating, and guiding these initiatives in an atmosphere of respect for the requirements of the general interest and national sovereignty. In other words, this doctrine gives a greater reliance on markets, especially international market forces, for guiding investment and output allocations in the country while at the same time gives the state interventionist powers to form state or parastatal enterprises to safeguard the sovereignty of the nation. From another standpoint, this doctrine acts as a safety valve, limiting state enterprises to run the traditional public utilities that support the directly productive sector.

From a political viewpoint too, planned liberalism regulates private enterprise (whether foreign or domestic) from attaining oligopolistic powers largely because unbridled economic liberalism may lead to economic imperialism, subvert Cameroon's embryonic development, as well as jeopardize national sovereignty. To regulate and control private enterprises, the state may decide to enter into partnership with such interests or create public or parastatal institutions through which it can stimulate, control, or direct the national economy as a whole and safeguard its own interests.

Self-Reliant Development

The transfer of power at independence involved primarily a handing over of the machinery of government. Since Cameroonian participation in the private modern sector was limited during the colonial period, it became obligatory for the state to satisfy both the social aspirations of self-reliance and control over the nation's economic destiny, as well as improving the living standard of the population. Since the mid-1960s, the economy has seen a significant overall growth, as depicted in Table 4.7.

One universally recognized feature of structural economic change is that, as countries develop, the proportion of gross domestic product (GDP) and employment accounted for by agriculture tends to decline. The reason for this is that improved living standards entail an increasingly personal consumption of goods and services other than food, and this necessitates a concomitant rise in the production of human and other resources allocated to nonagricultural production. In 1960, 87.8 percent of the economically active Cameroonians were engaged in agriculture, while by 1970 there had been a 17 percent reduction, with approximately 70 percent of the population engaged in agriculture. This notwithstanding, however, agriculture continues to provide the bulk of the GDP, some 35 percent, and employs a third of the active population (Table 4.8).

The assumed relationship between industrialization and development has led many unsuspecting developing countries to adopt negative policies toward agriculture and thereby to transfer a disproportionate amount of government-controlled investable resources into industry. Fortunately, Cameroon, unlike many of its neighbors, has placed agriculture in the forefront of development. This concept is captured in the self-reliant development doctrine espoused at the 1975 CNU Party Congress held in Douala.

Growth in the realm of agriculture can be attributed largely to the efforts of private individuals (who are small-scaled rather than plantational or industrial) and mostly small subsistence-oriented farmers. However, the government has acted as a catalyst in this self-reliant development approach by implementing policies that do not penalize small holder farmers, including a production policy that gives greater consideration to domestic demand. This is a policy of increased productivity and self-suffi-

Table 4.7. Total Real Annual Growth of the Cameroon Economy (in Constant 1979 CFA Francs)

Period	*Total*
1966–1967	1.8
1967–1968	6.4
1968–1969	5.0
1969–1970	3.0
1970–1971	3.8
Average of second plan (1966–1971)	4.0
1971–1972	-0.4
1972–1973	8.8
1973–1974	11.2
1974–1975	-1.7
1975–1976	5.0
Average of third plan (1971–1976)	4.4
1976–1977	8.0
1977–1978	8.5
1978–1979	8.1
1979–1980	3.0
1980–1981	1.6
Average of fourth plan (1976–1981)	5.8
1981–1982	4.8
1982–1983*	7.0
1983–1984	n.a.

Source: Ministry of Economic Affairs and Planning, 1981b.
*Based on the projected growth rate of the GDP.

ciency in food, which at the same time encourages increased cash crop production by the constant increase in the prices of these crops, especially during periods of world market commodity slumps. Additionally, the government has pursued a financial and monetary policy geared toward the mobilization of domestic savings; a trading policy based on the active promotion of selective exports and imports of capital and consumer goods; a policy of rigorous exploitation of national resources and reorientation of industry and employment: a wage policy that follows the pace of development requirements and of objectives pursued through development; and an intensive research policy adapted and geared toward the realization of national objectives.

Table 4.8. Distribution of the Gross Domestic Product (GDP) by Sector, 1980—Cameroon

Sector	*Millions CFA Francs*	*Percentage*
Agriculture, fisheries	305,400	34.5
Mines	4,200	0.5
Manufacturing industries	87,400	9.9
Electricity, water, and gas	11,700	1.3
Construction and public works	46,600	5.3
Commerce	154,100	17.4
Transport and communication	65,900	7.4
Public services	70,700	8.4
Other services	139,200	15.7
TOTAL	885,200	100.0
Customs duties	54,600	
GDP at market prices	939,800	

Source: Ministry of Economic Affairs and Planning 1981b.

The principle of self-reliant development and the policies generated from it have had far-reaching consequences. It cannot be overemphasized that Cameroon has made private peasant production the main plank of agricultural development. Though the government has tended to stay clear of direct state production in agriculture, there is no lack of public investment in infrastructure, research, marketing, extension, and credit facilities. Thus it is noteworthy that agriculture received more than 30 percent of total public investment in the third (1971–1976) and fourth (1976–1981) plan periods, while FONADER (National Fund for Rural Development, set up in 1973) was formed as a bank capable of handling deposits in order to improve its role as a "banker for peasants." Since its creation, the government has been shifting investment priorities and making loans available to rural small holder farmers. For example, the government supplied fertilizers to farmers at an import cost of 2.12 billion CFA francs in 1977–1978 and almost 4.5 billion CFA francs in 1980–1981. An interesting postscript of the policy of self-reliant development is its long term objective of making Cameroon the "store-house of Central Africa."

Balanced Development

Simply put, the doctrine of balanced development upholds the idea that equal attention should be paid to the different sectors of activity in the economy; to the regions, towns, and countryside; and to men, women, adults, and youths. Given Cameroon's economic, social, cultural, geographical, historical, and linguistic diversity, it has been felt that it would be unfair to concentrate development efforts in only one part or area of the country. Because missionary and colonial penetration into the inland and northern areas of Cameroon was slow, difficult, and often unsuccessful, many regions and rural areas have remained comparatively impoverished. Consequently, balanced development is an attempt by the government to redress regional inequalities by providing education, infrastructures and the public amenities necessary for bridging the country and the town.

The government has made considerable efforts to give concrete form to this principle in a number of ways. In recognizing the rural sector as carrying the bulk of the nation's population (about 80 percent) and its agricultural production, both peasant and commercial, the Third and Fourth Five-Year Development Plans outlined steps to ensure the implementation of various projects in rural areas, establishing credit facilities and rationalizing and marketing food crops produced to meet increased urban demand.

Making the rural areas attractive to youth would stem the flow of unemployed school graduates drifting into the towns and cities. Since the majority of the population depends for its livelihood on agriculture, and since a large percentage of exports and thus of GDP comes from agricultural commodities and industries related to agriculture, jobs for the unemployed must be generated in the rural sector. To this end, agricultural estates, pioneer villages, development areas, and other rural projects are being used to encourage the settlement of young people in rural areas. Such integrated rural development schemes that have been launched by the CNU would contribute enormously to the balanced development of Cameroon's varied regions.

The secondary sector, which concentrates on semi-manufactured, manufactured, and petroleum products, is also given full attention in the doctrine of balanced development. Measures are taken to ensure that the locations of industries are not concentrated within a single town or region. Cameroon has been lucky to discover large deposits of petroleum and gas. Rather than committing these resources lavishly to consumer development projects, the government is using them in areas that are least developed to benefit the people by providing rural public health care facilities and clean drinking water, extending farm-to-market roads, and supporting cash croppers in times of falling prices.

Finally, the manifestation of the principle of balanced development is reflected in the educational sector. Cameroon has clearly committed itself to education as a national priority, devoting some 25 percent of the national budget to this sector. The decision to decentralize the disciplines and faculties of the University of Yaounde, relocating them in the various provinces to develop into new universities, will expand the number of such institutions, reduce enrollment and overcrowding problems at the University of Yaounde, and mitigate the problem of regional inequality in the access to higher educational institutions.

Social Justice

The doctrine of social justice aims at redistributing the fruits of development equitably among different groups and giving each citizen an equal opportunity within the framework of national solidarity. This concept implies distributive rather than commutative justice and carries with it the notion of reform. At times when overall productivity in the economy is increasing, there is little justification for not distributing the national cake equitably. Policies designed to increase smallholder productivity and income include hard decisions on exchange rates, tariff structures, formal sector wages (such as the 1983 salary increase in all sectors), retail price controls, and agricultural producer prices. It makes little sense to increase the purchasing power of rural incomes through such policy reforms if failures in the distributive systems conveying manufactured consumer goods to the hinterland subvert the use of increased incomes for increased purchases. So implementing the concept of social justice means improving physical transport infrastructure, especially feeder roads and storage facilities, and increasing the operating efficiency of credit (FONADER), marketing (MIDEVIV), and transport intermediaries.

GOVERNMENT POLICIES AND THEIR IMPLEMENTATION

The state is of fundamental importance in attaining development objectives, but it could also be a major limitation to overall development. There are two issues here: (1) whether the state is actively oriented toward promoting sustained growth and development, and (2) whether it is capable of implementing such a program. The first condition is easily met since most government leaders recognize that some form of development is necessary for their survival (citizens now expect it from them). They may also find that development could bring in a lot of foreign capital through loans, aid, grants, and other investment commitments, which is usually not contrary to their immediate interests.

The implementation of development plans in Cameroon, as in most third world countries, relies heavily on special institutional and regulative factors. These are usually fostered by the government rather than by market mechanisms. They were designed originally to increase the supply of capital to nascent industries, to increase the share of indigenous capital formation and accumulation, and finally to provide local businesses with less decentralized and better informed entrepreneurial guidance. Thus, given its repressive and integrative functions, the state is in a position to provide the preconditions for the process of production and overall economic development.

One of the functions of the state in the process of indigenous capital accumulation is to formulate regulations and make credit available to local business enterprises. Since the early 1960s, foreign and domestic investors have been assisted through liberal legislation with the result that at present there is a preponderance of quasi-majority interests in industries in the country, which were taken out in the form of foreign private capital. All this has been made possible by the Cameroon Investment Code, promulgated as part of the state's program to foster the expansion of domestic and foreign business. It consists of four categories:

(1) Preferential Treatment A permits duty-free entry of the required raw materials and capital goods for a period of up to ten years and allows reduced rates of, or exemption from, indirect taxes (for example, the single tax on production) on finished products for a period of up to three years, including exemption from new taxes and changes in the rates of existing ones.

(2) Under Preferential Treatment B, enterprises may be eligible to obtain, in addition to the benefits under Preferential Treatment A, exemption for a period of up to five years from taxes on profits and, in the case of mining and timber companies, from the payment of royalties. They are also eligible for many benefits from new tax laws that might be introduced during the first ten years of their operation.

(3) Under Preferential Treatment C, large corporations may conclude an agreement with the government under which they may receive all or part of the privileges of Preferential Treatment B. The agreement in each case will also define other government guarantees in the legal, economic, and financial fields, including the undertaking to assure stable conditions for financial transfers and the marketing of the enterprise's goods for a period of up to 25 years. The enterprise in turn must guarantee a minimum volume of production and grant to its employees certain minimum social benefits, including housing.

(4) Preferential Treatment D, which applies to enterprises making investments of particular importance to the long-term economic development of the country, gives to the enterprises all the benefits of Preferential Treatment C, as well as a guarantee that new taxes and tax rates will not apply to such enterprises for up to 25 years.

One of the effects of this legislation has been the low contribution by nationals to the formation of the capital of industrial enterprises because of the high foreign exchange costs incurred by local industries. In general, the Investment Code does not define the areas of the economy in which foreign and domestic private capital can be channeled, with the result that domestic public investment and foreign private capital have given rise to financially unstable businesses. Even joint ventures with prospects of local ownership have not led to the power structure's passing into local hands. In Preferential Treatment C, provisions that require a minimum volume of production (in other words, jobs and training) to be made available to nationals and other social benefits are rarely enforced.

Ironically, foreign economic agents (F) not only win contracts that are financed by international organizations but also projects that are sponsored by the state's own revenues. This may account partially for the growth of foreign business in the construction and public works sector in Cameroon. Cameroon's Investment Code serves to promote such a growth; whereas these foreign firms import machinery on a tax free basis, this same privilege is refused Cameroonian businessmen.

Credit facilities for local enterprises have been greatly expanded as a conscious effort by the state to develop domestic capitalism. Up to the mid-1970s, a number of public institutions were created to make more credit and guidance available to local entrepreneurs:

- The Ministry of Planning and Territorial Development;
- The Centre for Information and Documentation of Economic Planning, charged with the responsibility of collecting data on the whole economy and reporting on the progress of development plans;
- The National Investment Society of Cameroon, responsible for some of the national development projects;[18]
- The Cameroon Development Bank (BCD) to finance projects in line with economic and social development objectives;[19]
- The Cameroon Investment Code designed to encourage the increase of private capital, both foreign and domestic;[20]
- The National Fund for Rural Development (FONADER), set up as a farmers' bank to offer credit to development activities located in the rural sector;[21]

- The National Centre for the Assistance of Small and Medium-Size Undertakings (CAPME) to provide artisanal enterprises with industrial and commercial character by coordinating the actions of business undertakings and to promote indigenous capital accumulation;[22]
- The Aid and Loan Guarantee Fund for Small and Medium-Size Undertakings (FOGAPE) as direct aid to small indigenous enterprises in the form of training, counsel, and guaranteed bank loans.[23]

The provisions of these financial institutions were meant to put a larger proportion of capital at the disposal of local businessmen. Unfortunately, some bad results have been recorded. The National Investment Corporation (SNI), for example, was created to enable the government to mitigate the shortage of private domestic investments by promoting joint ventures. Most enterprises in which SNI has shares are running at a loss (4.6 billion CFA francs worth of losses in 1977–1978 and, in 1981–1982, 5 billion CFA francs).[24] This may be partly due to the inefficient management of some of our parastatal enterprises. However, in 1982, the SNI, a parapublic institution, participated in 62 undertakings in the primary, secondary, and tertiary sectors of the economy with total investments (net of taxes) of more than 46 billion CFA francs.[25]

Another important achievement of the 1970s is the large scale expansion of state credit institutions such as the BCD, FONADER, and FOGAPE. The BCD has been the source of state finance to the local commercial and industrial sectors. The bank, with a capital of 6 billion CFA francs, is funded 82 percent from Cameroon government sources, 10 percent from the French Caisse Centrale de Cooperation Economique (CCCE), and 8 percent from loans from the Bank of Central African States.[26]

The objectives of BCD are essentially to support the economic development efforts of the state by financing local enterprises and commerce, agro-industry, and small- and medium-size undertakings, and to participate in large industrial projects with financial institutions such as SNI, FONADER, and FOGAPE. The credits meted out in 1982–1983 amounted to 29.63 billion CFA francs.

During this period, particular attention was given to small- and medium-size undertakings with the disbursements to 104 local enterprises amounting to 6.02 billion CFA francs, an annual credit growth of 20.3 percent.

In order to intervene better in the rural sector, FONADER, an agricultural credit institution, now transformed into an agricultural credit bank, has specific funds placed at its disposal by the state or international financing bodies to enable it to grant credit to farmers or stock-farmers as part of special development projects. This is the case with credits granted for projects such as SOCAPALM, High Plateau of the West, North-West

Benoue, SEMRY, Special Fund for Rural Action, and Meat Plan. The state provides financing for major rural development projects so that various economic groups of the rural sector may have production credits of a special nature (housing, school, etc.). The total amount of credits granted by FONADER increased from 2 billion CFA francs in 1980 to 6 billion in 1983.[27]

As was FONADER, which caters to the rural sector, FOGAPE (created in 1975) was designed to assist indigenous traders and businessmen who for one reason or another had difficulties in securing bank loans. In 1983, FOGAPE intervened on behalf of 251 businesses requiring bank loans of 5.49 billion CFA francs while guaranteeing 3.58 billion CFA francs (see Table 4.9).

Table 4.9. FOGAPE Credit Disbursement to Enterprises by Sector of Activity, 1983

Categories	*Number*	*Total Credit Requested in Million F/CFA*	*Total Amount Guaranteed in Million F/CFA*
Individual Large-Scale Credits			
Professionals	28	495.3	341.0
Agro-pastoral	16	242.2	172.1
Sub Total	44	737.5	513.2
Credit to Entrepreneurs			
Industrial Enterprises	132	3,753.2	2,418.5
Commercial Enterprises	17	181.9	142.6
Others	58	826.7	510.6
Sub Total	207	5,499.3	3,071.7
TOTAL	251	6,236.8	3,584.9

Source: L'Economie Camerounaise: Bilan de l'exercice 1982–1983, p. 155.

Of the 251 operations processed by FOGAPE in 1983, 114 requested 3.7 billion CFA francs which was to be financed by BCD while the remaining 137 enterprises had to seek credit from commercial banks. In the industrial sector, 132 proposed ventures required a record credit of 3.7 billion CFA francs, approximately 68 percent of projected investment capital.[28]

These regulations and credit facilities have all helped to increase state participation in industrial and agricultural enterprises in the country. With the extension of the state's interest, it has been possible for it to monitor and ensure that industrial and agricultural development conform to its policies.

CONCLUSIONS

This chapter began by examining Cameroon's development policies within a conceptual framework of the triangular relationship between the state, indigenous capitalists, and foreign economic agents. In spite of stated development policies, foreign capital plays a dominant role in Cameroon and has not been greatly affected by the growth of indigenous capital or even the extension of the state sector. Although the economy has witnessed a successful period of economic growth since independence, largely because of its policy of planned liberalism, which strongly encourages private initiative with the state guaranteeing the general interest, an independent indigenous industrial bourgeois class of capitalists has yet to become a permanent feature of the economy.

The state's intervention has generally favored large-scale foreign enterprises, although the recent trend is to diversify increasingly the source of foreign investment, as illustrated by the past four five-year development plans. Indigenous businessmen have acquired wealth from commercial retailing, urban property, and real estate, while those in the import and distributive trades are still dominated by foreign capitalists. However, there is a small group of Cameroonian entrepreneurs who have established large-scale industries usually in association with foreign partners and the state.

Until 1975, one could count certain viable and prosperous indigenous businesses such as CETRIC, BURETIC, SOPPO, and NANGAH and Company. Whereas the investment budget for the 1975–1980 period increased by 28 percent, indigenous business was going through a survival crisis. However, some Cameroonian businessmen are determined to fight against this trend through UNECAM, which was created in 1974.[29] Whereas UNECAM's membership is mostly Cameroonian, there is a parallel union made up mostly of foreign businessmen. Out of this union's 57 members, only 3 are Cameroonians. At the general assembly of UNECAM in October 1983, it was established that over 80 percent of Cameroonian entrepreneurs had no jobs or were folding. These figures are in great contrast to the report of the parallel union, which talks of a growth in their business. But this is not surprising since state firms such as SONEL and SOCAPALM, which also put out bids for contracts, are also members of the parallel union.

Indigenous capitalists have yet to provide an effective challenge to or even to supplant foreign capital. Typically 80 percent or more of industrial value-added is in import-substituting activities, which in Cameroon includes food and beverage processing, textiles, garment manufacture, wood products, paper, and printing along with a sprinkle of capital intensive projects in petroleum refining, cement, and fertilizers. Petroleum and its by-products are having a significant impact on the development of the country. Since 1977, the revenue obtained from oil has been able to offset the high cost of industrialization, as well as to initiate the structural transformation of the economy.

The decade of the 1970s saw a huge increase in state ventures. Through its liberal development policies, investment codes, legislations, and credit facilities, many parapublic corporations have been formed, thus making it possible for the state to move gradually from a mediating position between domestic and foreign economic agents to become an instrument that is increasingly used by the bureaucratic and managerial elements of the bourgeoisie class to accumulate capital.[30]

The 1980s find the overall capital product, especially in industry, regulated and subsidized by the state. Although oil revenue has recently made a decisive difference, industrial expansion continues to rely on revenue from exports of agricultural products and foreign investment capital. The revenue from exports of agricultural products is largely collected by marketing boards that subsidize such state-protected monopolies as power, water, and transportation (Cameroon Airlines, Railways). Other industrial sectors, where a few local businessmen have been able to enter (building construction, furniture, motor vehicle importation and distribution, food processing, etc.), have generally depended on foreign management and technology. It has been necessary for such investments to occur as joint ventures, collaborations between foreign investors and indigenous capitalists.

The function of the state has been precise. The vacuum created by the absence of an independent industrial bourgeoisie has been filled by the bureaucratic and managerial elements within the state who have been able to use it to form an alliance with foreign capital. A number of industries that were already working before independence have more than tripled their output in the past two decades, especially beer, soda waters, cocoa butter, plywood, cottonseed oil, and furniture. Examples of new industries that have been successfully established either by indigenous proprietors and/or foreign investors include footwear, clothing, aluminum sheeting, plastic, and utensils. However, it is hoped that such regulations (Investment Code) and institutional facilities as the Cameroon Development Bank, FONADER, CAPME, and FOGAPE would be able to reverse the bias against emerging small-scale indigenous investors and have a profound impact on the rate of domestic capital formation and accumulation in Cameroon.

NOTES

1. In 1981, the World Bank reclassified Cameroon from a low-income to a middle-income country (with a GNP per capita income of more than $560). Although the growth rate of the economy throughout the 1960s was disappointingly low (an average of 4 percent), its political stability and the legacy of planned liberalism bore positive fruits in the 1980s. See *West Africa* 1983, pp. 596–597.

2. For a useful summary and an African application of Sunkel and Fuenzalida's 1974 transnational thesis, see Godfrey and Langdon 1976.

3. "Foreign economic agents" is a generic term used to refer to transnational firms, expatriate groups resident in a country, foreign governments, and international financial agencies. See UNCTAD Doc. TD/B/AC. II/21 of June 19, 1979, p. 11. In this context, our focus would be mainly on transnational companies and other foreign businesses.

4. Historians tell us that Fernando Po, a Portuguese sailor, landed on the shores of Cameroon in 1472. Because of the great quantity of prawns, he is said to have named the river "River dos Camerones," (river of prawns), from which the name Cameroon is derived. For details, see Le Vine 1961.

5. Adam Smith, quoted in Kamark 1967, p. 7.

6. This company represented one of the biggest private French interests in Africa—Societe des Plantations Reunies de l'Afrique Occidentale (SPRAO).

7. *L'Industrie Camerounaise,* Douala 1981, p. 21.

8. *L'Industrie Camerounaise,* Douala 1981, p. 21.

9. It should be pointed out that the CDC employs more than 50 percent of the West Cameroon labor force and accounts for over half of export trade. However, it has contributed little to the industrial development of the region since its concentration has remained in the export of primary products.

10. The CDWF was the counterpart of the French FIDES, except that there was no such explicit planning structure as the one in East Cameroon.

11. *L'Industrie Camerounaise en 1980–1981,* Douala 1983, p. 2.

12. In the case of the first plan (1960–1965), the gap was about 60 percent, while for the 1966–1971 plan, 73 percent of the total planned investment was to come from external sources (36 percent from direct private foreign investment and 37 percent from public foreign grants and loans).

13. Cameroon, Ministry of Economic Affairs and Planning 1981.

14. The 1971–1972 year was decisive for Cameroon's development policies, which are relatively centrist and experimental compared to other Francophone countries. They played an active role in building regional economic links through both membership of the Central African Economic Union (UDEAC) and in developing routes to the sea and sources of manufactures for its land-locked neighbors, Chad and the Central African Republic.

15. Cameroon, Ministry of Economic Affairs and Planning 1981, p. 160.

16. *L'Industrie Camerounaise,* 1981, p. 21.

17. The political instability, which marked the decade preceding independence in 1960, slowed the economic development of Cameroon. The government had to exert tight control on the economy (for example, in its labor policy) or on the investment programs of foreigners and thus was able not only to limit the oc-

currence, frequency, and diffusion of strikes but also to select the entrepreneurs it deemed to be desirable in the country.

18. Now known as the National Investment Corporation, or Societe Nationale d'Investissement (SNI), it was created in 1964 by the government to mitigate the shortage of private domestic savings by promoting joint ventures. It therefore plays the role of a government merchant bank complementing the action of an investment bank by financing large bodies.

19. The Cameroon Development Bank or Banque de Developpement Camerounaise (BCD) was created in 1960 with a status approved by decree Number 60/247 of December 29, 1960 and replaced on March 3, 1976 by decree Number 76/89.

20. This legislation, which was first promulgated on June 29, 1960, and was later revised in 1964 and 1966 provides four categories of preferential treatment that may be granted to eligible entrepreneurs, foreign or domestic undertakings approved in forming new industrial or agricultural projects in the country. For further details, see Ministry of Industrial and Commercial Development, 1972.

21. The National Fund for Rural Development or Fonds National de Developpement Rural (FONADER) was created by decree Number 73/24 of May 29, 1973, and modified by law Number 77/5 of July 13, 1973.

22. The National Centre for the Assistance of Small and Medium-Size Undertakings or Centre National d'Assistance aux Petites et Moyennes Entreprises (CAPME) was created by the government in 1970 as a national body coordinating the actions of the above institutions.

23. In spite of the various national institutions and credit facilities (FONADER, CAPME, BCD, and SNI), indigenous businessmen continued to have difficulties in obtaining bank loans. Through decree Number 75/238 of April 1975, the government created a national body to mitigate the difficulties encountered by small- and medium-size undertakings. This body is known as Aid and Loan Guarantee Fund for Small and Medium-Size Undertakings or Fonds d'Aide et de Garantie des Credits aux Petites et Moyennes Enterprises (FOGAPE).

24. Cameroon, Ministry of Economic Affairs and Planning 1981, p. 164. The figure of the 1981–1982 period was obtained from an interview with an SNI official in February 1984.

25. Societe Nationale d'Investissement 1981.

26. Cameroon Development Bank 1982.

27. Groupement Interprofessionnel pour l'Unite et de Coordination des Interets Economiques au Cameroun 1984, pp. 145–152.

28. Groupement Interprofessionel pour l'Unite et de Coordination des Interets Economiques au Cameroun 1984, p. 155.

29. For a critical appraisal of Small and Medium-Size Undertakings in Cameroon, see a recent article "Pour l'Integration des P.M.E. Camerounaises a l'Economie Nationale," *Cameroon Tribune,* March 14, 1984.

30. Another political move by the government to concentrate power was to curtail labor movements. In 1971, the country's three major trade union confederations were formally dissolved and reconstituted into the trade union wing of the party.

5

THE PRACTICES OF A LIBERAL POLITICAL ECONOMY: IMPORT AND EXPORT SUBSTITUTION IN CAMEROON (1975–1981)

Jean-Claude Willame

Under President Ahidjo's iron rule, Cameroon has traditionally been regarded as a paradigm for African development. Until recently, most international banks gave the country the unique distinction of being the sole African state to be granted a triple A credit rating. Cameroon was touted as an agricultural success story for maintaining its population on the land: self sufficiency was said to be reached in the realm of food production. It has also become a favorite son of oil companies: offshore oil output jumped from 1.4 million tons in 1979 to 4.3 million in 1981. Much vaunted was the government policy of keeping the oil boom under strict surveillance (as well as under strict secrecy) by underplaying the importance of that commodity in a traditionally agricultural economy.

President Biya's arrival in power has coincided with the discovery of some hard facts about the real economic situation in Cameroon. The "green revolution" launched with fanfare in 1972 has failed to live up to expectations. The pace of the rural exodus has accelerated as in many African countries: 16 percent of the population lived in the urban centers around 1970, 34 percent in 1980, and 65 percent could do so by 1990. This is one of the fastest rates of urbanization in the third world. The social situation in such cities as Douala has become explosive with crime and poverty rampant and an insufficiency of housing for newcomers.

The traditional export crops of Cameroon—coffee and cocoa—have not been doing well for the last three years. Not only are the forecasts of the Fourth Five-Year Plan far from being met, but the production of these "stimulating" crops has been falling since 1980. In 1982, a report from the Finance Commission of the French Assembly (rapport Vivien) observed that "without oil, the trade balance of Cameroon would show a substantial deficit" (*Cameroon Selection,* November 30, 1982).

The rate of inflation has greatly escalated—more than 20 percent according to recent estimates. As a consequence, industrial activity has severely dropped while some state enterprises are close to bankruptcy.

Oil has indeed become a major asset for the Cameroonian economy. It represents about 60 percent of exports, but, contrary to Ahidjo's unrealistic wishes, the effects of the oil boom have been disruptive in many ways: profiteers have made quick and immense fortunes especially in the construction business at Douala, Limbe, and Yaounde, while trusting bankers discovered at their own expense that credit was suddenly available without guarantee to well connected people. Additionally, the oil boom may be a short-lived phenomenon: oil exploration has come to a standstill, and the huge LNG project has been postponed.

This chapter attempts to demonstrate that the "Cameroonian miracle" has been based on unsound practices of import and export substitution in both agriculture and industry. These practices were established when the growth of the once slow-moving and nonintegrated Cameroonian economy suddenly accelerated and overheated through a process of disruptive expansion. Note that, as in many other African countries, lack of efficient planning has been mostly responsible for these ill practices. Planned liberalism, the key term in the official language, was supposed to supplement defective private initiative with state intervention in the economy. In fact, the doctrine of planned liberalism was more a shopping list of desirable public sector investment projects for interested financing bodies and industrialists than the rigorous exercise in integrated financial, economic, and social allocation it was theoretically intended to be. As one economic commentator has recently noticed, "it is a helpful vademecum for the new investors who are now beating a path to Cameroon's door" (*African Business,* April 1982, p. 23).

AGRO-BUSINESS VERSUS RURAL DEVELOPMENT

In Cameroon, agro-industries have been conceived of as the key instruments to enhance rural development and as a means of escape from a too strong dependency on traditional crops (coffee and cocoa). While the peasant sector was favored in the First and Second Five-Year Plans (by, for example, reinforcement of the cooperatives and support for integrated agricultural projects), one could notice a sudden reversal of this trend from the third plan onward. In that plan, 60 percent of public investment was poured into agro-industrial ventures; this percentage grew to 63 percent in the fourth plan. With the fifth plan, and despite the rhetoric of support to the Cameroonian peasant, willingness to transform the rural mode of production through agro-industrial complexes is more evident. In an interview with *Afrique Agriculture,* the minister of agriculture declared that agro-industries should become "poles of development of the rural space thanks to the improvement they bring to the working and living conditions of all the peasants" (*Afrique Agriculture,* December 1982). The truth was, however, quite different.

The Case of State Ventures in Agriculture

Support for agro-industrial ventures initiated by the state already started in 1968 with the creation of the Cameroonian Palm Grove Company (SOCAPALM), which was to produce and sell palm oil from an estate of 220,000 hectares. The beginnings of that company were slow and painful; it was not until 1978–1979 that production really got started. The Cameroonian Palm Grove Company was in the red for most of that time, except in 1980 when it made a small profit. The company is listed in *Bilan diagnostic du secteur agricole*—a critical but official study on agricultural development in Cameroon since the 1960s—as an agro-industrial investment too costly for the country: in 1981, investments at SOCAPALM had reached a record of 33 billion CFA francs, 60 percent of which came from several international loans and aids (such as The World Bank) (Ministere de l'Agriculture, March 1980; *Fichier Industriel de l'Afrique Noire,* 20 July 1981).

Despite massive external aid, the profit-earning capacity of SOCAPALM is in doubt; as had many of its "colonial" counterparts—Cameroon Development Corporation (CDC) and PAMOL—SOCAPALM had severe difficulties in recruiting palm cutters and workers, and company plans for creating village plantations have notoriously failed. The *Bilan diagnostic* mentions that yields could not go over 8.2 tons per hectare whereas they should normally reach 12–13 tons.

Inadequate management has also been said to be a major problem for SOCAPALM. After an investigation, the World Bank recommended in 1981 "to strengthen the company, including the recruitment of new staff for certain key posts" and "to defer new investments" (International Development Association 1981, p. 31).

Hevea-Cameroun (HEVECAM), was created in 1975, is also an important state venture in the realm of agro-industry (15,000 hectares of rubber plantations): its origin lies in the sudden increases of rubber prices during the mid-1970s. It is also a costly project: in 1975, investment was estimated at 20,597 million CFA francs, and in 1980 it had jumped to more than 30 billion. Overruns were due to underestimations in feasibility studies and labor costs. As has SOCAPALM, HEVECAM will most probably depend on continuous external aid (from the World Bank and Caisse Centrale de Cooperation Economique) for its survival. However, its profitability relies on an uncertain premise: the increase of world prices of rubber, a product that must compete more and more with synthetics. Another recurrent problem is hiring labor. The company has little, if any, impact on its environment: in 1979, only 6.6 percent of the labor force came from the area where the plantations had been established. The company was thus forced to recruit young and often unstable workers from distant regions (the West and South-Center of Cameroon).

Another agro-industrial venture initiated by the state and receiving a lot of publicity is the national rice project in northern Cameroon (SEMRY). The rice project was supposed to enhance agricultural revenue in a poor area and to limit cereal imports at the national level. The rice project started initially in 1971 on a small scale (SEMRY I): rice production in 1976–1977 went up to 24,000 tons, while initial hopes did not forecast more than 12,000. In the same period, the net revenue for one family rose to 218,000 CFA francs against 50,000 for other ordinary peasants. However, before the consolidation of the project, the second phase of SEMRY received (in 1977) the green light from the national authorities as well as from its major financial backer, the World Bank. The second phase of the rice project (SEMRY II) was particularly ambitious; it aimed at developing 15,000 hectares of rice cultivation (as opposed to 5,000 for SEMRY I) and included costly expenses in technical assistance—63 percent of the personnel costs—infrastructure, and heavy equipment. The total cost reached 13 billion CFA francs (against 2.2 billion for SEMRY I). Table 5.1. illustrates the rather meager results of the national rice program in northern Cameroon.

Table 5.1. Production, Marketing, and Cultivated Surfaces of SEMRY, 1976–1981

	1976	*1977*	*1978*	*1979*	*1981*
Cultivated surfaces	4,503	5,327	4,940	5,188	6,217
Production	25,353	25,969	25,433	27,586	26,350
Commercialized production	23,140	18,565	18,865	20,506	—
Local consumption	1,692	4,730	4,202	4,060	—
Sales on the black market (Nigeria)	521	2,674	2,361	3,020	—

Source: Ministere de l'Economie et du Plan 1981.

There are several explanations for the stagnation, or even failure, of SEMRY. The first is the high capital cost of the project, which makes prohibitive the marketing of rice in Cameroon; according to a U.S. Agency for International Development (USAID) document (USAID 1981) the price of Cameroonian rice in the northern part of the country is 50 percent higher than the world price. Secondly, the government did not take adequate measures to fight against the competition of local rice importers. To be sure, the national authorities took some measures to encourage local rice consumption by obliging each merchant to buy Cameroonian rice first before authorizing the merchants to import. However, that measure did not succeed. According to interviews in Yaounde in 1982, we learned that merchants ordered their national rice quotas but did not accept deliveries and continued importing rice from India and Pakistan. One of the prime goals of the rice program—to restrict cereal imports—could thus not be met. Between 1976 and 1979, rice imports grew dramatically and reached the same level as before SEMRY started: 41,00 tons in 1979, that is, more than half of the national consumption, as opposed to 23,000 in 1976 (Ministry of Agriculture 1980b). Undoubtedly, world prices went down from 1975 onward, but this decrease cannot explain the doubling of rice imports against which the national authorities were unable to react.

A third explanation for the failure of SEMRY lies in deficiencies in the initial feasibility studies, particularly at the socioeconomic level. It was known since the early 1970s that rice cultivating was among several economic activities of the northern peasants (ONAREST n.d., Number 16). Once started, that cultivation became popular in the northern area, but the mistake was to overemphasize rice at the expense of all other crops and activities. Moreover, the revenues drawn from rice were not high. Although the price paid to the producers doubled between 1973 and 1980, the amount of money spent by the peasants of SEMRY to buy fertilizers, tools, and other supplies had almost tripled during the same period (Tchala 1982, pp. 165–170). According to a 1981 investigation, many rice producers complained that they did not have enough labor for rice crops, mostly when they were busy with other crops. They refused to grow rice during the rainy season because they would earn more money fishing (Sissom and Ahlers 1981). To many, SEMRY as well as other "societes de developpement" (state ventures) have appeared as bureaucratic and monopolistic marketing agencies that imposed themselves on the peasantry rather than adapt to the peasants' own needs (Thijs and Willame 1983, p. 98).

The Case of Deceptive Joint Ventures

Planned liberalism in Cameroon was supposed to stimulate important initiatives in the private sector. The question is to what extent were those private initiatives more successful than the state ventures in agriculture. Taking into account all the main joint ventures that started around the mid-1970s, the answer is undoubtedly negative.

All of these joint ventures were undertaken in a less populated zone along the trans-Cameroonian railways that linked the poor and untapped northern part of the country to the southern part where most of the natural resources were concentrated. The underlying idea was to create a new pole of development in the North by limiting its imports of food (sugar and wheat) or by enhancing its local resources (skin and leather). This made sense in theory but did not work in practice.

The Cameroon Sugar Company

The Cameroon Sugar Company (CAMSUCO) was created in March 1975 following an agreement signed between the government and the French multinational Grand Moulin de Paris (GMP-SOMDIAA), which also happens to be the main shareholder of the other sugar plant of Cameroon, the Societe Sucriere du Cameroun (SOSUCAM). According to the agreement, GMP was to build sugar plantations and a refinery with a capacity of 50,000 tons per year at Mbandjok, quite near SOSUCAM. Grand Moulin de Paris did not take much risk in that venture since it subscribed to only 3.5 percent of the assets. All the other shares—and the risk—were divided between three Cameroonian parastatals, the Societe Nationale d'Investissement (SNI), the Office National de Commercialisation des Produits de Base (ONPCB), and the Caisse Nationale de Prevoyance Sociale (CNPS).

The Cameroon Sugar Company was considered at the time a priority for the economic development of the country. In November 1976, it received major fiscal exemptions given its importance for the national economy and the importance of the investment.

Investments were indeed big: in the middle of 1981 they amounted to 24 billion CFA francs, while those of the sister company, SOSUCAM, which could produce 30,000 tons of sugar per year, did not exceed 6 billion in 1980. These investments were supported by credits from such large financial institutions as Chase Manhattan, Banque Nationale de Paris (BNP), and Caisse Centrale de Cooperation Economique, representing more than 75 percent of the total investment.

A major justification given by the national authorities, as well as by the foreign promoters, was the alleged shortage of sugar in Cameroon. The possibility of extending the capacity of the sister company was never seriously envisioned, although this made more sense given the size of the Cameroon market (50,000 tons of sugar per year). This argument was summarily dismissed by the partisans of CAMSUCO who argued that any excess of production would be exported after 1980. This was very poor economic reasoning, since the major western customers—especially the EEC—were already taking protectionist measures to fight against third world competition in the sugar industry and since neighboring countries (i.e., Ivory Coast) were making similar plans to increase sugar production on a large scale.

The decision to go ahead with another sugar refinery coincided with a purely artificial boom on the international sugar market. At the same time, Ivory Coast had launched, also with the assistance of the French GMP, a huge sugar plant that was to become a major catastrophy after 1980 when sugar prices went down again: Ivory Coast is currently stuck with an excess capacity of 200,000 tons of unsaleable sugar. The Cameroon Sugar Company was not confronted with the nightmarish difficulties of the sugar industry in Ivory Coast; but, the economic and financial balance sheet of the company was not encouraging (see Table 5.2).

Table 5.2. Balance Sheet of CAMSUCO

	CAMSUCO (%)		*Sector Average (%)*	
	1977–1978	*1978–1979*	*1977–1978*	*1979–1980*
Financial charges—turnover	52	101	35	39
Net result/turnover	-419	-58	-25	-21
Total debts/liabilities	82	125	48	105
Cash flow plus Finance charges plus taxes/total assets	11	17	4	16

Source: Societe Nationale d'Investissement 1979 and 1980.

The report of the main shareholder, the Societe Nationale d'Investissement (SNI), emphasized that the survival of CAMSUCO in 1980 was dependent on new financing, an increase in sugar prices, and protection of the national sugar industry. This meant that CAMSUCO sugar was going to be more expensive than imported sugar and that fraudulent exports from Nigeria were expected to increase.

On the other hand, CAMSUCO has not been able to meet the initial target of 50,000 tons after the first five years of operation; production between 1980 and 1982 had not reached the level of 29–33,000 tons per year.

The Societe de developpement de la production du ble

The Societe de developpement de la production du ble (SODEBLE) is another initiative of the French multinational GMP and another big failure in the practice of import substitution. The wheat complex also started in 1975 following a visit to Cameroon of the president of GMP who was said to be well connected with President Ahidjo's entourage.

Wheat experiments had already been made before 1970 in Cameroon but had not produced expected results. Between 1970 and 1975, however, new experiments took place under the supervision of a French agronomist of the Societe Camerounaise de Minoterie (SCM), a subsidiary of GMP. In 1975, these experiments were said to be conclusive and, before expecting further results on a larger scale, the SODEBLE project got started. It was to produce 125,000 tons of wheat per year over 50,000 hectares (10,000 for the first three years). The project foresaw that Cameroon could meet its wheat needs by 1983 and make a substantial savings in foreign exchange (more than 1 billion CFA francs per year, according to SODEBLE experts). An agreement was eventually signed between GMP representatives and the Cameroonian authorities; here too, GMP, which was both the consultant and the constructor, did not take any risks in the venture and even refrained from taking any shares in the new company's assets. The results were very soon damaging as Table 5.3 shows:

Table 5.3. Production of SODEBLE, 1975–1982

Year	*Cleared (hectares)*	*Sowed (hectares)*	*Harvested (hectares)*	*Production (T.)*
1975–1976	500	—	12	120
1976–1977	1,000	610	610	400
1977–1978	3,000	2,506	130	800
1978–1979	5,500	4,851	4,500	104
1979–1980	6,500	—	2,000	1,542
1981–1982	—	—	600	900

T = Tons

Source: Afrique Agriculture, November 1, 1979, p. 51; *Cameroun Selection,* March 9, 1982.

Results were very far from the initial forecast. Instead of the expected 10,000 hectares, the harvested surfaces reached only 4,500 in 1978–1979, then dropped to 2,000 in 1979–1980 and 600 in 1982. Yields did not reach 10 quintals per hectare, although 25 were initially forecasted. In 1978, it was announced by the major shareholder, the SNI, that SODEBLE was on the verge of bankruptcy. The SNI explained that feasibility studies had been undertaken without too much care: weather conditions were not in fact favorable for wheat cultivation in the Adamaoua plateau, none of the chosen varieties of seeds could flourish in local conditions, and erosion had not been taken into account. Even an agronomist of GMP conceded that new experiments were required; he was not too optimistic about SODEBLE, saying that wheat would always be marginal in Cameroon and that "it will take a revolution for it to reach the peasants" (*Afrique Agriculture,* November 1, 1979, p. 49). Moreover, no study had been conducted on the sociological impact of the introduction of the new crop: no one paid much attention to the fact that the Adamaoua plateau was mostly inhabited by cattle raisers who, having been expropriated, came to clash with SODEBLE workers (Barbier, Courade, and Tissandier 1980, p. 251).

It is thus no wonder that the SODEBLE project was virtually left aside at the end of 1981 and reoriented toward maize and soya production. At that time, 4 billion CFA francs had been spent in the project and the new necessary financing for maize and soya was estimated at another 5 billion.

In addition to the factors that the hastily done feasibility studies overlooked, the wheat project could not compete with the powerful French lobby of cereal importers and indeed with GMP itself. The SCM, the subsidiary of GMP in Cameroon, had increased significantly the capacity of its wheat mills; in 1980, the SCM announced that a new mill was going to be built in the North to be fed with French wheat. Furthermore, wheat started to be imported on a large scale precisely at the time when the SODEBLE project was launched (*Marches Tropicaux et Mediterraneens,* November 7, 1980). This seems to imply that, willingly or unwillingly, the right hand of the French "partner" to SODEBLE was ignoring what the left hand was in fact doing.

The Societe des Tanneries et Peausseries du Cameroun (STPC)

The third agro-industrial project launched around the mid-1970s is the STPC, specializing in the production of skin and leather in the neighborhood of Ngaoundere. The origin of that project dates back to the beginning of the 1970s with the projected creation of a leather factory by the firm BATA of Cameroon. BATA had planned to use Cameroonian leather and skins in order to make local shoes. This project was, for obscure reasons, dropped and replaced in 1975 by another that aimed at combining exports of skin and leather (70 percent of production) with their utilization for the internal market (30 percent of production).

As was the case with other agro-industrial ventures, the French partner, the Tanneries Paul Vaillant et Fils, took a limited risk by subscribing to only 10 percent of the assets. This percentage fell to 5 percent in 1980, when it was clear that STPC was on the verge of bankruptcy. On the other hand, STPC was heavily financed by external loans; Cameroon's intervention was limited to 330 million CFA francs for a total investment of nearly 3 billion CFA francs.

The agreement signed between the French operator, Paul Vaillant, and Cameroonian authorities (SNI, Ministry of Finance, and Office National pour la Commercialisation des Produits de Base) stipulated that the Tanneries Vaillant was to build a factory and seven collecting centers all over Cameroon by 1977.

The factory started in March 1978 after almost a year of delay. Six out of the seven collecting centers had been created, but only in the northern part of the country unlike what was initially foreseen in the agreement.

One year after its opening, STPC was already in deep trouble. According to the 1979–1980 report of SNI, the company, in addition to excessive indebtedness, suffered from a sudden price decrease of its finished products on the international market (30 to 40 percent). Its total debt amounted to 5.2 billion CFA francs for assets of 3.9 billion. Financial charges and amortizement represented 75 percent of the net loss, which amounted to 1.2 billion. "Its only chance for survival lies for the time being in the selling of raw skins on the international market" (Societe Nationale d'Investissement, 1980, p. 18). The factory eventually closed down in 1981.

The explanation of SNI for the losses encountered by STPC was, however, far from complete. First, the project was risky from the start since most of the output (70 percent) depended on the widely fluctuating prices on the world markets. In addition, Cameroon had very limited experience as a skin and leather exporter (1,500 to 3,000 tons a year at best). Second, the STPC dossier was obviously ill prepared. The plant should have been settled after the consolidation of the newly created collection centers, especially in an area where most people regarded cattle as a means to increase their social status and where more modern shepherds drew greater profit from selling livestock to urban markets and slaughter houses in the South.

Agriculture and Technocratic Development

As the case studies have shown, agro-industry, be it public or semipublic, has failed to meet the expectations of Cameroonian technocrats backed by foreign consultants, constructors, and financiers. Their initial choice was obviously dictated not only by a disappointment with the performance of small scale agriculture, but above all by a distrust of peasant production, which was regarded as too "traditional," that is, too archaic. Ironically enough, these "archaic" and "traditional" peasants who did not matter much in these modern and highly capital intensive ventures took their revenge by turning their back on these agro-industrial projects.

Agro-industry also failed completely in substituting national products for food imports, as was clearly demonstrated in the cases of the sugar, wheat, and rice projects. As a matter of fact, it had been impelled to answer the growing demands of an urban market, rather than to make the rural environment more dynamic and thus to check rural exodus, which is the real problem to overcome in such a country as Cameroon. Finally, their low performance failed completely to feed local manufacturers; in that respect, it has been pointed out that such traditional crops as cotton, cocoa, and tobacco, which were peasant productions, were much more integrated in the industrial environment than were palm oil, rubber, rice, and wheat (Thijs and Willame, 1983, p. 103).

Eventually all the agro-industrial ventures have had a negative impact on the Cameroonian agriculture. Not only have all of them been a sort of waiting place for an unstable rural subproletariat that was expecting to find better opportunities in the big cities, but they drew money away from the rural peasantry through "caisses de stabilisation" and marketing boards, which were all financially involved in agro-industry, instead of playing the role they were expected to perform: that of stabilizing prices and sustaining peasant production. According to a recent survey (*Marches Tropicaux et Mediterraneens*, May 7, 1982), the amount of money that the cocoa producers were required to pay in taxes and other levies to the main Cameroonian marketing board, the Office National de Commercialisation des Produits de Base, was higher than the money they earned. In 1978 and 1979, the former was twice as high as the latter. Coffee producers were similarly penalized. These taxes and levies could have been justified had they been reinvested in sound projects. Such was not the case, as the above examples have shown.

THE COLLAPSE OF IMPORT AND EXPORT INDUSTRIAL SUBSTITUTION PROJECTS

In quantitative terms, the industrial sector in Cameroon has developed quickly since independence. Before 1960, there were only three important industrial plants in the country: a brewery, a cigarette factory, and an aluminum plant. As in most central African countries, industrial integration was virtually nonexistent at the end of the 1960s: the sector of consumption goods existed side by side with that of the processing industry without any apparent links between the two (Schamp 1978, pp. 243–266). As Table 5.4 indicates, the spectacular increase of the industrial sector started after 1974–1975 and especially from 1978 onward with the beginning of the oil boom in Cameroon.

Table 5.4. Contribution of the Primary and Secondary Sectors to the GNP in Cameroon (1959–1960 = 100)

	1959–1960	*1963–1964*	*1970–1971*	*1974–1975*	*1978–1979*
Primary	100	118	191	396	742
Secondary	100	180	561	759	1,627

Source: Marches Tropicaux et Mediterraneens, 1980, p. 2758.

The three industrial ventures that are analyzed in the following sections date back to that period of industrial soaring. All of them were celebrated as major steps in the industrialization process and the increasing self-dependency of Cameroon. They demonstrate, however, the artificial nature of Cameroon's industrial expansion (Schamp 1978, p. 248).

The Societe Camerounaise des Engrais

The proposal of creating a fertilizer plant in Cameroon is already old; a project had been proposed at the end of the 1960s by the French Societe d'Engrais et Produits Chimiques d'Afrique Equatoriale (SEPCAE), a subsidiary in Cameroon of the industrial group Societe Commerciale des Potasses et d'Azote (SCPA), which was a major exporter of fertilizer in Africa. That proposal could not be qualified as an import substitution project since most of the production, which was heavily dependent on foreign input, would have been exported. A German engineering firm; Kloeckner, presented another more ambitious project more directly related to the satisfaction of the Cameroonian market, which came into competition with SEPCAE's project. Kloeckner's project was linked to the development of a new industrial zone near Douala, Bonaberi.

In 1973, the German firm signed a convention with the Cameroonian authorities to set up a "turn-key" fertilizer factory, the Societe Camerounaise des Engrais (SOCAME). This investment was regarded as a high priority and accordingly received special fiscal privileges. It was initially announced that Kloeckner would take a majority of the shares of SOCAME (51 percent). However, later on, SEPCAE joined the consortium and was entitled to 10 percent of the assets.

For almost three years, however, the SOCAME project lay dormant. The reason seems to have been a disagreement between SEPCAE and Kloeckner. It could not be overcome and, at the time the plant started production, SEPCAE had finally withdrawn from the company. At the same time, the German engineering firm had substantially reduced its participation in SOCAME assets (25.5 instead of 51 percent). This was already a clear indication that something was amiss within the joint venture.

The plant started to become operational in 1976; five billion CFA francs had already been spent. The capacity of SOCAME was set at 90,000 tons of ammonia, phosphate, NPK fertilizers, and sulfuric acid during the first fiscal year, which was half of the nominal capacity of 180,000 tons. Quite suddenly, the plant stopped producing in December 1977 after having delivered 47,401 tons. One year after this unexplained halt it was announced that the subsidiary of SEPCAE would come back to SOCAME in order to put the plant on a sounder footing. The German director of SOCAME left Cameroon while Kloeckner definitively withdrew from the company by selling its shares to European Fertilizer Corporation (EFC). Thereafter, Cameroon became the majority shareholder of SOCAME (with 75 percent of the shares) and injected an additional 2 billion CFA francs to save the company from immediate bankruptcy. The Societe Camerounaise des Engrais was then discharged from all the marketing operations that were entrusted to SEPCAE. The latter undertook for several months to sell the stock of fertilizers accumulated by SOCAME, which continued, however, to suffer from heavy loss (1 billion for half a year). The financial balance of SOCAME two years after beginning operation is summarized in Table 5.5.

Table 5.5. Balance of SOCAME Accounts, 1978–1980 (in Percent)

Financial charges/turnover	198	221.6
Added value/turnover	20	-97.5
Net result/turnover	-674	-679.8
Total debt/total liability	110	151.2
Cash flow plus financial charges plus taxes/total assets	-13	-2.4

Source: Societe Nationale d'Investissement 1983.

Despite emergency financial aid from the government, SOCAME was forced to close down for the second time in December 1981 after having produced no more than 50,000 tons of fertilizer. This closure became official and definitive the following month. For Cameroon it was a heavy loss in terms of money and employment while, for SCPA, the losses amounted to a little more than 600,000 FF. In its 1981 annual report, the French group wrote that "after having decided to start again the activities at the fertilizer plant which is a technically sound venture, Cameroon has not dared to keep on providing the necessary help that could have made SOCAME a competitive enterprise" (*Afrique Information,* July 7, 1982).

The explanation given by SCPA officials about the closing of SOCAME is far from convincing. The report did not say a word about the strong initial reluctance of the French group about the SOCAME venture in a country where SCPA has traditionally been the major exporter of fertilizer. At the time SOCAME started to operate, SCPA was held responsible for a major dumping maneuver; this was confirmed by the fact that fertilizer imports suddenly increased from 41,000 tons in 1976 to more than 100,000 tons in 1978.

The conception of SOCAME was deficient. It was heavily dependent on raw material (including phosphates, sulphur, and liquid ammonia) the prices of which have known unpredictable and wide fluctuations since the 1973 oil price increase. In 1979, for instance, the prices of some chemical components of fertilizers were sometimes higher than the values of the finished products. The Societe Camerounaise des Engrais also used imported supplies, such as packing bags from Indonesia, even though Cameroon had its own packing bag factory.

The marketing of SOCAME products was also inefficient; it aimed mostly at satisfying a small group of powerful customers (parastatals and a few private companies) rather than the large group of peasants that could have absorbed 130,000 to 150,000 tons per year.

Moreover, the expenses for technical assistance weighed heavily on the financial balance of SOCAME. Wages spent for expatriate workers represented 41.8 percent of the personnel cost in 1978 (against 29–30 percent spent by other companies for the same sector). During the same period, the amount spent on salaries was 96 percent on the company turnover.

Finally, from an economic point of view, SOCAME was too small a venture to compete for exports with the huge companies in operation all over the world. The Societe Camerounaise des Engrais was doomed to fail to the extent that it could not find an outlet on the internal market.

Cellulose of Cameroon

Cellulose of Cameroon (CELLUCAM) represents the most important venture ever made in Cameroon in terms of capital investments: its total cost has been estimated at more than 80 billion CFA francs. Its purpose was to develop the local wood industry through the processing of timber into paper pulp.

The origin of CELLUCAM can be traced back to the second national plan which allocated 8 billion CFA francs for the project. With the third plan, the value of the pulp factory rose to 14 billion.

The project was born at a time when a certain optimism was the rule concerning paper pulp factories in Africa south of the Sahara. Several similar projects existed "on paper" in the beginning of the 1970s: whether in Gabon, Congo, or Ivory Coast, they were all very costly projects, varying between 80 and 110 billion CFA francs. This optimism was based on the idea that the African rain forest had unlimited resources and that the raw materials should be processed rather than merely exported. In Cameroon, the project started in May 1974 with the signing of a convention between the national authorities and an Austrian engineering firm, Voest Alpine. According to that convention, Voest Alpine would be the leader of a consortium charged with the building of a turn-key factory with a capacity of 122,000 tons of paper pulp per year during a first phase, and of 240,000 to 480,000 tons in later stages. It was forecast that, later on, 40,000 to 50,000 tons would feed the local or regional market and would necessitate the building of big paper factories in Cameroon.

The capital of the company was set up at 8 billion CFA francs, which was only about one-eighth of the total investment. The participants in the venture were, on the one hand, the state, various Cameroonian parastatals (SNI, ONPCB, Caisse de Stabilisation des Hydrocarbures), and individuals, and, on the other hand, a consortium of financial or industrial companies. The leader of the foreign participants, Voest Alpine, took only 10 percent of the shares in the venture: it had no experience in the building of paper pulp plants. Strangely enough, the Swedish company that was to be the marketing agency for CELLUCAM, Svenska Cellulose Aktiebolaget (SCA), was not among the shareholders and had no representation in Cameroon. Another noticeable fact was that by the time CELLUCAM started to operate, Voest Alpine had given up 25 percent of its shares.

Construction of the factory started in June 1976 and went on until November 1980. Several foreign and local contractors were involved in building CELLUCAM: The equipment was delivered by no less than 15 companies. The variety of that equipment made the venture a highly complex one, especially at the level of maintenance. On December 31, 1980, the plant was ready to operate. However, there were rumors about CELLUCAM having financial troubles. The Austrian director of the company declared that "as any new investment, we have to overcome a difficult period during the first years; for such a project, it is necessary to finance the usual losses of the starting period. Moreover we have to support the financial charges related to social and infrastructure investments. . . . If price structure stays the same as today and *if one does not lose the courage to keep on investing* [our emphasis], the competitive capacity of CELLUCAM will not be in doubt" (*Cameroun Selection,* June 10, 1980). In other words, the CELLUCAM leadership was announcing that new expenditures were going to be necessary while more than 75 billion CFA francs had already been invested. The director of CELLUCAM omitted saying that the prospects of paper pulp world prices were not good at all; however, according to data from the famous French Centre Technique Forestier Tropical, one could have forecasted that prices were going to be stagnant for years to come.

Cellulose of Cameroon became operational at the end of January 1982. Two months after the plant opened, two explosions completely destroyed the departments that were essential to the plant's bleaching process. CELLUCAM started to operate again four weeks later, but it was at that time impossible to produce bleached pulp. Production thereafter concentrated only on an unfinished product, the crude pulp. The report on the accident—it was apparently due to a "wrong maneuver"—was never officially released.

At the end of 1983, CELLUCAM was said to be on the verge of bankruptcy. Several hundred workers and employees were fired, and there were talks about closing the plant, though this was considered politically unacceptable given the amount of investment already made.

It is difficult to believe that the problems at CELLUCAM are related either to a major accident or to an unfortunate conjuncture. From the start, risks were too high with respect to the costs involved. As one French specialist wrote, "for such a heavy industry the right to make mistakes does not exist" (Renard 1981, p. 514).

The economies of CELLUCAM are not advantageous for Cameroon. The project is highly dependent on foreign input. If one takes into account the cost of such expensive imports as caustic soda and chlorine dioxide, financial charges, and technical assistance expenditures, the total of foreign costs represents more than 35 percent of the company turnover. On the other hand, one must question whether the plant, which is export oriented, is not handicapped by its small production capacity. According to recent estimates, to be viable, a paper pulp factory should have a capacity of 150,000 to 300,000 tons, which the CELLUCAM plant does not have. Finally, the paper pulp market is increasingly in competition with such other markets as plastic sheets and the audio-visual industry. To be successful, it is not enough for a company just to produce paper pulp, which today must be of the purest quality: the product must be aggressively and efficiently marketed. This does not seem to be the case with CELLUCAM, since its marketing agency is located 1,000 miles from the factory and is not even among the shareholders of the venture.

In addition to being a poor economic project, CELLUCAM is strongly disadvantaged by heavy financial charges as Table 5.6 illustrates.

Table 5.6. Balance Sheet of CELLUCAM on June 30, 1980 (in Millions CFA Francs)

	CELLUCAM	*Average Within the Sector*
Personnel costs		
local	738	2,845
expatriates	435	85
Investments	69,525	76,010
Long and midterm debts	62,443	66,274
Financial charges		
local	—	417
foreign	3,082	3,352

Source: Societe Nationale d'Investissement 1983.

With respect to other companies of the wood industry (including COCAM, SOFIBEL, and ECAM), CELLUCAM holds the record for financial costs. Wages of the expatriates represents 37 percent of the total wage bill (against 27 percent for the wood industry). This percentage represents the salaries of some 49 foreigners hired by CELLUCAM. Debts and foreign financial charges are at a very worrisome level: they come to 80 percent of the average of the wood and paper industry in Cameroon.

From a technical standpoint, there are clear indicatioans that feasibility studies have not been undertaken with care. According to CELLUCAM managers, the company was to be a world leader in processing timber on a vast scale (250,000 hectares per year). But there is no policy of replanting in Cameroon, and this will probably be a serious ecological problem for the country in the future. Second, the rainy season, which is long where CELLUCAM was built, makes it difficult if not impossible to run the factory at a sufficient capacity level for several months at a time. (It can be run at 40 to 50 percent of capacity during the rainy season according to CELLUCAM's own estimates.) Moreover, during that season, the heavy Berliet trucks used for conveying timber are not adapted to the local feeder roads. Third, the tropical forest in Cameroon is composed of a large variety of timber, both in terms of size and quality. According to a French specialist, it does not seem that CELLUCAM has taken the necessary steps as far as stockyards and cutters are concerned (Renard 1981, p. 514). Additionally, the quality of the finished products is questionable, since it is not clear whether pulp from trees that vary in quality can compete with pulp from high quality trees. The quality of pulp is important in the paper industry. Finally, after visiting CELLUCAM two years after its opening, the French expert found that many technical problems had not been overcome: the capacity of the stockyard had been underestimated; the pulp consumed much more timber than was expected; there were severe problems in the barking of trees due to a faulty initial design; bad filtering posed many problems; and water pipes and tubes corroded quickly (Renard 1983).

The Societe Nationale de Raffinage

Another major industrial joint venture in Cameroon is the new oil refinery, which started operating in 1981. Refineries built in Africa south of the Sahara have most often produced disappointing results. Most of them have been "white elephants" continued for political reasons (as were) steel plants, they were regarded as symbols of industrialization) rather than for economic purposes. Very few African countries have a market large enough to justify an integrated oil industry. When they are export oriented, African refineries are confronted with the constraints of an integrated marketing system that they do not control. Finally, many of them are functioning at a low capacity level and have been through difficult times for a variety of reasons (*West Africa,* February 28, 1983).

The construction of a national refinery in Cameroon is an old project: it was already announced as being imminent in 1971. In January 1973, an agreement was signed between the government and the French Petroleum Company (CFP-Total) about the creation of the Societe Nationale de Raffinage (SONARA). Thereafter, there was a long period of silence, which can be explained by several reasons. It was argued at the time by the oil industry that Cameroon was too small a market (425,000 tons of refined oil in 1975–1976 corresponding to 600,000 tons of crude) to justify building a refinery. The major French company operating in Cameroon, Elf-Acquitaine, was also opposed to the idea, given that it was a majority shareholder in the Gabonese refinery of Port-Gentil, which supplied Cameroon with refined oil.

In 1976–1977, however, it became clear that the government was strongly pressing to build its own facilities and was showing signs of impatience with the reluctance of the oil companies. During a visit to Mobil Oil sites, the minister of mines declared: "the government wishes that discovered oil be exploited as soon as possible for the local market: the problem of marketing arrangement and export is a secondary issue that should be studied later on" (*Marches Tropicaux et Mediterraneens,* March 21, 1976). At one point the government even threatened publicly to cancel exploration permits of the big oil companies and to call for smaller ones saying that it could not tolerate their reluctance to develop the oil potential of Cameroon.

In January 1977, the SONARA project eventually received the green light and a contract was signed between Cameroon and CFP-Total concerning the technical assistance to be provided to the new refinery. The major oil companies took a minority share in SONARA (8 to 10 percent), which seemed to demonstrate their reluctance to participate fully in the venture. Their participation could be interpreted as a gesture of "good will" toward the Cameroonian authorities whom they did not wish to alienate. At any rate, one of the Elf directors declared later on that Cameroon had no use for a refinery for the time being: "one should be able to count on production that could feed the refinery for almost 20 years. This is not the case in Cameroon today" (*Cameroun Selection,* March 1981, p. 435).

The Societe National de Raffinage became operational in May 1981 and, as expected, showed signs of economic and financial stress from the start. First there was the issue of the costs involved. In 1974, investments had been estimated at 20 billion CFA francs. Two years later they jumped to 32 and next to 38 billion and eventually reached the record amount of 72 billion. The Societe National de Raffinage is probably the most costly refinery recently built in Africa as Table 5.7 below shows.

In a report released just before starting SONARA, World Bank experts pointed out that the capacity of the Cameroonian refinery was too small to be really profitable and that the infrastructures linked to the plant were too large and too costly. To make a profit, the experts estimated that SONARA would have to produce 100,000 barrels a day instead of the 40,000 barrels a day that it produces now.

Table 5.7. Costs of Some African Refineries (Estimates)

	Cost (in million dollars)	*Capacity (in million tons)*
Refinery of Nouadhibou (Mauritania)	110 (1981)	1
Refinery of Togo	80 (1978)	1
Refinery of Pointe Noire (Congo)	112 (1982)	1
Refinery of Limbe (Cameroon)	275 (1981)	±2

Source: West Africa, February 28, 1983.

The cost of the Limbe refinery is astonishing in that it is a rather unsophisticated plant—of a topping-reforming type—which does not even have a cracking unit that would produce an output with a higher level of octane, nor an asphalt unit that would have been helpful for Cameroon's road construction program. As far as its output is concerned, SONARA is not even adapted to the Cameroonian market: as Table 5.8 shows, 70 percent of the plant's product is fuel-oil and diesel, which is of little use in the country.

Table 5.8. SONARA Production and Oil Consumption in Cameroon, 1980

	Consumption (%)	*Production (SONARA) (%)*
Gasoline	28.9	14
Kerosene	10.4	11
Jet fuel	10.1	—
Gas oil	36.5	—
Diesel	0.2	20
Fuel oil	8.6	50
Others	4.5	—
TOTAL	100.0	100.0

Source: World Bank 1980b.

Before the refinery became operational, World Bank experts had also forecasted that the refined products of SONARA would probably be more costly for the economy than the alternative of importing oil (World Bank 1980b, p. 26). This forecast was confirmed two months after the opening of the refinery when the government announced a price increase of gas. To reduce losses to a minimum, national authorities were confronted with two choices: either reduce the delivery prices to SONARA or increase the retail price of oil. The government could not proceed with the first option, since this would have meant breaking the agreement with the oil operators who, in addition to being shareholders in SONARA, were the only exporters of Cameroonian oil. The second choice was thus the easiest one; it was also the most costly for the customer. To be sure, even before SONARA started to operate, the retail price of oil in Cameroon was already 60 to 95 percent more expensive than world prices (World Bank 1980b).

As noted earlier, the oil business exists in quasi-secrecy in Cameroon, and it is not easy to discover what is really happening at SONARA now. There are, however, some disturbing facts that seem to prove that the refinery is indeed in trouble. At the end of 1982, imports of refined products at the harbor of Douala continued to represent 25 percent of the total imports of the country: 621, 870 tons in 1979, 685,850 in 1980, 736,950 in 1981, and 732,212 in 1982. On the other hand, the government has always declared that SONARA would be fed by Cameroonian crude, but, according to reliable sources, the refinery did not process more than 300,000 tons of local crude in 1982, which represents approximately 15 percent of the capacity of the plant (*Afrique Information,* December 23, 1981). Since 1982, news about SONARA has become scanty if not nonexistent.

SOME CONCLUDING REFLECTIONS

The different case-studies that have been presented in this chapter do question the celebrated wisdom of the economic decision-making process in Cameroon. As noted at the outset, economic planning suffers from major flaws: World Bank experts have recently, in their polished language, pointed to the contrast between "the anticipated growth of public investment programs" and "the limited experience of local administration in management." Their report more particularly stresses the shortage and high turnover in qualified Cameroonian staff who find more attractive working conditions in the commercial or private sector (International Development Association 1981). In this context of poor performance, the decision-making process has been pervaded by a lot of corruption generated at all levels, including the top of the administration, which was highly successful in this case in keeping government business under tight secrecy. While ordinary business complained about pervasive bureaucracy and corruption, this was not the case with some local and foreign investors, namely the contract hunters, who could easily prosper provided they would have direct access to what is nowadays called the "Ahidjo system." According to some observers, recent changes in the contract award system made by the new president might have directly threatened some interest groups that drew their economic power from the presidency and have been at the root of political tension in Yaounde. To be sure, the same observation could be made for most African countries. In the case of Cameroon—and this would seem to apply to other countries that went through oil, copper, or other types of booms—mismanagement and corruption were all the more damaging because of the country's poorly integrated economy, which was in a matter of four to five years suddenly and artificially overheated.

One of the major negative impacts of the industrial and agro-industrial failures that have been presented here is Cameroon's growing indebtedness since 1977. The total debt has reached more than 2 billion dollars in 1982 against only 544 million dollars in 1976 (World Debt Tables 1983). World Bank estimates have been quickly outrun: in 1980 the projected 1985 debt of Cameroon was about 1.5 billion dollars, and a year later it was estimated that Cameroon would owe 3 billion dollars in 1985. The level of debt servicing expenses is worrisome. It has increased from 25.4 million dollars in 1974 to 200 million dollars in 1981. According to recent estimates, the debt service ratio would have crossed the fateful level of 20 percent, which would normally entitle the International Monetary Fund (IMF) to intervene. It is true however that Cameroon is relatively, though artificially, protected by the safety net of the franc zone.

In terms of employment, the 1975–1980 industrial ventures have created significant distortions; investments in these ventures have had the effect of making employment rarer instead of stimulating it. In Cameroon, the capital/labor ratio has indeed reached extraordinary proportions at the expense of the latter as Table 5.9 illustrates. Cameroon must today cope with a tremendous unemployment problem. Thousands of people, mostly youngsters, are flowing from an impoverished rural milieu to big cities in search of better opportunities. In 1977–1978, a confidential World Bank report estimated that 40 percent of rural people lived below the threshold of poverty against 15 percent in the big cities (World Bank, 1980a).

Finally, one must emphasize another negative impact of the 1975–1980 overheated "industrialization" process in Cameroon. Most of the time, investments in that country have taken the form of deceptive and nonrisk capital accumulation. As has been noticed in most of the so-called joint ventures, foreign entrepreneurs have taken little if any shares in the assets of the projects to which they contributed and which they promoted through their consultancy agencies and other means. As a matter of fact, it is even difficult to describe the entrepreneurs' involvement as investment: it would be more accurate to say that they merely sold technology in the form of turn-key projects. Our case studies have clearly demonstrated that capital intensive technology was neither appropriate nor adapted to Cameroon's technical, financial, economic, and social conditions and that it mostly benefitted "contract hunters" and their immediate entourage who were able to accumulate large profits on the side.

Table 5.9. Investments and Employment in Cameroon: Some Meaningful Cases

Company or Project	*Cost of Investment (in Billions CFA Francs)*	*Number of Jobs Created*	*Cost per Job (in Dollars)*
SOCAME	9	380	112,781
CELLUCAM	75	1,200	297,619
ALUCAM	23.2	77	1,434,735
HEVECAM	7.7	2,250	16,431
CAMSUCO	23.7	3,126	36,102
SODEBLE	4	50	380,952
SEMRY (11)	13.6	7,000(prev.)	9,252
SONARA	66	302	1,040,681

Source: M. Thijs and J.C. Willame 1983, p. 315.

It is not quite clear whether the "new regime" headed by President Biya has perceived the need to reverse some ill practices of planned liberalism in Cameroon and to come back to a more common sense political economy, especially in rural development and infrastructure, which have been neglected during the oil boom. This eventually leads us to a political conclusion; that a common sense policy will depend on a more transparent economy, which requires in turn less politics, fewer group rivalries, and more democracy.

6

AGRICULTURAL PRODUCTIVITY IN CAMEROON

Virginia DeLancey

Agriculture has been the dynamic force behind the development of the Cameroon economy. The production of export crops, especially cocoa, coffee, groundnuts, cotton, palm products, bananas, tobacco, and rubber, has provided foreign exchange to finance the import of capital goods and services for the development of the economy as a whole. The production of food crops has allowed Cameroon to remain basically food self-sufficient, even as the population has continued to increase and become more urbanized, and it has saved foreign exchange that would otherwise have been required to import food.[1] The continued growth of agriculture has supported the development of industries, particularly those industries such as textiles and processed foods, which use domestically produced raw materials. It has also provided a market for the products of many of those industries. Thus, a growing, developing agricultural sector has supported the development of the Cameroon economy in general. That is, between 1970 and 1982, agricultural production grew at an annual average of 3.4 percent while Gross Domestic Product (GDP) grew at an annual average of 7.0 percent and population grew at 2.2 percent (World Bank 1984, p. 220).

Cameroon is one of the few sub-Saharan African countries to achieve such success. Only nine other sub-Saharan African countries, on the continent, were able to equal or exceed such growth of the agricultural sector. Of those countries that were able to do so, only Botswana was able to equal or exceed such growth of GDP (Table 6.1), although it is not certain that even this would be true if more recent, comparable data were available for that country.[2]

Indeed, Cameroon compares favorably with the rest of Africa. In the past, most African countries were able to feed their populations; today most are no longer able to do so. Table 6.2 shows that only ten sub-Saharan African countries on the continent were able to provide 100 percent of the daily, required, per capita calorie supply in 1981 (Benin, Cameroon, Ivory Coast, Lesotho, Liberia, Niger, Senegal, Sierra Leone, Somalia, and South Africa). Only four of them (Benin, Cameroon, Ivory Coast, and South Africa) were also able to maintain or increase per capita food production. The other six (Lesotho, Liberia, Niger, Senegal, Sierra Leone, and Somalia) were able to provide the minimum required number of calories, but the index of per capita food production had decreased over the last ten years to as low as 60 for Somalia (1969–71 = 100). As a result of the declining per capita food production, by late 1983, there was a list of more than 24 African countries that were then unable to feed their populations.

Table 6.1. Growth of Production: Average Annual Growth Rate, 1970–1982 (in percentages)

Country	*Growth of Agriculture (%)*	*Growth of Gross Domestic Product (%)*
Cameroon	3.4	7.0
Mauritania	3.4	2.0
Liberia	3.5	0.9
Mali	3.8	4.3
Malawi	4.1	5.1
Kenya	4.1	5.5
Sudan	4.1	6.3
Ivory Coast	4.5	5.7
Gambia	7.0[a]	2.8[a]
Botswana	8.5[b]	13.5[b]

[a]Figures are for 1970–1979.
[b]Figures are for 1970–1978.
Sources: World Bank 1984, p. 220; World Bank 1981, p. 144.

Most African countries have become increasingly dependent on food imports and/or food aid, and thus on the world economy to feed their citizens. They must now earn foreign exchange to purchase food in addition to purchasing capital for development, or else they must divert foreign exchange from the purchase of capital goods and services to the purchase of food. This is because the growth of food production, which has averaged 1.5 percent per year for the entire continent, has been well below the annual growth of population, which has increased from an average of 2.5

Table 6.2. Per Capita Calorie Supply and Index of Agricultural Production per Capita, Selected Sub-Saharan African Countries

Country	*Daily per Capita Calorie Supply (Percentage Required, 1981*	*Average Index of Food Production per Capita (1969–1971 = 100), 1980–1982*
[a]Benin	101	100
[a]Cameroon	102[b]	102
[a]Ivory Coast	112	107
Lesotho	111	84
Liberia	114	88
Niger	102	88
Senegal	101	93
Sierra Leone	101	81
Somalia	100[b]	60
[a]South Africa	118	193

[a]Countries that provided 100 percent of the Required Daily Per Capita Calorie Supply and that have also maintained per capita food production since 1969–1971.

[b]Data are for years other than those specified.

Source: World Bank 1984, pp. 228–229, 264–265.

percent per year during 1960–1970 to an average of 2.7 percent per year during 1970–1981 (World Bank 1981, pp. 45–47). In Cameroon, food production grew at an annual rate of 3.3 percent (World Bank 1981, p. 167). The population growth rate has been well below that, but it has increased from 1.8 percent per year from 1960 to 1970, to 2.2 percent from 1970 to 1981 (World Bank 1983, p. 184). Recent estimates indicate that the population growth rate has increased to at least 2.7 percent (Population Reference Bureau 1984), but that it may even be as high as 3.1 percent (World Bank 1984, p. 256). Various projections show that annual growth could be 3.5 percent between 1980 and 2000 (World Bank 1984, p. 254) and that it could be 3.65 percent by the year 2010 and 3.92 percent by 2025 (The Futures Group 1983, p. 4).

In addition to the increasing population growth rate, there is also increasing urbanization, and a rural exodus, throughout the continent. For example, in 1960, 11 percent of sub-Saharan Africans lived in urban areas. By 1981, 21 percent of sub-Saharan Africans lived in urban areas. Cameroon has been urbanizing more rapidly than the average. In 1960,

14 percent of Cameroonians lived in urban areas. By 1981, 36 percent of Cameroonians lived in urban areas and, by 1982, 37 percent lived in urban areas that had been growing at an annual average of 8.0 percent from 1970 to 1982 (World Bank 1983, p. 190; 1984, p. 260).

The increasing urbanization has several implications. First, there are proportionally fewer farmers remaining in the rural areas, and those that remain are growing older. Yet they must be increasingly productive in order to feed the growing urban population as well as to maintain or increase traditional export crop earnings. Second, when individuals move to town, they change their food preferences; they increase their demand for rice and wheat and decrease their demand for traditional staples such as plantains, cassava, yams, cocoyams, maize, millet, and sorghum. Yet, in Cameroon, as in most of sub-Saharan Africa, rice cannot yet be grown on an internationally competitive basis, and wheat is technically difficult to grow on a large scale. This leads to increased imports of food grains, which can lead to serious trade imbalances and future payment problems, particularly as the prices of food imports increase. Even using the World Bank estimate (perhaps an optimistic one) that wheat production can be increased by 4.5 percent per year, it is estimated that it will be necessary to import 506,000 metric tons of wheat in the year 2010 compared to the 113,000 tons that were imported in 1980 (The Futures Group 1983, p. 56).

Anticipating future problems of sufficient food production, former President Ahidjo launched the "Green Revolution" in March 1973 and committed the government to a policy of maintaining food self-sufficiency in Cameroon (Ahidjo 1973, pp. 17–18, 34). But not only does Cameroon want to remain food self-sufficient; it would like to become the "storehouse of central Africa," to export food surpluses to all of the surrounding countries, particularly since all are food deficit countries. In addition, although Cameroon now earns considerable foreign exchange from its oil, it is determined to continue its policy of encouraging production of traditional export crops to increase foreign exchange earnings. Such policies of increasing production of both food crops as well as export crops may be difficult to pursue simultaneously, particularly with an increasing population growth rate and a high rate of rural-urban migration.

Of particular relevance, Cameroon has been cognizant of the difficulties encountered by Nigeria, which has suffered from a case of "Dutch disease" contracted from policies related to the rapid growth of its oil export sector.[3] Those difficulties have included the deterioration of the agricultural sector to the point where Nigeria is no longer a net exporter of agricultural products but is now an importer of food. Cameroon has resolved to quarantine that economic malady, while exploiting its own recently discovered petroleum wealth. Thus far, it has been more successful than Nigeria was. But, it is still searching for the best way to inject oil revenues into the economy without causing runaway inflation and the rapid destruction of other sectors of the economy. It has begun to use those resources to reduce its dependence on foreign aid in implementing its current economic development plan, a plan that has increased the relative investment in agriculture. But, to achieve its goal of increasing production of both food crops as well as export crops, the challenge for Cameroon is to invest its resources in ways that will increase the productivity of the agricultural sector.

AGRICULTURAL PRODUCTIVITY: THE PAST RECORD

Agriculture fulfilled its role adequately in the past, because Cameroon has had relatively favorable geographic and demographic conditions compared to many other African countries. Cameroon has a varied climate that ranges from tropical rain forest along the coast to desert conditions in the far north. Between these two extremes, there are fertile, volcanic soils on the slopes of Mount Cameroon, cool plateaus in the west and northwest, and warm savanna elsewhere. Such diversity has been able to support the production of many different types of crops, saving Cameroon from the problems typical of monoculture countries.

In the past, Cameroon also had vast areas of arable, uncultivated land. And, because it falls within a belt of human subfertility in Africa, it had a comparatively small population that grew relatively slowly. Consequently, although the population density varied throughout the country, the overall population density was low. With the possibility of land-extensive farming in most parts of the country, by a rural-based, agriculturally oriented population, it was relatively easy for that population to feed itself. Food production per capita was sufficient.

Because there was little pressure on the land, there was less concern, in the past, about yields per hectare, except on the large, commercial plantations. Nevertheless, the data that exist indicate, in general, that yields were higher than they are now. This was probably a result of several factors: the cultivated land was less depleted; the perennial crops such as cocoa and coffee were younger, less diseased; and the recurrent, prolonged droughts of recent years had not begun. Long-term government policies, particularly those related to producer prices and investment in the agricultural sector, for example, may have prevented agriculture from reaching its full potential then as they have today. Nevertheless, in spite of government policies, agricultural production was adequate in the past, because agricultural, demographic, and climatic conditions were more favorable in earlier years than they are now. Today, for production to continue to be adequate, there is need for greater concern about agricultural productivity.

Although agricultural production appears to be growing well, the overall rate covers up certain variations and trends within the sector. It is difficult, however, to obtain accurate and complete data for the agricultural sector. The last agricultural census was conducted in 1972–1973, but it did not include data from farms on which employed labor was important. A new census is just being completed, but the data are not yet available. The Ministry of Agriculture has been gathering data over the years, but those data are difficult to use because the statistical base was changed in 1976. Furthermore, the traditional method of intercropping makes it difficult to determine production and area figures for specific crops (World Bank 1980c). Such problems make it almost impossible to determine productivity variations and trends. Yet, it is certain that as the percentage of the economically active population in agriculture decreases, while the total population increases, it is essential that those remaining in agriculture become increasingly productive in order to achieve the goals set by Cameroon for the agricultural sector.

Evidence from the Ministry of Agriculture

While the available evidence is sparse and somewhat questionable, the Ministry of Agriculture expressed concern about productivity trends after conducting a major analysis of the agricultural sector, from 1960 to 1980, in order to prepare the Fifth Five-Year Economic, Social and Cultural Development Plan for 1981–1986 (Cameroon, Ministry of Agriculture, 1980, pp. 75–88).

Coffee

Between 1962–1963 and 1977–1978, the Ministry of Agriculture found that yields for arabica coffee had dropped from 400 kg./ha. to 200 kg./ha. While yields for robusta remained stable at 320 kg./ha. overall, yields in four of the seven provinces that existed at that time (the West, Southwest, Northwest, and Littoral) had decreased (Cameroon, Ministry of Agriculture, 1980, p. 75).

Cocoa

During this same time period, yields for cocoa remained nearly stable, increasing from 261 kg./ha. to 267 kg./ha. But, after disaggregating the figures, significant growth (nearly 1 percent per year) was found in the favorable zones, particularly the Center-South and net negative growth was revealed in the marginal zones (Cameroon, Ministry of Agriculture 1980, p. 75).

Cotton

Cotton showed increasing productivity as land-intensive methods were introduced. Yields increased from 379 kg./ha. in 1960 to 844 kg./ha. by 1970. They decreased to 455 kg./ha. in 1973–1974 when the Sahelian drought touched Cameroon, but they subsequently increased dramatically to 1,262 kg./ha. in 1978–1979 (Cameroon, Ministry of Agriculture 1980, p. 76).

Groundnuts and Cassava

Yields for groundnuts and cassava decreased between 1960 and 1980 because of deterioration of the genetic material and an increase in plant diseases. The ministry assumed that there might be a similar trend for other food crops, except for rice and maize for which considerable research has been conducted (Cameroon, Ministry of Agriculture, 1980, p. 76).

Palm Products, Sugar, and Wheat

The Ministry of Agriculture did not report productivity trends for such crops as palm products, sugar, and wheat—crops grown by specialized societies, usually parastatals. It merely noted that actual yields were always lower than the objective yields set by those parastatals (Cameroon, Ministry of Agriculture 1980, p. 76).

Evidence from the FAO and the USDA

Production figures and indexes, as well as productivity data, provided by the UN Food and Agriculture Organization (FAO) show some variation from those reported by the U.S. Department of Agriculture (USDA). Both differ from those of the World Bank and from those discussed in the *Bilan Diagnostic du Secteur Agricole de 1960 a 1980.* Using 1969–1971 as a base, the FAO and the USDA agree with the other sources that total agricultural production and total food production in Cameroon have shown substantial growth in recent years; however, they do not agree on whether per capita production has been maintained (Table 6.3). The most recent FAO indices (1982) use 1974–1976 as base years, and thus cannot be compared to the earlier indices (UN, FAO, 1983). Yet, they show continued growth of both total food and total agricultural production.

Per capita indexes are more significant when considering Cameroon's goals of maintaining food self-sufficiency. The FAO indicated that total production in Cameroon has been growing fast enough to maintain per capita production, even with a rapidly growing population. For agricultural production, it reported a per capita index of 101; for food production, it reported a per capita index of 102. The USDA, however, reported lower indexes. It found that in 1983 agricultural production and food production were lower, per person, than they were in 1969–1979 and the same or lower than in 1981.

The most recent FAO indexes, using the revised base years of 1974–1976, showed a slight recovery from 1981 to 1982 of per capita agricultural production and nearly stable per capita food production (UN, FAO, 1983). But the per capita index for agricultural production was only 92.7, and that for food production was only 91.7. Thus, according to the FAO, in 1982, agricultural production and food production were lower, per person, than they were in 1974–1976.

Table 6.3. Production Indexes (1969–71 = 100)

	Total				*Per Capita*			
	Agriculture		*Food*		*Agriculture*		*Food*	
Year	*FAO*	*USDA*	*FAO*	*USDA*	*FAO*	*USDA*	*FAO*	*USDA*
1981	128	128	130	125	101	98	102	95
1983	—	127	—	130	—	93	—	95

Source: United Nations, Food and Agriculture Organization 1982; United States, Department of Agriculture data bank (n.d.).

Recent productivity figures, as questionable as they are, are interesting to compare. Of the 18 crops for which the FAO provided data on yields per hectare for Cameroon in 1982, two thirds of the crops had yields lower than the average for those specific crops in Africa, and African yields are generally lower than world-wide yields. Only paddy rice, millet/sorghum, dried beans, sesame, seed cotton, and tea had yields that were equal to or higher than the average in Africa. Wheat, maize, potatoes, sweet potatoes, cassava, groundnuts, tomatoes, onions, sugar cane, coffee, cocoa, and tobacco had yields lower than the average. Productivity trends are more difficult to examine because the FAO data and the USDA data differ in some respects.

Coffee

Neither the FAO nor the USDA distinguish between robusta and arabica coffee. But, as does the Ministry of Agriculture, the FAO shows lower yields from 1979 to 1982 than the average for the base years 1969–

1971. Similarly, the USDA reported consistently lower yields from 1980 to 1983 than from 1972 to 1974.

Cocoa

The Ministry of Agriculture reported similar yields for cocoa in 1962–1963 as in 1977–1978, but it suggested that there was substantial growth in certain zones. However, the FAO and the USDA suggested that overall yields increased from 1969 until 1975, after which they returned to those reported in 1962–1963.

Cotton

The FAO, as does the Ministry of Agriculture, reported dramatic increases in seed cotton yields in the late 1970s compared to those of the 1960s and the early 1970s. Similarly, the USDA showed increased productivity for cotton lint from 1979 compared to figures from 1965 to 1978.

Groundnuts and Cassava

The Ministry of Agriculture used groundnuts and cassava to exemplify the decreasing yields of food crops in general. Similarly, the FAO reported that groundnut yields from 1979 to 1982 were much lower than for 1969–1971. Yet, it reported that cassava yields from 1979 to 1982 were slightly higher than for 1969–1971, even though there have been disease problems affecting cassava. The ministry considered maize and rice to be exceptions to the declining yields of other food crops because so much research has been done on them. Yet, the FAO reported maize yields that were lower from 1979 to 1982 than in 1969–1971. Rice, however, is indeed different; yields in 1982 were triple the average for 1969–1971.

Sugar and Wheat

The crops grown by large, government-owned, parastatal, specialized societies have shown varying results. According to the Ministry of Agriculture, actual yields may be lower than objective yields for all such crops; yet, the FAO reported sugar cane yields that were much higher from 1979 to 1982 than for 1969–1971. Wheat, however, has not fared well. The yields averaged 492 kg./ha. from 1974–1976. By 1979, they had increased to 1,000 kg./ha. But by 1980–1982, they had dropped to half of that, to 500 kg./ha. As a result, production of wheat was cut back, and diversification of crops was begun within SODEBLE, the parastatal originally set up to develop wheat production.

Summary

Yields reported by the FAO and the USDA, in general, have not been high over the years. Cocoa, one of the most important export crops, has shown continued decline of yields. Wheat, one of the four most important imports, has simply not succeeded on a large scale in Cameroon. Other crops have shown decreased yields, with some, but not complete, recovery. These are maize, potatoes, groundnuts, sesame, tomatoes, onions, coffee, and tobacco. Among these, coffee, groundnuts, and tobacco are exports, and maize is an important staple. A few crops have shown increased yields. These include sugar cane, millet/sorghum, and sweet potatoes (which still have low yields), although yields have remained stagnant for two or three years. Only cotton, rice, tea, cassava, and dried beans have shown steadily rising yields.

CAUSES OF LOW PRODUCTIVITY

Certain factors have probably contributed more than other factors to the decreased and fluctuating yields of crops.

Neglect of the Agriculture Sector

Over the years, the agricultural sector in Cameroon has contributed annually more than 30 percent of GDP; yet, typical of many developing countries, the government has always reinvested in the sector a much lower percentage. For examples, investment in agriculture during the Third Development Plan (1971–1972 to 1975–1976) was 12.5 percent. Investment in the sector during the Fourth Development Plan (1976–1977 to 1980–1981) was planned at 12.7 percent but was actually only 10.3 percent (U.S. Agency for International Development 1982, Addendum p. 17). Thus, although the agricultural sector has not been fully developed, much of the value generated in that sector has been reinvested in other sectors, perhaps prematurely, in an effort to develop the economy in general but especially the urban areas where political power is based. That power base has always been more concerned about such urban issues as consumer food prices, unemployment, and the amenities of city life than about such rural issues as producer prices for farm crops, improvement of agriculture, and rural welfare and development in general. Despite the low investment, however, during the 1970s and early 1980s, agricultural production continued to grow faster than the growth of population and better than in most other sub-Saharan African countries. Yet, it did not grow as rapidly as the overall economy. The relative neglect of the agricultural sector, in terms of investment, in favor of other, politically important sectors contributed to that slower growth and probably also to declining productivity.

Drought

The weather also has not cooperated with the agricultural sector. Cyclical climatic conditions in Africa were brought vividly to the world's attention by the Sahelian drought of the early 1970s. That same drought affected agriculture in Cameroon, as well. During the past three years, the drought has begun to return. Although cotton yields actually increased slightly from 1981–1982 (1,260 kg./ha.) to 1982–1983 (1,280 kg./ha.), total production decreased because less hectarage was planted as a result of lack of rain (*Africa Research Bulletin,* March 15–April 14, 1983, p. 6815). However, the acreage planted in perennial crops, such as tree crops, is more difficult to alter. Thus, yields are more likely to decrease in those areas most affected by the drought. For examples, as production of cocoa decreased from 68,200 tons in 1981–1982 to 57,200 tons in 1982–1983, it is likely that yields were also lower. Similarly, export of coffee for the first 11 months of the year decreased from 25,000 tons in 1982 to 13,500 tons in 1983. Exports of bananas and palm oil were also lower. And production of groundnut oil and sugar was less (*Jeune Afrique,* February 8, 1984).

Producer Prices

Most of the export crops, such as coffee and cocoa, are sold by farmers to the Office National de Commercialisation des Produits de Base (ONCPB), the National Produce Marketing Board (NPMB). The ONCPB pays the farmers a producer price fixed each year by the government, ostensibly for price support and stabilization purposes, and sells the crops on the world market. The producer prices have generally been lower than world prices. Thus, over the long run, farmers have received less than the value of their crops, with the surplus being retained by the government. Some of that surplus has been reinvested in the agricultural sector, into development of infrastructure, research, or subsidization of farm inputs. But a large part has gone into the national budget for general development purposes, rather than being reinvested in the agricultural sector. Eventually, it was determined that prices being paid to farmers were too low to provide a real incentive to produce. Many farmers had begun to neglect export crops because it had become relatively more profitable to produce food crops. Yields, as well as production of export crops, were dropping. To encourage export crop production, producer prices were increased dramatically for several years; but it soon became difficult to continue to do so because, by 1978, world prices had begun to decline. Furthermore, as producer prices for export crops were increased, concern grew that farmers would begin to neglect food crops because, in the past, the Ministry of Agriculture had observed a trade-off between the production of export crops and the production of food crops in Cameroon, depending on relative prices (Cameroon, Ministry of Agriculture 1980).

Aging Plantations

Over the years, as farmers neglected their coffee and cocoa farms because of the profitability of producing food crops, the average age of the coffee and cocoa farms increased, and their condition deteriorated from lack of maintenance and investment. Yields for groundnuts and cassava decreased because of aging and increasingly diseased genetic materials. There has been evidence of lower yields for other food crops, as well, particularly staples such as cocoyams and plantains.

Lack of Insecticide and Herbicide Treatments

The agricultural census of 1972–1973 estimated that 73 percent of the land cultivated for industrial crops and 96 percent of that cultivated for food crops did not receive insecticide or herbicide treatments. As cultivated areas have increased and new varieties have been planted, the risks of infestation by insects and sensitivity to disease have increased. Because of this, the Ministry of Agriculture believes that increases in both production and productivity depend, to a great extent, on use of insecticides and herbicides (Cameroon, Ministry of Agriculture 1980, pp. 78–79). The government has encouraged the use of such inputs on export crops by subsidizing their application. They are still not used extensively for food crops.

Little Use of Fertilizer

Historically, agriculture in Cameroon has been land extensive. Land that had been cultivated for several years was then allowed to remain fallow until it became rejuvenated. Over time, agriculture has become more intensive. The same land is cultivated year after year, with shorter and fewer fallow periods. Yet, fertilizer has not been used to fully compensate for this. Fertilizer use has been extremely low in the past, particularly by food crop farmers. For example, the agricultural census in 1972 found that 91 percent of land cultivated in food crops and 62 percent of the land cultivated by export crop farmers had never been treated with fertilizer (Cameroon, Ministry of Agriculture 1980, p. 84). This has improved, however. In 1970, only 28 kgs. of fertilizer were used, on the average, per hectare of arable land; by 1981, 60 kgs. were used per hectare (World Bank 1984, p. 228). Yet, this is still very little.

Summary

The low and declining yields of crops in Cameroon can be attributed to multiple causes. The most important ones in the past have been the general neglect of the agricultural sector in favor of other sectors considered important to overall development (particularly those politically important in the urban areas), drought, producer prices that did not provide incentives to produce, the consequent aging of the plantations, the lack of insecticide and herbicide treatments, and little use of fertilizer.

STRATEGIES TO IMPROVE PRODUCTIVITY

Concern with productivity may have begun to grow during the early 1970s, particularly from 1973 when former President Ahidjo initiated the "Green Revolution" in Cameroon. But little real action was taken until recently to improve productivity. It is possible, however, that during the Fifth Development Plan, real progress may yet be made toward improving agricultural productivity.

Greater Emphasis on Agriculture

Certainly, there is greater potential for improving productivity in the agricultural sector during the Fifth Development Plan (1981–1986). The actual sum, as well as the percentage of total investment, is to be increased. The Fifth Development Plan anticipates that 23.7 percent of the investments will be made in the agricultural sector. This is more than twice that of the Fourth Development Plan. The emphasis of the plan is on agricultural development in particular and rural development in general, because it is now believed that the economic development of Cameroon must be based on agriculture. One of the seven main objectives of rural development policy, is to "give highest priority to increase in productivity in the agricultural sector" because

> It is known . . . that only a steady increase in productivity will in future raise production especially as there will be a decrease in the proportion of the population actively involved in agriculture in many areas (Cameroon, Ministry of Economic Affairs 1981b, p. 64).

The plan admits that there had been expectations that productivity would rise because of the establishment of state-managed agricultural undertakings using modern techniques and trained managerial staff. However, despite huge investments, there was little success. In fact, there was even a negative impact on peasant farm production. Many peasant farmers became temporary wage-earners and eventually permanent urban dwellers. After taking office, President Biya initiated a general policy of examining state enterprises in all sectors of the economy, in search of ways to make them more efficient and productive.

To increase productivity in the agricultural sector, the Fifth Development Plan proposed five subobjectives:

1. "All farmers should have easy access to technical information and should be given all the inputs and the required means of production in time and in sufficient quantities and at an encouraging price" (Cameroon, Ministry of Economic Affairs and Planning 1981b, p. 64). This relates to agricultural extension, access to inputs, and price policies.
2. "Law and regulations governing land tenure will be amended with a view to facilitating access to land by initial settlers, young farmers and businessmen involved in the field of agriculture so as to ensure for the latter lasting custody over land they have developed" (Cameroon, Ministry of Economic Affairs and Planning 1981b, p. 64).
3. "In agronomic research, absolute priority will be given to increasing the productivity of small holdings considering their special constraints" (Cameroon, Ministry of Economic Affairs and Planning 1981b, p. 64). Emphasis is to be on crop research, particularly food crop research, and on mechanization. Experimental farms will be set up in the "support centres" in order to provide a framework for the research and an opportunity for agricultural extension services to establish a link with agronomic research. There will also be experiments with integrating agriculture and cattle rearing.
4. "Government agricultural undertakings will maintain what has been achieved until it reaches a satisfactory level of productivity before embarking on extension programmes" (Cameroon, Ministry of Economic Affairs and Planning 1981b, p. 64).
5. "The State will promote the opening of medium-sized agricultural farms . . . that will be most viable in technical and economic terms" (Cameroon, Ministry of Economic Affairs and Planning 1981b, p. 65).

Some of these general policy objectives are being implemented through the following specific interventions.

The National Food Plan

The new emphasis on food crop production is evident in the development of a long-term national food plan, which was included in the Fifth Development Plan. Among the many priorities of the food plan, those most likely to affect productivity as well as total production are:

1. Systematic introduction of a food crop component in all development projects;
2. Priority to distribution of selected, high yield seeds and seedlings;
3. Effective stabilization of prices of such particularly important products as maize and sorghum along with the creation of adequate storage facilities;
4. Intensification of programs aiming to reduce postharvest losses;
5. More frequent granting of credit to private entrepreneurs who want to create predominantly food crop farms in areas near urban centers;
6. Intensification of research and experimentation, particularly with respect to furnishing high yield, disease- and pest-resistant seeds and seedlings; to developing the best systems of production for savanna areas, including mechanization that will not destroy the soils; to finding ways to reduce the long fallow period in the forest zones while preserving soil fertility; and to creating experimental orchards and setting up technical support structures, especially for citrus fruits;
7. Encouraging the resettlement of youths who have received extensive agricultural training in food crop farming (Cameroon, Ministry of Economic Affairs and Planning 1981b, pp. 65–66).

Achieving these objectives may increase yields significantly.

Renewal of Cocoa and Coffee Plantations

Because yields of many cocoa and coffee plantations have been low due to long-term neglect and aging of the trees, a program was initiated in 1978–1979 to encourage replanting of the old trees. Allowances are paid to participating cocoa farmers (for two years) and coffee farmers (for three years) in order to compensate them for the loss of earnings before the young trees begin to produce (Cameroon, Commission Nationale du

Comite Agro-Pastoral 1981, p. 15). Unfortunately, the allowances have not been a sufficient incentive to encourage the desired amount of replanting.

Land Intensive Cultivation

From its introduction in 1951 until the 1970s, cotton was grown in the North on an extensive, low-input basis with no fertilizer. Yields were low, averaging 500 kg./ha. After reaching a maximum cultivated hectarage in 1968, farmers began to decrease the area planted, because of low producer prices and drought. They replaced cotton with food crops; cotton production decreased. In 1974, world prices increased and remained high for cotton. At that time, following the drought, La Societe de Developpement du Coton (SODECOTON), a parastatal, was established to take over the operation of the French development company CFDT, which had originally developed cotton in the area. La Societe de Developpement du Coton attempted to increase the profitability of cotton as an intensively grown cash crop, using pesticides and fertilizer, and reorganizing the farming system to regroup farmers' fields in order to facilitate rotation of cotton with other crops. It also increased the producer price. In response, yields rose from 500 kg./ha. to 1,420 kg./ha. in 1979, while total area devoted to cotton continued to decline until 1978. Efforts are now being made to develop other cash crops, such as maize and groundnuts, in the areas where cotton is no longer grown. Efforts are also being made to increase the productivity of staple food crops, especially sorghum, in those areas. Thus, increasing intensification of cotton production has allowed increasing concentration of the production of food crops as well.

Irrigation

There are three, large, irrigated rice projects in various locations in Cameroon. The oldest, La Societe d'Expansion et de Modernisation de la Riziculture de Yagoua (SEMRY), which began operations in 1971, has achieved relatively high yields, partly as a result of a very costly system of irrigation. Another project, La Societe de Developpement de la Riziculture dans la Plaine des Mbos (SODERIM) began operations (as MIDERIM) in 1973, experimenting with rain-fed production and irrigation that did not require extensive infrastructure. Problems of low yields led to a reorientation of the project toward more extensive irrigated rice culture, beginning in 1979. The FAO estimates that about 10,000 hectares of land were irrigated in 1980 throughout Cameroon. Irrigation may need to be expanded in the future, particularly in the northern areas, but attempts must be made to keep the schemes relatively simple, for maintenance purposes, and also cost efficient. Although largely because of the cost of transport, SEMRY rice, in particular, cannot compete price-wise with imported rice; at this time, a complicated *jumelage* system prevents stockpiling of expensive domestic rice.[4]

Intensified Use of Inputs

Farmers are being encouraged to use more insecticides, herbicides, and fertilizer. In the past, fertilizer was sold at subsidized prices, but only for export crops. Recently, this privilege has been extended to food crops as well. However, the general policy of subsidized input prices is being questioned. Because it can lead to excess demand for "cheap" inputs, it can result in allocation of limited quantities on other bases, more likely to powerful, large-scale farmers, leaving none for smaller-scale farmers. Thus, Cameroon is considering a policy of gradually reducing input subsidies, hoping that the profits from the higher yields produced with input use will be an incentive and will be sufficiently high to cover the full cost of them.

Slow bureaucratic administration of input subsidy programs often delays delivery of the inputs, preventing them from reaching farmers at the time they are required. Farmers with sufficient resources may pay black market prices to get fertilizer when they need it, but others may have to suffer without it. Thus, the government is organizing new input distribution channels through decentralized "service centres" in the field. Research has shown, however, that farm inputs are often supplied more efficiently by private enterprise than by state-owned institutions. Thus, action should be taken to analyze the alternatives more thoroughly in Cameroon to determine the optimum public/private input supply mix.

The National Seed Plan

New, high-yielding pest- and disease-resistant seeds and plant materials are being developed to replace old, genetic materials now being used. The Fifth Development Plan foresees restructuring the Food Development Authority (MIDEVIV) and discharging it of its former responsibilities in order to administer a newly developed national seed plan. This is as much a reaction to the lack of success of MIDEVIV in its former operations as it is a response to new priorities. Some of the most important crops to be covered by the seed plan are grains (maize and rice), fruit, groundnuts, plantains, and yams. Coffee and cocoa are covered by another project.

Research and Technology

The little agricultural research that was conducted in the past was carried out mainly on export crops. Efforts are now being made to produce technical packages that can be extended to food crop farmers as well. Most success has been achieved with maize and varieties of irrigated rice. Some success has also been achieved in better-yielding yams, cassava, plantains, and pineapples. Nevertheless, results have been insufficient compared to the needs.

The Fifth Development Plan envisions further research into sorghum, groundnuts, soya, beans, and fruits,[5] with research on vegetables expected to begin in 1984. A National Soils Centre was recently opened to coordinate soil research (Eckebil 1983, pp. 86–88). In general, the theoretical side of research into crops and soils is going fairly well, according to Dr. Jacques-Paul Eckebil, Director of Cameroon's Agricultural Research Institute, but the same cannot be said for farming systems, where a real effort is called for in order to produce improved production systems for the peasant farmer (Eckebil 1983, p. 88).

Technological research is also being conducted. The Centre National d'Etudes et d'Experimentation du Machinisme Agricole (CENEEMA) was created in 1974 to support the gradual mechanization of agriculture with emphasis on technology appropriate for Cameroon farms. Since its creation, it has been constructing or adapting relatively simple farm and food processing equipment to increase the productivity of many small- and medium-scale farmers. Some of this technology is made available through the "Young Farmers Settlement Program," which provides Cameroonians between the ages of 18 and 35 with allowances to set up a farm as well as a reimbursable, interest-free advance to acquire agricultural equipment, with priority being given to those who have attended one of the various agricultural schools or training programs. Nevertheless, there is still a wide gap between the development of technology and the large-scale adoption to it. Greater educational efforts, perhaps through the agricultural extension system, must be made to convince farmers of the benefits of such technology.

Credit

Adoption of technology and use of inputs requires not only knowledge of the benefits of such technology and inputs, but also the ability to acquire them. Acquisition, for most farmers, must be on a credit basis. Thus, access to credit is essential for increasing productivity.

Large-scale farmers have always had greater access to credit than small-scale farmers because they are judged as more creditworthy. Because small-scale farmers and women seldom have access to bank credit, they have had to rely more on various types of traditional savings and loan associations such as *njangis, tontines,* and "country meetings," or money lenders.[6] Less than 20 years ago the cooperative credit union movement was established. Since then, it has grown rapidly. If current efforts to strengthen it are successful, it has great potential for becoming one of the most important sources of credit for small farmers by bridging the gap between traditional institutions and formal banking institutions.

The National Fund for Rural Development (FONADER) was set up in 1973 to promote and accelerate economic and social development in rural areas, particularly through provision of agricultural credit. The amount of credit it has been able to provide has always been insufficient, and it seldom has reached small-scale farmers. To make it more accessible to farmers, FONADER has been decentralizing its offices throughout the provinces. In addition, the Fifth Development Plan has proposed to transform FONADER into a true agricultural bank in order to increase the funds available for credit operations. Progress has not been rapid.

Agricultural Extension

Agricultural extension services must link the results of agricultural research and technology development with the farmers in the fields. In the past, extension services were provided mainly through the Ministry of Agriculture and directed toward export crops. Although women have traditionally grown food crops, very little extension was directed toward food crops in general and toward women farmers in particular. The newly created regional, integrated development authorities such as the Northwest Development Authority (MIDENO) and the Union Centrale des Cooperatives Agricoles de l'Ouest (UCCAO)—which administers the integrated development project for the West province, as well as the transformed sectoral development societies such as SODECOTON, operating in an integrated development context—are increasingly taking over extension work in their areas. As all of these institutions now include a food crop component, secondary though it may be to the emphasis placed on export crops, there is greater potential for reaching all farmers in the area.

The former extension system is also being reorganized to operate uniformly, using the "Training and Consultation Method" similar to that developed by Daniel Benor. To support that system, a network is to be set up, comprised of "Service Centres" for supply of inputs and credit and "Support Centres" situated near the "Service Centres" to house agricultural extension services, including demonstration farms.

Within the extension system, transportation remains one of the most difficult, everyday problems for most extension agents. Too many extension agents are confined to their offices for lack of transport; too few are physically able to reach the farmers in the fields.

Appropriate Education

To enable the extension system to operate effectively and to improve the agricultural sector in general, appropriate education is essential. Formal educational institutions have increased the number of agricultural technicians, technical agents, and cooperative specialists from five in 1965 to 1,625 in 1979, and there are plans to double or triple the number each year (Cameroon, Ministry of Agriculture 1980, p. 120). This is being facilitated by a major project to develop the University Center for Agriculture at Dschang.

At the farm level, there are several programs to train young farmers. The National Civic Service for Participation in Development Centers teach modern agricultural practices and stimulate complementary employment in rural areas by training carpenters, masons, blacksmiths, and other skilled craftsmen. The Centers for Training Farm Families (CTFF) were established to develop a network of agricultural innovators in the North who would diffuse modern methods of agricultural production to their neighbors (International Union for Child Welfare, n.d.). Unfortunately, many participants leave the rural areas after training, or do not otherwise diffuse the techniques (Agbor-Tabi, n.d., c. 1981).

In general, agricultural education still suffers from the image that agriculture is not a prestigious occupation. Too many potential students prefer to study subjects that are far less practical for a developing country. Too few women opt for agricultural education in preparation for a career or, because of earlier training, are unable to meet the prerequisites if they reach higher educational levels. Some have also accepted the belief that agriculture, except for the home economics and domestic science aspects, is a male occupation. Many of these obstacles and stereotypes must be overcome.

Land Tenure

Land tenure problems may become more acute in the future as population growth puts more pressure on the land. There is some evidence of this occurring already in the more highly populated areas of the West province. Over the generations, plots may become more fragmented and scattered through heredity if possibilities for consolidation do not exist.

Yields will probably drop as a result. The land tenure ordinances of 1975 allow the state to redistribute lands not under cultivation to those who apply to use them for productive purposes. And there is now a land registry system that allows persons farming by usufruct to obtain title to the land. This may encourage efficient, productive, larger-scale farming. But it may also discriminate against less-educated farmers who do not understand the legislation and who are unable to complete the necessary paper work. Many of those farmers are the ones producing most of the food. Furthermore, research shows that small-scale farmers are often more productive than large-scale farmers.

In addition to traditional land tenure and private ownership, the state may also take over land, with compensation. This has been done for resettlement schemes, for some large-scale development projects, as in the case of rice, or for such programs as the "Settlement of Young Farmers."

Revitalization of Village Communities

One of the highest priorities of the Fifth Plan is the revitalization of "village communities." This is to improve the general quality of life in the rural sector by providing many of the social services of urban areas. It would include improving the infrastructure to facilitate communication with markets, improving or building schools and health clinics, extending electricity to more locations, providing better access to safe water, and developing rural industries. It is hoped that this program will slow down the rural exodus, particularly that of potential, young farmers, thus reversing the current trend toward an aging farm population and thus increasing the overall productivity of farming by encouraging vigorous, young Cameroonians, trained in agriculture, to remain in the rural areas to farm.

SUMMARY AND CONCLUSIONS

Cameroon has been wise to base its development on agriculture. The agricultural sector produces exports that earn foreign exchange, which is used to import capital for development. It produces food crops that, in contrast to most other sub-Saharan African countries, have thus far been able to feed the population of Cameroon. And it produces other crops that are processed domestically to develop local industry. As a result, the agricultural sector has been influential in stimulating the economy throughout the years. Gross Domestic Product has averaged a respectable annual growth rate of 7.0 percent.

Agricultural production, too, has been growing, although not as rapidly as GDP. It has been growing at an annual average of 3.4 percent, faster than the present population growth rate of 2.7 to 3.1 percent. As a result, Cameroon has been able to remain basically food self-sufficient. However, further analysis reveals causes for concern about the agricultural sector.

The population of Cameroon has continued to grow. More serious, the population growth rate has also continued to grow, increasing over the past 24 years from an average of 1.8 percent to 2.7 percent and possibly as high as 3.1 percent per year. In addition, Cameroon has a high and increasing rate of urbanization, presently 8.0 percent, which is rapidly draining the countryside of the young, potentially productive farmers and greatly increasing the demand for food in the urban areas. The challenge for Cameroon is to find some way to increase agricultural production in order to feed a growing, increasingly urbanized population. In the short run, it must do this with a farm population that is becoming proportionately smaller and older every year. The only way to succeed in the short run is to help farmers to become more productive.

The healthy appearance of the economy and the growth of the agricultural sector cover up the fact that agricultural productivity may be much lower than it should be and than it could be, and that it may have decreased in recent years. It is difficult to obtain accurate productivity data, data that can be compared over time, or even data that can be compared among the various institutions attempting to gather it. Certainly, however, when analyzing past performance of the agricultural sector, the Ministry of Agriculture expressed concern about productivity, particularly for the two main export crops, coffee and cocoa, but also for food crops in general, other than for maize and rice. The ministry noted, also, that yields for such crops as palm products, sugar, and wheat, grown by parastatals, were always lower than those projected by the parastatals.

The data that are currently available seem to indicate that, in general, except for a few crops such as rice, millet/sorghum, dried beans, sesame, cotton, and tea, yields per hectare in Cameroon are below the average for Africa, and African yields are not high. Data from the FAO and the USDA confirm the concerns of the Ministry of Agriculture. Those data show that cocoa, an export crop, has had continually declining yields, and wheat, an important import, has not been able to progress much beyond the experimental stage. Most other crops, including such important ones as coffee, maize, groundnuts, and tobacco, have exhibited lower yields than in 1969–1971, although they have recovered to some extent from 1979 through 1982. A few crops, including sugar cane, millet/sorghum, and sweet potatoes have increased yields since 1969–1971, although they have remained stagnant for the last two or three years. Only cotton, rice, tea, cassava, and dried beans have shown steadily increasing yields over the years.

Although there may be many factors that have caused productivity to drop, some have been more influential than others. Drought has been a problem throughout the continent, one that has been difficult to counteract. Other influences have been largely related to government policies. For example, over the years, typical of many developing countries, investment in the agricultural sector, in general, has been relatively low compared to the contribution it makes to GDP. This has been accomplished by paying government-fixed producer prices for export crops that have been lower than world prices—until the recent drop in world prices for several crops decreased the gap. The difference between the producer prices and the world prices has not always been used to stabilize farm prices; much of it has gone into a general budget category. As a result, much of the contribution of the agricultural sector has been reinvested in other sectors of the economy, especially in the urban areas where political power is based. Because low prices failed to provide sufficient incentive to produce, it is believed that farmers began to neglect their export crops, causing lower production and also lower productivity as farms became older and were not maintained. In addition, over time, the need for insecticide and herbicide treatments has increased, yet there has been little use of them except by export crop farmers who received subsidized applications. Similarly, the need for fertilizer has increased as cultivation has become more intensive over the years. Yet, too little has been used, except by export crop farmers who were able to purchase it at a subsidized price. Such subsidies have not been available to food crop farmers until recently, when they were given subsidized access to fertilizer. But most small-scale farmers still are not sufficiently convinced of the benefits of those inputs to use them on food crops on a large scale; there is a large, educational challenge that must be met by the agricultural extension system.

Cameroon has observed the difficulties experienced by other African countries that have not emphasized agriculture, especially Nigeria, another oil-producing country. The resulting concern of the Cameroon government has produced some policy changes that are intended to stimulate the agricultural sector and to base overall development on agriculture. Some of those policy changes have already helped to reverse decreases in productivity. Greater emphasis on agriculture is evident from both the actual as well as the percentage increase in investment in the agricultural sector within the Fifth Development Plan. Specific objectives are also aimed at increasing productivity. In particular, a national food plan was included in the Fifth Development Plan. Although results have been discouraging, farmers are being encouraged to replant cocoa and coffee plantations. More encouraging has been the adoption of intensive cultivation of cotton. Introduction of irrigation, particularly for rice, has increased yields, but it has been expensive. Use of inputs such as insecticides, herbicides, and fertilizer is increasing, but slowly. The price of fertilizer for all crops, not just for export crops, is now subsidized. This may encourage more farmers to experiment with it, particularly if extensive efforts on demonstration plots can provide solid evidence of the benefits. A national seed plan has been prepared to promote the development and distribution of improved varieties of seeds and seedlings, but its success has not yet been evaluated. Research on crops and development of small-scale farm technology is increasing, but adoption on a wide scale is still lacking. There are plans to increase the availability of credit to allow farmers to invest in their farms, but the resources are still insufficient and the innovations too slow to meet the needs. Improved methods of agricultural extension have been devised, but budgets must allow implementation. Changes have been made in land tenure laws, but, in the long run, these could have either beneficial or detrimental effects. There is recognition that changes must be made in the education system. Some of those changes are already being implemented, but they will impact only over time. Finally, revitalization of village communities is a general priority of the Fifth Development Plan, in order to decrease the rate of urbanization and to encourage young, vigorous, trained farmers to remain in the rural areas, but it is difficult to show concrete progress in this area.

In conclusion, Cameroon has been able to maintain solid economic growth as well as acceptable growth in the agricultural sector. However, Cameroon is now at a crucial turning point with respect to per capita production. The government is aware of the need to increase agricultural productivity in order to maintain per capita production, and it has already made some progress in reversing the downward trend for some crops. Furthermore, it has prepared elaborate plans that have been included in the Fifth Development Plan. Yet, plans are not always implemented. In fact, only 51.2 percent of the planned investment in the agricultural sector was actually made during the Fourth Development Plan (United States Agency for International Development 1982, p. 18). The time period of the Fifth Development Plan is now more than half completed, yet there has been little action toward achieving some of the objectives. Implementation must proceed more rapidly. Strategies of the government, private investors, and international donor organizations should be directed toward increasing not only agricultural production, but agricultural productivity as well, in order to assist Cameroon to achieve its dual goals of increasing foreign exchange earnings from agricultural exports and maintaining self-sufficiency in food crops in order to sustain the long-term development of its economy.

NOTES

1. Although food imports have been increasing and becoming more diversified, until recently they were composed mainly of wheat, rice, sugar, and hops. There has been little food aid.

2. The figures for Botswana are from 1970–1978, not as recent as those for the other countries in Table 6.1. They do not reveal the effects of changed international economic conditions and several years of serious drought that are reflected in the figures for the other countries.

3. "Dutch disease" was identified during the rapid expansion of natural gas exports in the 1960s in the Netherlands. The boom caused upward pressure on the exchange rate and destroyed the competitiveness of other exports, especially as the tax revenues from those exports were returned to the economy in ways (such as large increases in transfer payments for welfare) that caused increased inflation, and eventually even greater dependence on that enclave export, natural gas.

In the case of Nigeria, as large quantities of foreign exchange were received from oil exports, the exchange rate was allowed to appreciate over time. This greatly increased the demand for imports as they became very cheap relative to domestic goods, and it made nonoil exports uncompetitive on the world market; domestic production suffered.

Although the oil sector is an enclave with only weak linkages to the remainder of the economy (because it uses little domestic labor or materials), its revenues are easily taxed by the government. In fact, at one time, 65 percent of Nigeria's revenues were derived from oil exports. If those tax revenues had been "sterilized" in overseas government deposits, most of the Dutch disease might have been prevented. But, as they flowed rapidly into the economy, they affected it in several ways. While they had little effect on the costs of the capital-intensive oil export sector, they had a very strong effect on the remainder of the economy, particularly when they were used to increase civil servants' salaries. The large increases in the money supply led to increased inflation. Within a few years, the overvalued exchange rate along with domestic inflation led to increased inflation, while the overvalued exchange rate along with domestic inflation led to increased unemployment and stagnation of the nonoil sectors of the economy, particularly agriculture, the sector most relevant to our discussion of Cameroon. Whereas Nigeria was formerly an exporter of agricultural products, the agricultural sector deteriorated to the point where it was no longer able to produce enough food to feed the population. Nigeria soon became a large-scale food importer (see Gillis et al. 1983, pp. 428; 529–36, for a more detailed discussion of Dutch disease).

4. Each time they order from abroad, importers are also required to purchase a specified quantity of locally produced rice in proportion to the quantity that they wish to import. A ratio of one kg. of local rice for every kg. of imported rice has been typical.

5. Citrus, avocados, mangoes, guavas, and grenadillos.

6. *Njangis* and *tontines* are forms of rotating credit associations common to many African countries. "Country meetings" often provide more general savings and loan services for their members, on a nonformal basis, in combination with other social functions, usually ethnically oriented. (See DeLancey 1978 for a more detailed description of such traditional savings and loan associations.)

Appendix 6.1. U.S.D.A. Data Commodity Production (1,000 Metric Tons) and Yields (kg./ha.)

	Rice, Paddy		*Cotton, Lint*		*Cocoa*		*Coffee*	
Year	*Prod.*	*Yield*	*Prod.*	*Yield*	*Prod.*	*Yield*	*Prod.*	*Yield*
1960	8	1,000	n.a.	n.a.	67	n.a.	37	n.a.
1961	4	571	n.a.	n.a.	74	n.a.	40	n.a.
1962	9	900	n.a.	n.a.	75	n.a.	43	n.a.
1963	11	786	n.a.	n.a.	76	n.a.	43	n.a.
1964	14	1,077	n.a.	n.a.	86	n.a.	47	n.a.
1965	13	1,182	15	205	93	n.a.	55	n.a.
1966	16	1,143	20	245	89	n.a.	63	n.a.
1967	22	1,467	20	222	87	n.a.	80	n.a.
1968	16	1,143	17	181	93	n.a.	82	n.a.
1969	18	1,200	24	224	105	n.a.	82	n.a.
1970	14	824	32	283	110	n.a.	88	n.a.
1971	15	938	13	125	115	n.a.	65	226
1972	11	647	15	150	123	n.a.	96	340
1973	12	600	16	181	107	334	94	331
1974	24	1,143	10	161	110	338	104	347
1975	30	1,304	14	232	118	359	80	220
1976	41	1,577	17	238	96	230	80	231
1977	41	1,519	17	280	106	259	66	175
1978	44	1,833	14	294	106	246	108	303
1979	47	1,958	21	441	123	281	110	307
1980	44	1,833	28	491	119	268	98	277
1981	50	1,923	30	500	118	266	98	265
1982	71	2,366	22	379	116	267	101	272
1983	n.a.	n.a.	28*	483*	n.a.	n.a.	101	270

*Estimate
Source: U.S.D.A.

Appendix 6.2a. FAO Data on Commodity Production (1,000 Metric Tons) and Yields (kg./ha.), 1969–1971, 1979, 1980, 1981

	Wheat		*Rice, Paddy*		*Maize*		*Millet/Sorg.*		*Potatoes*		*Sweet Potatoes*		*Cassava*		*Beans, Dry*		*Groundnuts*	
Year	*Prod.*	*Yield*	*Prod.*	*Yield*	*Prod.*	*Yield*	*Prod.*	*Yield*	*Prod.*	*Yield*	*Prod.*	*Yield*	*Prod.*	*Yield*	*Prod.*	*Yield*	*Prod.*	*Yield*
1969–1971	—	—	13	844	355	1,151	343	719	54	2672	134	3,212	637	3,965	59	578	206	845
1979	2[a]	1,000	15	866	408	748	414	834	24	968	130[a]	3,421	1,000[a]	4,348	95[a]	625	108	303
1980	1[b]	500	55	2,391	490[b]	907	400[b]	889	50[b]	2,000	130[b]	3,421	1,000[b]	4,292	98[b]	636	110[b]	314
1981	1[b]	500	55[b]	2,391	490[b]	926	400[b]	889	60[b]	2,400	135	3,512	1,011[b]	4,283	100[b]	633	120[b]	343

	Sesame		*Seed Cotton*		*Tomatoes*		*Onions, Dry*		*Sugar Cane*		*Coffee, grnd*		*Cocoa*		*Tea*		*Tobacco leaves*	
Year	*Prod.*	*Yield*	*Prod.*	*Yield*	*Prod.*	*Yield*	*Prod.*	*Yield*	*Prod.*	*Yield*	*Prod.*	*Yield*	*Prod.*	*Yield*	*Prod.*	*Yield*	*Prod.*	*Yield*
1969–1971	6	365	58	561	70	5,916	4	2,492	224	20,394	90	373	127	328	1	1,283	4	617
1979	5	182	80	1,421	31	3,127	6	1,896	720[a]	36,000	101	282	123	287	2	2,212	3	605
1980	8[b]	267	89[a]	1,401	40[a]	4,000	10[a]	2,500	790[a]	35,909	102[a]	300	120[a]	282	2[a]	1,978	3[b]	600
1981	10[b]	333	65[b]	1,300	50[a]	5,000	15[a]	2,500	580[a]	34,118	105[b]	293	110[a]	259	2[b]	2,088	3[b]	588

[a]Unofficial
[b]Estimate
Source: U.N., FAO, *1981 FAO Production Yearbook,* 1982.

Appendix 6.2b. FAO Data on Commodity Production (1,000 Metric Tons) and Yields (kg./ha.), 1974–1976, 1980, 1981, 1982

	Wheat		*Rice, Paddy*		*Maize*		*Millet/Sorg.*		*Potatoes*		*Sweet Potatoes*		*Cassava*		*Beans, Dry*		*Groundnuts*	
Year	*Prod.*	*Yield*	*Prod.*	*Yield*	*Prod.*	*Yield*	*Prod.*	*Yield*	*Prod.*	*Yield*	*Prod.*	*Yield*	*Prod.*	*Yield*	*Prod.*	*Yield*	*Prod.*	*Yield*
1974–1976	—	492	34	1,445	539	1,102	389	899	78	3,008	143	3,508	842	4,348	75	597	256	758
1980	1[a]	500	55	2,391	490[a]	907	400[a]	889	50[a]	2,000	130[a]	3,421	1,000[a]	4,223	98[a]	636	110[a]	314
1981	1[a]	500	55[a]	2,391	500[a]	926	400[a]	889	60[a]	2,400	130[a]	3,421	1,040[a]	4,462	103[a]	648	120[a]	343
1982	1[a]	500	59[a]	2,545	500[a]	926	406[a]	893	60[a]	2,400	130[a]	3,421	1,077[a]	4,491	108[a]	657	120[a]	343

	Sesame		*Seed Cotton*		*Tomatoes*		*Onions, Dry*		*Sugar Cane*		*Coffee, grnd*		*Cocoa*		*Tea*		*Tobacco leaves*	
Year	*Prod.*	*Yield*	*Prod.*	*Yield*	*Prod.*	*Yield*	*Prod.*	*Yield*	*Prod.*	*Yield*	*Prod.*	*Yield*	*Prod.*	*Yield*	*Prod.*	*Yield*	*Prod.*	*Yield*
1974–1976	9	535	46	695	91	6,069	21	3,299	411	28,698	92	283	100	272	2	2,043	3	543
1980	8[a]	267	89[a]	1,401	40[a]	4,000	10[a]	2,500	790[a]	35,909	102[b]	300	120[b]	282	2[b]	1,905	3[a]	600
1981	10[a]	333	65[b]	1,300	50[a]	5,000	15[a]	2,500	580[a]	34,118	90[b]	256	115[b]	262	2[a]	2,259	3[a]	600
1982	10[a]	333	70[b]	1,426	50[a]	5,000	15[a]	2,506	580[a]	35,902	105[b]	291	120[b]	264	2[a]	2,277	3[a]	606

[a]Estimate
[b]Unofficial

Source: U.N., F.A.O., *1982 FAO Production Yearbook,* 1983.

7

OIL REVENUES AND THE CAMEROONIAN ECONOMY

Nancy C. Benjamin and Shantayanan Devarajan

During its first 18 years as a nation, Cameroon enjoyed modest but steady economic growth, with an average annual growth rate of Gross Domestic Product (GDP) of 5 percent. The agricultural sector dominated the economy, accounting for 32 percent of GDP and employing over 80 percent of the labor force. Moreover, of the 1.1 billion dollars of export earnings in 1981, 72 percent came from agricultural exports—mainly coffee and cocoa. A manufacturing sector, based on processing indigenous raw materials, had gradually developed to about 25 percent of GDP. While the nontradable sectors—construction, services, public administration—were growing rapidly, poor infrastructure and low levels of education were frequently cited as obstacles to the country's development. One of the wealthiest countries in sub-Saharan Africa, Cameroon still relied on foreign capital (aid and borrowing) for its investment. Finally, the country enjoyed a degree of political stability almost unparalleled in the region.

We thank Iradj Alikhani, Clive Bell, Jeffrey Lewis, Frank Lysy, Robert Weiner, and Derek White for comments on an earlier paper, from which the present paper draws heavily. The World Bank does not accept responsibility for the views expressed herein, which are those of the authors and should not be attributed to the World Bank or to its affiliated organizations. The findings, interpretations, and conclusions are the results of research supported by the bank; they do not necessarily represent official policy of the bank. The designations employed, the presentation of material, and any maps used in this document are solely for the convenience of the reader and do not imply the expression of any opinion whatsoever on the part of the World Bank or its affiliates concerning the legal status of any country, territory, city, area, or of its authorities, or concerning the delimitation of its boundaries or national affiliation.

The discovery of oil off the west coast of Cameroon and its subsequent production beginning in 1978 could significantly alter this pattern of development. On the one hand, with annual oil revenues exceeding 1 billion dollars, the country would no longer be dependent on coffee and cocoa exports for its foreign exchange. Moreover, the 750 million barrels of reserves represented a pool of savings that could finance badly needed investment projects. In general, this windfall could launch the economy on a path of higher growth and increasing productivity.

On the other hand, the experience of some exporters has shown that oil revenues can be a mixed blessing. The rapid infusion of oil income raises domestic prices to a point where the traditional traded goods sectors are no longer competitive in world markets. In Cameroon's case, this would translate to putting the agricultural export and import-substituting manufacturing sectors in jeopardy. At the same time, the added demand induced by the oil income results in a boom in the nontradable sectors. When coupled with the contraction of the traded goods sectors, this results in major structural changes to the economy. The syndrome, known as the "Dutch disease," can lead to an economy that is heavily dependent on oil for its foreign exchange, where construction and services are the only other activities and all other goods are imported. Such a scenario can be particularly troubling to Cameroon the reserves of which are limited and which therefore has to prepare for the post-oil era.

The purpose of this chapter is to analyze the actual and probable impact of the oil sector on the Cameroonian economy. After six years of production, we can look at whether the expected effects have in fact taken place. Has Cameroon succumbed to the Dutch disease? If not, why not? Since the bulk of the oil revenues have yet to be spent, we attempt to anticipate the effects of this expenditure. What will be the impact on traditional exports, nontradables, and the distribution of income? Using a model of the Cameroonian economy, we simulate various expenditure patterns and discuss the implications of the results for public policy.

The first part of the chapter is a description of the oil sector—its size, scope, and links with the rest of the economy. As the oil sector is surrounded by official secrecy in Cameroon, some of this information is speculative. Nevertheless, we conclude that a significant portion of the oil revenues are being saved abroad. In the second part of this chapter, we trace the evolution of the oil economy since 1979. We show that by not spending the bulk of its oil revenues, Cameroon has avoided the drastic structural changes experienced by other oil exporters. We then ask the question, "how will the economy evolve should the oil money be spent in larger proportions?" To answer this, we describe a model of the economy, use it to perform experiments related to the oil sector, and interpret the results. The conclusion summarizes the salient points and draws some policy implications from our analysis.

THE OIL SECTOR

Cameroon is a small oil producer, with ultimately recoverable reserves estimated at 100 million tons or 750 million barrels (Nicod 1983). These figures are smaller than those of any OPEC member and about half the size of Gabon's reserves. All the oil is in the Rio del Ray basin, which has been heavily explored over the past ten years. Hence, no new discoveries are expected.

Oil production began in 1977 under a joint venture between the French company Elf-Aquitaine and the Cameroonian public corporation, the Societe Nationale des Hydrocarbures (SNH). Since 1983, two other multinational companies, Total and Shell, have entered into joint ventures with SNH to produce oil from the Victoria and Lokele fields, respectively. Total crude oil production, which was less than a million tons in 1979, is expected to peak in 1984 at 7.6 million tons (equivalent to 150,000 barrels per day) and taper off by the mid-1990s (Nicod 1983). The forecast production profile is given in Table 7.1.

Table 7.1. Cameroonian Oil Production, 1982–1990

Year	*Production (million tons)*
1982	5.2
1983	6.3
1984	7.6
1985	7.6
1986	7.3
1987	7.0
1988	6.7
1989	6.4
1990	6.1

Source: Nicod 1983.

Until 1981, all of Cameroon's oil was exported. Since the construction of a domestic refinery, about 25 percent is now diverted to producing petroleum products, some of which are also exported (Societe Nationale d'Investissement 1983). From the production figures in Table 7.1, this amounts to exports of about 5 million tons. Annual export earnings now exceed 1 billion U.S. dollars—well over 15 percent of GDP. The United States is by far the largest buyer of Cameroonian oil (82 percent) with the

Rotterdam spot market and France running a distant second and third (Direction de la Statistique 1982).

Despite its small size by world standards, Cameroon's oil sector has grown to play a major role in the domestic economy. The impact on employment and demand for domestically produced goods, however, has been minimal: production of offshore oil is an extremely capital intensive activity, using imported materials and foreign labor. The significance of the oil sector, therefore, lies in its contributions to the government's treasury and the country's foreign exchange earnings.

Where public finance is concerned, the government earns from oil production in two ways: from its participation in the joint ventures and from royalties paid by the foreign companies. Under the joint venture agreements, SNH pays 50 percent of exploration, development, and production costs, and receives a fraction of the output that varies from 60 to 70 percent. Since SNH is an autonomous public corporation, none of these revenues enter the government's budget directly. They are deposited outside the Cameroonian banking system. When they are drawn on to finance investment expenditure, the expenditure is listed as an extrabudgetary item (*hors budget*) in the government accounts. In 1981, extrabudgetary expenditures were almost twice the actual investment expenditure of the government. Revenues from royalties and corporate income tax paid by the foreign companies are, however, entered directly in the government budget.

On the foreign exchange side too, there appears to be an effort to keep the oil earnings separate. The figures for oil exports cited above are based on independent estimates of production, refinery production, and Cameroonian oil imports by its main trading partners. The government's official trade statistics report earnings from crude oil exports in 1982 to be 154.8 billion CFA francs (Direction de la Statistique 1982). This translates into an export volume of 1.87 million tons, which is only 45 percent of our independently estimated figure of 4.13 million. If the official figures are adjusted for this discrepancy, the 1982 trade deficit of 67.7 billion CFA francs changes to a surplus of 119.6 billion CFA francs.

All this seems to indicate that the Cameroonian government is accumulating sizable foreign exchange reserves abroad. There is some evidence that they are being held outside the Bank of France, probably in U.S. banks. By its membership in the Central African Currency Union (Banque des Etats de l'Afrique Centrale), Cameroon is obligated to keep its official reserves in the Bank of France. However, in 1982, these reserves increased by 45.8 billion CFA francs, which is half the trade surplus estimated above.

In sum, while the size of the oil sector has grown rapidly since 1977, the government has followed a cautious policy with respect to oil revenues. Instead of spending on consumption and investment, the

Cameroonian government has chosen to save the bulk of its oil money. What have been the effects of this strategy? In the next section, we attempt to answer this question by looking at the evolution—both actual and hypothetical—of the Cameroonian economy in the wake of an oil boom.

THE IMPACT OF OIL ON THE REST OF THE ECONOMY

The Cameroonian Economy, 1979–1982

Over the past four years, the growth rate of the oil sector has dwarfed that of the other sectors of the economy. Whereas the nonoil sector's real GDP grew at about 8 percent in 1980 and 1981 and 3 to 4 percent the two subsequent years, the oil sector registered growth rates of over 40 and 20 percent in the same period.

Consequently, the oil sector's contribution to the economy has increased substantially. As a share of total GDP, oil has grown from 4.3 percent in 1980 to 14 percent in 1984. Perhaps more significant is its contribution to total exports. Crude oil exports have risen from one-fifth to two-thirds of total merchandise exports in the last five years. Finally, the government's revenue base has become increasingly oil-dominated. In 1980, less than 5 percent of revenues were oil related; by 1984, the comparable figure was 40 percent. It is important to note, however, that these figures are low when compared with other oil exporting developing countries. For example, the share of oil in nonmining GDP for Ecuador, Indonesia, Nigeria, Trinidad and Tobago, and Venezuela rose to an average of 30 percent in the first five years of production (Conway and Gelb 1984). In Cameroon, this share rose to only 15 percent over the same period.

How has the rapid growth of the oil sector affected the rest of the economy? As we said earlier, a large part of the oil revenues are being saved abroad. We would expect, therefore, that the country has not yet contracted the Dutch disease. Nevertheless, it is worth asking how the other sectors have performed in light of the observed expansion of the oil sector. First, since some of the oil revenues have been spent on investment projects, the nontradable sectors—particularly construction and public works—have enjoyed high rates of growth (nearly 20 percent a year in current prices). Second, the tradable sectors—agriculture and manufacturing—continued to expand in the first few years of the oil era but have suffered in the last two years. Due to severe drought, agricultural output of both food and cash crops fell in 1983 and is expected to decline again this year. Similarly, industrial output, suffering from a worldwide recession and shortages of raw materials from the drought, declined 2 percent in 1983 and is expected to decline by another 3 percent this year. Meanwhile, industrial wages rose by 21 percent in 1983 while employment fell 4 percent.

It is interesting to note that the government's reaction has been to use the oil revenues to offset the deterioration in the tradable sectors. For example, the public investment program has emphasized industrial ventures. In addition, transfers from the government have enabled the National Produce Marketing Board (Office Nationale de la Commercialisation des Produits de Base), which sets producer prices for coffee and cocoa, to keep increasing those prices despite softening world markets in these commodities. Thus, the incentives to produce the cash crops have been maintained.

In short, the Cameroonian government's cautious approach to the oil revenues appears to have prevented, up to now, the severe dislocations that often accompany an oil boom. Nevertheless, the pressure to spend more of the oil income may become irresistible in the near future. Moreover, as the oil sector matures, the share of oil revenues that is repatriated is bound to become larger. What impact will this have on the domestic economy? In the next section, we attempt to answer this question with some simulations with a multisector, general equilibrium model of the Cameroonian economy.

A Model of the Cameroonian Economy

In order to simulate the effects of an oil boom on the economy, it is plain that we need a model that distinguishes between tradable and nontradable sectors—that is, a multisector model. Also, prices in such a model should be endogenous, for the essence of the Dutch disease lies in the impact of oil income on relative prices. Lastly, the model should be general equilibrium, since income effects feature critically in the mechanisms we are attempting to describe. The model to be presented here exhibits all three of these characteristics. In addition, it has been tailored to suit certain distinctive features of the Cameroonian economy. For example, imports and domestically produced goods in the same sector are taken to be imperfectly substitutable, reflecting quality differences between the two. The labor market is modeled with certain rigidities that are reminiscent of the Cameroonian reality. Most importantly, the model has been estimated using Cameroonian data (for the fiscal year 1979–1980). In what follows, we present a heuristic description of the model, its major assumptions, and essential economic mechanisms that drive it. For a more complete description of the model, the reader is referred to Benjamin and Devarajan (1984).

Our computable general equilibrium model is a descendant of Johansen's (1960) pioneering work on the Norwegian economy. It follows more closely the applications of Computable General Equilibrium (CGE) models to developing countries by, among others, Adelman and Robinson (1978), Taylor et al. (1980), and Dervis et al. (1982). Specifically, the model is a variant of that developed by Dervis, et al. (1982) and used by Michel and Noel on Ivory Coast (in Zartman and Delgado 1984).

All CGE models attempt to simulate a market economy where prices and quantities for goods and factors adjust to equate supply and demand. The equations that govern supply and demand behavior, in turn, are based on individual optimizing behavior by agents in the economy: producers maximize profits and consumers maximize utility. The set of equilibrium conditions that any solution to a CGE model must satisfy is a set of equations balancing supply and demand in each sector. Supply consists of domestic production and imports. The different components of demand are intermediate demand, consumer demand, investment demand, government demand, and export demand. Since this equilibrium is achieved by adjustment of prices, it is important to specify how each of the components of supply and demand depend on prices.

We begin with imports. In the classical theory of international trade, a traded good is assumed to be one for which (1) the country is a price taker in the world market and (2) domestically produced, is a perfect substitute for that sold in world markets. This specification leads to the result that the domestic price of a traded good is equal to its world price. Now, for such a country as Cameroon, the second assumption is particularly troublesome. First, quality differences are frequently observed between imports and domestic substitutes. Second, at a level of aggregation of 11 sectors, each sector represents a bundle of different goods. For example, the capital goods sector includes some goods (such as machine tools) produced in Cameroon and others (such as heavy machinery) that are not. Clearly, these two types of goods are not perfect substitutes. In our model, we resolve the problem by relaxing the second assumption for imported goods. Instead, we postulate that, for any traded good, imports and domestically produced goods are imperfect substitutes. This formulation implies that consumers will choose a mix of imports and home-produced goods depending on their relative prices. Also, as a result of this specification, the domestic price is no longer equal to the world price. However, the link between the two prices becomes stronger the more substitutable the two goods are.

Exports are also affected. Classical trade theory assumes that a small country faces a perfectly elastic demand for its exports. Again, this assumption may not be realistic for many developing countries. While they may not be able to affect the world price with their exports, such countries may register a declining market share as, say, their domestic prices rise. To reflect this, we specify Cameroon's exports as facing a downward sloping demand function.

Domestic supply of each good is produced according to a production function using as inputs intermediate goods, labor (three skill types), and sector-specific capital. Demand for labor, then, is determined by setting the wage equal to the value of the marginal product of labor in each sector. The wage is that which clears the market for labor in each skill class, with labor supply exogenously given.

Intermediate, consumer and government demand shows different effects. Intermediate demand for any good is determined by a fixed-coefficients relationship to outputs of all the sectors that use that good in their production. We assume there is one representative household in the economy that buys consumer goods according to fixed expenditure shares. Thus, when the price of a good rises, households consume less of it, ceteris paribus. Total consumption expenditure is taken to be a fixed fraction of disposable income that, in turn, is total factor earnings less direct taxes. We assume the government keeps the nominal level of expenditure fixed. Hence, when the price of something the government buys increases, the government demands less of it.

In the comparative statics experiments, capital stocks in each sector are held fixed. Therefore, investment does not add to the capital stock. Nevertheless, we assume investment goods are produced and financed by the level of savings in the economy. The composition of investment goods demanded is assumed to be analogous to that in the base year. Savings are the sum of private and public savings. Public savings include foreign savings, which are exogenous. Since they are exogenous, we vary them to represent different levels of expenditure out of oil income. By Walras' Law, foreign savings are also the difference between the value of imports and value of exports. Hence, it is not surprising that an increase in foreign savings will lead to an increase in imports and decrease in exports.

Equilibrium in this model is defined as a set of prices (one for each sector) and wages (one for each skill class) such that supply equals demand for goods in each sector and workers in each skill class. Simulations with the model are carried out by perturbing an initial equilibrium by changing the value of an exogenous variable or parameter. A new equilibrium is solved for, and the resulting values compared with those of the initial equilibrium.

Simulations with the Static Model

The model just described was estimated for the Cameroonian economy for 1979–1980. Of the model's 11 sectors (see Table 7.2), only two—

construction and public services—are "pure" nontradables. Of the remaining nine, five are net exporters (mainly primary goods and private services), while four manufacturing sectors are net importers. In general, the substitutability between foreign and home goods is higher for primary and consumer goods than for intermediate and capital goods.

Table 7.2. Estimated Model of the Cameroonian Economy, 1979–1980

Sectors	*1979–1980 Net Trade (Billions of CFA Francs)*	*Export/ Production Ratio*	*Imports/Domestically Produced Supply Ratio*
1 Food crops	2.133	1.39	0.76
2 Cash crops	117.026	95.14	125.88
3 Forestry	22.314	75.71	0.32
4 Food processing	5.490	32.56	36.98
5 Consumer goods	-31.198	4.95	32.98
6 Intermediate goods	-37.241	35.63	75.70
7 Cement and base metals	-39.115	30.73	209.63
8 Capital goods	-130.881	37.27	209.63
9 Construction	0.000	0.00	0.00
10 Private services	7.187	13.26	13.94
11 Public services	0.000	0.00	0.00
TOTAL		19.27	29.19

The assumption of imperfect substitutability between home and foreign goods is an important one. For example, if the prices of domestic goods rise relative to the prices of foreign goods, consumers do not instantly switch all their purchases to imports. Rather, some of the demand is still satisfied by domestic production. Also, an import tariff will have a milder effect on the domestic economy than classical trade theory would predict. Since the domestically produced good is only an imperfect substitute, it does not register as strong an increase in demand, and hence in output, when a tariff is levied on the import.

There are three categories of labor in the model, and their employment pattern in the various sectors is shown in Table 7.3.

Finally, the intermediate flows and the structure of demand are given in Tables 7.4 and 7.5.

Table 7.3. Categories of Labor in the Cameroonian Economy, 1979–1980

Sector	*Rural*	*Urban Unskilled*	*Skilled*	*Total*
1 Food crops	.91	.09	—	1
2 Cash crops	.89	.10	.01	1
3 Forestry	.76	.18	.06	1
4 Food processing	.52	.38	.10	1
5 Consumer goods	.36	.48	.16	1
6 Intermediate goods	.42	.38	.19	1
7 Cement and base metals	.42	.38	.19	1
8 Capital goods	.44	.39	.17	1
9 Construction	.39	.49	.12	1
10 Private services	.39	.41	.20	1
11 Public services	—	.72	.28	1

We present first the results of some comparative static experiments where, from the base year, the model is driven to a new equilibrium by changes in some exogenous or policy variables. In these experiments, the capital stock and labor supply are held constant, whereas in the dynamic experiments they are updated in each period. We use the comparative statics experiments to explore the effects of an increase in expenditure of oil export revenues (this could also represent the patriation of other types of foreign earnings or a sudden injection of foreign exchange from any source) and the institution of an industrial policy that increases import tariff protection for intermediate goods and construction materials.

Since oil revenues were very small during the base year of the model, they provide a base case against which comparative statics experiments with high oil revenues can be evaluated. We simulate increased earnings from oil exports by injecting a specific amount of foreign earnings into the economy. This amount can be varied in order to reflect different levels of patriated foreign earnings. In testing this model for possible Dutch disease-type effects, we experiment with 500 million dollars or 105 billion CFA francs of oil revenues. This amounts to half the annual export earnings from oil sales or approximately twice the amount actually repatriated.

In the Cameroon model, oil revenues are channeled directly into the total savings pool available for investment. As a result of the first experiment, investment increases across sectors by an average of 41 percent;

Table 7.4. Intermediate Flows (in Billions of CFA Francs)

Sector	*1*	*2*	*3*	*4*	*5*	*6*	*7*	*8*	*9*	*10*	*11*	*Total*
1	10.07	0.00	0.00	21.80	0.24	0.00	0.00	0.00	0.00	25.37	0.00	57.48
2	0.00	2.00	0.00	1.47	1.33	1.90	0.00	0.00	0.00	0.00	0.00	6.70
3	0.00	0.00	0.00	0.18	0.00	5.99	0.00	0.00	0.00	0.00	0.00	6.16
4	1.13	0.83	0.00	2.33	1.46	1.43	0.00	0.00	0.00	0.57	2.51	10.26
5	0.00	0.00	0.00	0.08	6.38	1.24	0.00	0.00	0.00	0.64	0.55	8.88
6	2.23	16.28	0.62	2.73	9.84	66.72	6.25	0.16	25.53	5.72	13.88	149.97
7	0.01	0.03	0.01	8.09	6.03	15.91	9.43	1.21	32.46	0.11	0.00	73.29
8	0.14	1.28	0.72	0.67	1.46	14.95	0.70	0.52	4.57	2.40	0.00	27.39
9	1.56	0.15	0.09	7.53	2.17	15.08	0.06	0.00	2.54	2.37	0.65	32.20
10	1.24	40.29	7.87	7.27	30.88	65.42	4.03	1.02	23.84	84.54	39.59	305.99
11	0.07	0.39	0.10	0.39	0.64	2.72	0.17	0.01	0.78	1.35	0.00	6.60
TOTAL	16.44	61.23	9.40	52.54	60.43	191.36	20.64	2.92	89.72	123.06	57.19	684.92

Key: 1, food crops. 2, cash crops. 3, forestry. 4, food processing. 5, consumer goods. 6, intermediate goods. 7, cement and base metals. 8, capital goods. 9, construction. 10, private services. 11, public services.

Table 7.5. Structure of Demand

Sector	*Intermediate Flows*	*Construction*	*Government*	*Investment Goods*	*Stock Change*	*Exports*	*Imports*	*Total*
1	57.48	260.13	0.00	6.71	4.03	4.59	2.46	330.48
2	6.70	4.22	0.00	0.00	3.51	125.07	8.04	131.45
3	6.16	0.00	0.00	0.00	1.02	22.34	0.02	29.50
4	10.26	53.08	0.00	0.00	3.19	23.45	17.96	72.02
5	8.88	133.65	0.00	0.00	7.10	5.86	37.06	118.43
6	149.97	168.15	0.00	0.00	3.49	101.33	138.57	284.38
7	73.29	0.00	0.00	0.00	0.00	10.50	49.62	34.17
8	27.39	0.00	0.00	113.36	0.43	3.84	134.72	10.30
9	32.20	3.79	0.00	138.13	0.00	0.00	0.00	174.12
10	305.99	302.61	0.00	0.00	0.00	81.63	74.44	615.79
11	6.60	22.35	135.03	0.00	0.00	0.00	0.00	163.98
TOTAL	684.92	947.98	135.03	258.20	22.78	378.61	462.89	1964.62

Key: 1, food crops. 2, cash crops. 3, forestry. 4, food processing. 5, consumer goods. 6, intermediate goods. 7, cement and base metals. 8, capital goods. 9, construction. 10, private services. 11, public services.

domestic prices rise 23 percent and nominal wages 26 percent (see Table 7.6).

It may be of interest to see how these aggregate figures change if instead oil revenues are distributed directly to consumers. Consumer demand for labor-intensive goods drives nominal wages up 36 percent and domestic prices increase by 32 percent. Investment grows by only 14 percent as compared with 41 percent in the case where new revenues are channeled into investment. This latter specification is the one used in all the experiments presented below. It provides a benchmark ideal scenario where the first-round use of oil revenues is for improvement in the capital stock as opposed to expansion of consumption.

Table 7.6. 500 Million Dollar Expenditure from Oil Earnings

Percentage Change in	*Oil Revenues Channeled to Investment*	*Oil Revenues Channeled to Consumption*
Investment	40.7	14.1
Domestic prices	23.2	31.5
Composite prices	18.4	24.8
Nominal wages	26.2	36.4

This aggregate picture of the investment boom in the first experiment, with rising prices and wages, coincides with a general worsening of the trade position. However, evidence of the Dutch disease is best indicated in the sectoral breakdown of price, output, and trade changes. Traded sectors show the smallest price increases because the traded component holds constant at the world price while only the price of the domestically produced and sold portion responds to rising domestic demand (see Table 7.7). Thus the increases in domestic prices and wages worsen the trade position of the country both because productive resources move to more profitable nontraded sectors (where prices are increasing faster) and because domestic traded goods face some price competition from foreign goods, depending on how substitutable they are, in both domestic and export markets. The investment boom generated in this experiment causes imports to grow by 23 percent and exports to fall by 12 percent.

Some parallel results occur in changes in the structure of production (see Table 7.8). Production grows most significantly in construction—both a nontraded and investment good—while it declines severely in cash crops, the traditional export sector, which loses competitiveness as domestic costs rise. But the expected pattern of output changes is broken by other tradable sectors, notably capital goods, which shows a high growth rate. This is due to the structure of demand for the capital goods sector as it supplies investment goods to the large investment boom. Another tradable sector, construction materials, does not suffer as much as might be expected given the importance of foreign competition, since the booming construction sector demands a large share of its output. The small expansion in two other tradable sectors, food crops and consumer goods, occurs because trade is so small in these sectors that they behave more as nontradables.

Table 7.7. 500 Million Dollar Expenditure from Oil Earnings

	Sector	*Percentage Change in Price*
1	Food crops	24.6
2	Cash crops	6.5
3	Forestry	11.3
4	Food processing	17.3
5	Consumer goods	15.6
6	Intermediate goods	12.7
7	Cement and base metals	5.8
8	Capital goods	1.4
9	Construction	33.4
10	Private services	20.8
11	Public services	17.9
	TOTAL	18.4

Finally, the production of public services falls only because nominal government consumption has been fixed while prices are rising and the government purchases the vast majority of the sector's output. A different experiment fixing *real* government consumption would solve this problem but would also alter the amount of new investment from a given level of oil revenue expenditures. Such an experiment conducted with this model and with the same 500 million dollar oil revenue inflow shows that investment increases only 29 percent (as opposed to 41 percent) while

Table 7.8. 500 Million Dollar Expenditure from Oil Earnings

	Sector	*Percentage Change in Output*
1	Food crops	2.8
2	Cash crops	-12.9
3	Forestry	-6.6
4	Food processing	-5.7
5	Consumer goods	3.1
6	Intermediate goods	-1.5
7	Cement and base metals	-1.6
8	Capital goods	12.2
9	Construction	27.7
10	Private services	0.1
11	Public services	-11.5
	TOTAL	0.8*

*Given our assumptions of fixed capital stock and a fully employed fixed labor supply, the *total* change in real output is insignificant in these comparative static experiments; only the intersectoral structure of output changes is relevant. These assumptions are relaxed in the dynamic experiments.

domestic prices rise by 28 percent and wages by 30 percent (see Table 7.9). Nominal government consumption must increase more than 27 percent to make up for inflation caused by the rising demand. And maintaining the size of government causes large increases in real wages for skilled and urban workers since the public services sector relies on them heavily.

The effect of oil revenues on foreign trade is as could be expected (see Table 7.10). Imports rise in all traded sectors and exports decline, both because productive resources are drawn into nontraded sectors and also because domestic traded goods prices, not perfectly tied to international prices, are allowed to rise.

Turning to the impact of oil revenues on the labor market, we find labor in general leaving the traded for the nontraded sectors. Those sectors diverging from this expected pattern are the ones experiencing exceptional growth rates for reasons explained above. With the assumptions of a constant labor supply and flexible wages, the reallocation of workers is shown in Table 7.11.

Table 7.9. 500 Million Dollar Expenditure from Oil Earnings

	Constant Nominal Government Consumption	*Constant Real Government Consumption*
Change in		
Investment (%)	40.7	29.2
Domestic prices (%)	23.2	28.0
Composite prices (%)	18.4	22.2
Nominal wages (%)	26.2	30.4
Level of government consumption (billions of CFA francs)	135.2	171.9

Table 7.10. 500 Million Dollar Expenditure from Oil Earnings

Sector		*Exports*	*Imports*
1	Food crops	-6.29	43.53
2	Cash crops	-13.22	6.41
3	Forestry	-7.94	1.99
4	Food processing	-15.73	30.56
5	Consumer goods	-7.50	32.10
6	Intermediate goods	-11.81	15.56
7	Cement and base metals	-10.27	16.36
8	Capital goods	-6.16	37.55
9	Construction	0.00	0.00
10	Private services	-10.96	10.83
11	Public services	0.00	0.00
	TOTAL	-11.87	23.18

Table 7.11.

	Sector	*Percentage Change in Labor Force*
1	Food crops	4.35
2	Cash crops	-20.69
3	Forestry	-20.71
4	Food processing	13.08
5	Consumer goods	5.24
6	Intermediate goods	-4.04
7	Cement and base metals	-4.08
8	Capital goods	16.70
9	Construction	61.64
10	Private services	-0.76
11	Public services	-15.06
	TOTAL	0.00

Real wages increase by 5.7 percent in the economy overall, but there is variation in the distribution across skill categories:

Change in Real Wage Rate	
Rural unskilled	5.7%
Urban unskilled	6.4%
Urban skilled	3.3%

While the wages for skilled urban workers rise at less than the average rate, it should be remembered that they are paid ten times as much as the other two labor groups at the outset. Also, the wage differential developing between urban and rural unskilled workers has serious implications for the effect of oil revenues on rural-urban migration and productivity in agriculture. Any differences in rural and urban household consumption patterns will multiply the effects of this shifting income distribution.

In this first experiment, we have seen how the structure of the Cameroonian economy and the features of the CGE model that express this structure have complicated the spending effect of an oil boom. Of particular importance is the assumption of imperfect substitutability among foreign and domestic traded goods, which allows domestic prices of these goods to rise above world levels while they maintain a share in total supply. In view of the importance of this assumption, we examine here the elasticities of substitution and the sensitivity of the model to them.

All of the experiments presented so far use relatively low elasticities of substitution between home and foreign goods—near the minimum of 0.4 for intermediate and capital goods and higher, though still relatively low, for primary and consumer goods. This restricts the rate at which imports can replace domestic production as local prices and wages rise during the investment boom. As a comparison, we repeat the base foreign earnings experiment changing only the elasticities of home/foreign good substitution for the food crops, intermediate goods, construction materials, and capital goods sectors (see Table 7.12). In each case this elasticity is raised to near the maximum of the possible range (about 4.0). The high elasticity case creates the same amount of new investment as the base foreign earnings experiment but generates a different kind of boom.

Table 7.12. Model Results under Assumptions of Low and High Elasticities of Substitution between Home and Foreign Goods (Percentage Change from Base Year)

	Sector	*Low Elasticity*	*High Elasticity*
		Domestic Prices	
1	Food crops	24.81	15.14
2	Cash crops	15.24	8.79
3	Forestry	11.31	2.10
4	Food processing	24.58	15.11
5	Consumer goods	21.38	12.69
6	Intermediate goods	22.91	8.27
7	Cement and base metals	18.79	6.13
8	Capital goods	32.12	11.38
9	Construction	32.42	24.31
10	Private services	23.85	13.86
11	Public services	17.93	10.63
	TOTAL	23.21	13.24

Table 7.12. (Continued)

Sector		Low Elasticity	High Elasticity
		Output	
1	Food crops	2.81	1.71
2	Cash crops	-12.89	-7.92
3	Forestry	-6.57	-5.58
4	Food processing	-5.66	-3.97
5	Consumer goods	-3.13	2.35
6	Intermediate goods	-1.48	-8.59
7	Cement and base metals	1.59	-6.46
8	Capital goods	12.16	-6.77
9	Construction	27.71	28.43
10	Private services	0.06	-0.19
11	Public services	-11.51	-7.28
	TOTAL	1.28	0.13
		Imports	
1	Food crops	43.53	78.93
2	Cash crops	6.41	2.71
3	Forestry	1.99	-6.86
4	Food processing	30.56	18.12
5	Consumer goods	32.10	19.23
6	Intermediate goods	15.56	22.75
7	Cement and base metals	16.36	17.89
8	Capital goods	37.55	38.00
9	Construction	0.00	0.00
10	Private services	10.83	6.20
11	Public services	0.00	0.00
	TOTAL	23.18	23.49

Table 7.12. (Continued)

	Sector	*Low Elasticity*	*High Elasticity*
		Exports	
1	Food crops	-6.29	-4.20
2	Cash crops	-13.22	-8.08
3	Forestry	-7.94	-4.92
4	Food processing	-15.73	-10.26
5	Consumer goods	-7.50	-4.12
6	Intermediate goods	-11.81	-11.38
7	Cement and base metals	-10.27	8.23
8	Capital goods	-6.16	-10.86
9	Construction	0.00	0.00
10	Private services	-10.96	-6.84
11	Public services	0.00	0.00
	TOTAL	-11.87	-8.57
		Labor	
1	Food crops	4.35	2.65
2	Cash crops	-20.69	-12.98
3	Forestry	-20.71	-17.82
4	Food processing	-13.08	-9.44
5	Consumer goods	5.24	3.73
6	Intermediate goods	-4.04	-18.11
7	Cement and base metals	-4.08	-13.30
8	Capital goods	16.70	-10.33
9	Construction	61.64	63.52
10	Private services	-0.76	-1.54
11	Public services	-15.06	-9.99
	TOTAL	0.00	0.00

The pattern of price increases is similar to that of the base "low elasticity" experiment but the magnitude is smaller (13 versus 23 percent) because of the greater competition from foreign goods imported at constant world prices. Those sectors whose home/foreign goods substitution elasticity has been raised show the most significantly smaller price increases. In the same way, the structure of output changes in the "high elasticity" experiment echoes that of the base foreign earnings case, but instead of the surprising expansion of capital goods we find a contraction, and the previously mild declines in intermediate goods and construction materials have become more severe. The pattern of changes in imports shows how foreign goods more easily replace domestic producers in these sectors as suppliers to the domestic investment boom. The declines in intermediate goods and construction materials contribute to the contraction in capital goods (which is actually quite small in nominal terms), since the one is the major purchaser of intermediate goods from this sector and they both rely heavily on this sector for investment goods.

In the food crops sector, with its low nominal level of imports, output grows slightly less than before. However, the food processing sector suffers less of a decline as its major input, food crops, has a much lower price increase. Several sectors show a smaller drop in their exports as the price of their inputs and their own prices diverge less from world levels.

The reallocation of labor among sectors reflects the pattern of output changes, and nominal wages rise only 16 percent as compared to 26 percent in the first experiment.

Thus, the elasticity of substitution between foreign and domestic goods has a significant impact on the character of an investment boom generated by 500 million dollars of newly patriated foreign earnings. It affects price and wage inflation, the relative structure of output changes, and the magnitude of trade changes.

In this first series of experiments on the impact of new foreign exchange inflows, we find that, while the model produces Dutch disease-type results in aggregate, the detailed sectoral results show some cases that differ from the predicted pattern. Of key importance is the assumption of imperfect substitutability between home and foreign goods. This enhances the role of the direct and indirect demand in the economy and leads to some traded sectors expanding in the course of the oil-generated investment boom, despite the real exchange rate appreciation. The pattern of output changes in those sectors associated with investment goods seems most affected. Two tradable sectors showing positive growth rates—food crops and consumption goods—sell mostly to growing private consumption. Yet the buoyancy of these sectors is aided more by their insulation from foreign competition by means of their changes in the relative prices between domestic and foreign goods.

Given that some of the tradable sectors suffer a decline as a result of the oil boom, it is reasonable to suppose that the government may attempt to protect some of these sectors. We simulate such a policy with an experiment that doubles import tariffs for intermediate goods and construction materials. Doubling the tariffs is one possible industrial policy that would seek to protect and encourage output in these two manufacturing sectors. While this policy succeeds in the case of construction materials, it fails for intermediate goods (see Table 7.13).

Table 7.13. Double Import Tariffs Sectors 6 and 7

	Sector	*Percentage Change in Output*
1	Food crops	0.07
2	Cash crops	-0.35
3	Forestry	0.29
4	Food processing	-3.00
5	Consumer goods	-1.50
6	Intermediate goods	-2.29
7	Cement and base metals	3.98
8	Capital goods	2.49
9	Construction	4.76
10	Private services	0.24
11	Public services	0.24
	TOTAL	-0.01

The pattern of output is mostly explained by the structure of demand for the two sectors targeted by this policy. About half of the composite good in sector 6 is sold to final consumption, while in sector 7, all of the composite good is sold to intermediate consumption. In the model, intermediate demand does not respond to price changes since it behaves according to fixed technological coefficients; price changes merely alter the cost of production. As the increased tariffs in sectors 6 and 7 raise the price of those composite goods, the intermediate demand for construction materials remains inflexible to this change while the consumption demand for intermediate goods falls in response to the price increase.

It is also worth noting that sector 6 is a major purchaser of its own output, absorbing nearly half of the total supplied to intermediate demand. Thus, raising the tariff on intermediate goods acts to increase the cost of producing them. This situation arises in part because of the diversity of the items that have been aggregated into sector 6. In contrast, the major consumer of sector 7's output, buying nearly half of its total supply, is construction, a sector that grows significantly in this experiment. The higher tariffs cause government tariff revenues to increase 38 percent, and, with government consumption fixed, this contributes to higher total savings and fuels an increase in total investment of 7 percent. This investment boom keeps demand for construction strong, so its output grows despite the fact that the sector must pay more for one of its inputs. The price changes reported in Table 7.14 reflect the influence of the new tariffs on the imported components of goods in sectors 6 and 7 and the pattern of direct and indirect demands in the economy.

Table 7.14. Double Import Tariffs Sectors 6 and 7

Sector		*Percentage Change in Composite Goods Price*
1	Food crops	-1.0
2	Cash crops	0.1
3	Forestry	-0.8
4	Food processing	1.3
5	Consumer goods	0.4
6	Intermediate goods	7.8
7	Cement and base metals	17.2
8	Capital goods	0.2
9	Construction	6.2
10	Private services	-1.1
11	Public services	-0.2
	TOTAL	2.0

The impact of the tariff increases on the pattern of trade shows that imports of construction materials are hardly affected, dropping less than 1 percent, while imports of intermediate goods fall by 7.3 percent.

Simulations with the Dynamic Model

In the previous section, we presented several results based on experiments with the CGE model of Cameroon. A crucial feature of the experiments was that they were comparative statics. The equilibrium solved for was one in which many variables were held fixed. For example, the large savings generated by oil revenues did not get translated into increases in the capital stock because the latter was fixed. In this section, we present some dynamic simulations with the model. We solve for a sequence of equilibria where after each equilibrium the capital stocks and other exogenous variables are "updated" before solving for the next. Our purpose is to illustrate the various uses of the dynamic model rather than to draw specific policy conclusions at this stage of the exercise.

As stated above, the dynamic version of the model involves updating variables that are exogenous in the static version. Before proceeding to the actual results, therefore, we must specify which variables are updated and by how much. In the static model, which is savings-driven, the level of savings determines the amount of investment goods produced. However, these investment goods do not add to the capital stock until future years. In the dynamic version, in a given year, the total capital stock is increased by about half the total amount of investment generated in the previous year. This assumes that while all the savings in the previous year are used to purchase investment goods, not all these goods become net additions to the capital stock in one year, because of gestation lags in production. The amount by which each sector's capital stock is increased is determined by that sector's share in the existing stock of capital and the price of capital goods. We assume the labor supply for the unskilled categories (rural and urban) is growing at 2 percent per annum. The number of urban skilled workers is growing at 1 percent per annum. In the static model, government consumption expenditure is the one component of demand that is exogenous. This is assumed to grow at 6 percent per year. Note that government investment expenditure is endogenous in this savings-driven model.

We turn now to a discussion of the results from experiments with the dynamic model. Each experiment was carried out for a five-year period, the initial year being the model's base year, 1980.

The first simulation is an attempt to study the dynamic effects of the 500 million dollar foreign capital inflow (qua oil revenues) that was simulated in the comparative static experiments. Therefore we allocate this 500 million dollars into five annual installments of 100 million dollars each and trace the evolution of the economy as government consumption and the labor force grow at the rates described above. In aggregate GDP terms, the economy grows at an average annual rate of 2 percent. Private consumption, too, grows at this pace. The 6 percent growth in government consumption squeezes the government's budget sufficiently that public investment falls sharply in the five-year period. Reflecting the real exchange rate appreciation, imports grow at a rate (1.5 percent) that is half a percentage point faster than exports.

Turning to the sectoral breakdown, we observe that the dramatic structural shifts of the comparative static experiments are dampened considerably by this smoothing of the foreign capital inflow (see Table 7.15). There are at least two reasons for this. First, since factor supplies are growing in this period, nearly all 11 sectors of the economy experience positive growth. Second, government revenues do not rise to keep pace with the 6 percent increase in government consumption. Thus, government investment falls, and the investment boom—which was responsible for the rapid increase in manufacturing output in the static case—simply does not occur.

Table 7.15. Average Annual Growth Rates of Domestic Output, 1980–1984, with $100 Million in Foreign Earnings

Sector		*Percentage Average Annual Growth Rate*
1	Food crops	2.4
2	Cash crops	1.0
3	Forestry	5.7
4	Food processing	1.0
5	Consumer goods	1.2
6	Intermediate goods	0.6
7	Cement and base metals	0.0
8	Capital goods	1.3
9	Construction	0.3
10	Private services	1.8
11	Public services	5.1

To distinguish between the effects of the infusion of foreign exchange and those of other assumptions in the model, it is instructive to simulate a different trajectory of foreign savings. An experiment where the annual incremental inflow of foreign capital increased by 20 million dollars a year (starting at 100 million dollars and ending with 180 million dollars) reveals that the pattern of sectoral output growth rates in Table 7.15 was not accidental (see Table 7.16). Notice that the cash crops sector does worse in this scenario (0.5 as opposed to 1.0 percent growth) and construction does considerably better (1.0 versus 0.3 percent). This experiment highlights the fact that, despite the expansion in factor supplies, infusions of foreign exchange will continue to have the effect of inhibiting growth in the traded goods sectors while giving a fillip to the nontradables.

Table 7.16. Average Annual Growth Rates of Domestic Output, 1980–1984, with Increasing Foreign Earnings

Sector		*Percentage Average Annual Growth Rate*
1	Food crops	2.5
2	Cash crops	0.5
3	Forestry	5.2
4	Food processing	0.7
5	Consumer goods	1.3
6	Intermediate goods	0.5
7	Cement and base metals	0.0
8	Capital goods	1.3
9	Construction	1.0
10	Private services	1.8
11	Public services	5.1

CONCLUSION

In this chapter, we have examined the impact of the oil sector on the economy of Cameroon. We have attempted to identify features that make Cameroon's oil boom distinct from those of other oil exporters.

First, Cameroon is traditionally not an oil producer, nor will it be one in about ten years or so. Its oil reserves are tiny by world standards. Yet, the oil sector has grown to play a major role in production, exports, and government revenues. Oil therefore represents a temporary but significant windfall in Cameroon's economic development.

Second, it appears as if the Cameroonian government is following an extremely cautious policy with respect to expenditure from oil revenues. In stark contrast to other oil exporters at the same level of development,

Cameroon is saving in foreign banks the lion's share of its income from oil sales. Consequently, the Dutch disease—the syndrome of rapid structural shifts that has afflicted other exporters—has not hit Cameroon.

Third, should the rate of expenditure out of oil revenues increase, the ensuing changes in the economy may be somewhat different from those predicted by the classical models of international trade. Using our model of the Cameroonian economy, we showed that while the tradable sectors as a whole are likely to contract and the nontradables expand, some tradable sectors may actually experience an increase in demand and hence output. Specifically, some import-substituting manufacturing sectors, because they are not perfect substitutes for imported goods, may grow in order to meet the investment demand generated by increased spending of oil income. The sectors producing agricultural exports, however, are most likely to suffer from this action since the almost inevitable domestic inflation will harm their international competitiveness.

Given these distinctive features of Cameroon's oil sector, what implications can we draw from our analysis for public policy? At one level, an argument can be made that no policy intervention is warranted. The structural change arising out of an oil boom is the result of a change in market prices or endowments, neither of which necessarily calls for a response from the government. In this way, any attempt to protect the traditional traded goods sectors from the Dutch disease may, in fact, be misguided.

However, for Cameroon, the case for public intervention can be made on the grounds that its oil revenues are temporary. The contraction in the traded goods sectors that accompanies the oil boom may not be the best preparation for the postoil era. The policy issue then becomes one of when and where to spend the oil revenues. Essentially, the problem is analogous to managing a portfolio with three assets: oil in the ground, oil revenues held as foreign reserves, and oil revenues spent in the domestic economy. Each of these assets earns a different rate of return and the portfolio manager has to balance the levels of these rates with the uncertainty associated with each. In this framework, our analysis sheds light on the returns associated with the third asset. Clearly, the benefits from spending the oil money domestically depends on where they are spent. Results from our experiments show that, if the monies are spent in the same manner in which investment resources are allocated presently, contraction in the agricultural export sectors and some—but not all—manufacturing sectors will result. To prepare for the postoil era, therefore, the government may do well to concentrate on the sectors likely to be harmed most by the Dutch disease, namely cash crops, and consumer and intermediate goods.

The foregoing does not address the question of how much of the oil money should be spent and how much saved. Answering such a question would involve an intertemporal optimizing framework, which goes beyond the scope of our analysis. Nevertheless, it is worth noting that the observed behavior of the Cameroonian government—of saving about 75 percent of each year's oil earnings—implies a certain valuation of the relative rates of return of the two options.

As it enters the second half of the 1980s, Cameroon appears to be at a crossroads. It has managed to maintain its balanced pattern of development while oil production has peaked and significant oil incomes continue to be accumulated. How these revenues are used will crucially determined whether the oil windfall launches the economy into a path of higher growth and increasing productivity or leads to an economy that is ill-equipped for a future with no more oil revenues. The track record of some of the other oil exporters has not been exemplary. But the distinctive features of Cameroon's oil sector and the cautious approach of its policy makers give one cause for optimism.

8

CAMEROON'S FOREIGN RELATIONS

Mark W. DeLancey

> Africa's response to an inheritance of dependence and underdevelopment can now be divided essentially into two contemporary types, reflective of the traditional choice between collaboration and confrontation: those countries and classes in favour of further incorporation into the Western system and those in favour of disengagement from it. The former, incorporationist variety of state and strategy may be called "state capitalism" whereas the latter, disengagement variety, can be subdivided into two further variations: "state socialism" . . . and socialism . . . (Shaw and Aluko 1984, p. 13).

Cameroon is a clear example of Shaw's first category, a capitalist-oriented state with a foreign policy based on cooperation and interaction with the Western, capitalist countries of the world. There is, of course, a strong relationship between the domestic economic system of the country and the foreign policy of the country, and there is a strong relationship between the colonial experience of Cameroon and the fact that the country follows a capitalist path of development. However, from the political economy perspective, there are options to choose from, and alternatives in foreign policy to consider for Cameroon decision makers. The range of such alternatives is limited by the choice of economic system and so, too, the development policy choices are limited. But such a statement applies to each of the categories of African states enumerated by Shaw; the economic philosophy or path chosen by (or imposed upon) a set of leaders strongly influences their foreign policy. One suspects that is more the case for such relatively weak, underdeveloped states as Cameroon than it is for such powerful, rich states as France or the United States.

This essay has been prepared with the assistance of Peter Schraeder and Samuel Haggar, to whom special gratitude is noted.

Shaw's essay does not clearly define the three types of states he identifies. Crawford Young has defined these rather more concisely in his *Ideology and Development in Africa,* where he uses the terms Afro-Marxist, Populist Socialist, and African Capitalist. He includes, and quite correctly, Cameroon in the latter category (Young 1982, pp. 3–4). According to Young, the capitalist state is characterized by having a significant place reserved for private markets: "capital is viewed as the crucial factor of production and important spheres are reserved for the private sector"; "a strong exchange relationship with the industrial economies is a presumed corollary"; "in the economic sphere predominantly Western relationships are viewed as perfectly natural" (Young 1982, p. 185); and "little opprobrium attaches to the accumulation of wealth" (Young 1982, p. 186). Young utilizes Sayre Schatz's concept of "nurture capitalism" in discussing the role of the African state in capitalist development. The concept of nurture capitalism includes the following points:

1. Private enterprise is expected to provide the basic developmental thrust in the directly productive sector.
2. For this to occur with the anticipated vigor, a congenial environment is assured for all capital, domestic and foreign.
3. At the same time, an awareness, from a nationalist perspective, of the risks of total foreign domination of the economy dictates strenuous promotion of indigenous capital.
4. The contradiction implicit in 2 and 3 triggers sharp and continuous conflict between multinational and national capital (Young 1982, p. 189 and Schatz 1977, pp. 1–3).

As suggested in point 4, Young mentions the idea that "nationalism intervenes . . . to render ambiguous the value of foreign capital" (Young 1982, p. 185). This seems to be one area where a capitalist state exercises choice. There is a significant point of differentiation between Cameroon, where foreign capital is warmly welcomed and indigenous capitalists feel—and correctly—that their interests frequently take second place after the interest of foreign capital, and Nigeria, where the influence of local capitalism is much stronger and the government has placed greater restrictions on foreign capital and the activities of foreign investors.

The characteristics of nurture capitalism outlined by Young suggest rather definite directions for foreign policy decision makers. And Shaw strongly believes that the differences between capitalist and socialist orientations affect foreign policy.

> Clearly the foreign, as well as development, policies of such different regimes would themselves be quite distinctive. The former, state capitalist

> type would tend to be less radical, less non-aligned and more open to transnational associations whereas the latter, state socialist or socialist type would tend to be more radical, more non-aligned and less open to transnationalism (Shaw and Aluko 1984, pp. 14–15).

Yet, in a chapter devoted to the question of the relationship between ideology and foreign policy behavior, Young concludes that "Ideology . . . takes us some distance to an understanding of African international relations. But only a small part of the way" (Young 1982, p. 269). There are common themes that unite African states: nonalignment, the demand for a New International Economic Order, and opposition to racist rule in South Africa are among these. Regional politics influence the foreign policy of particular states, but "the tightly circumscribed choices in international economic relationships considerably reduce the impact of ideological perspective" and "there is simply no alternative to primarily Western linkages in trade and in access to capital" (Young 1982, p. 292).

In this chapter we shall examine the origins of Cameroon's foreign policy through an analysis of those aspects of the colonial experience relevant to the choice of a capitalist path of development by Cameroon's leaders. We shall then examine the foreign policy choices made within the boundaries established by that capitalist path of development in the 24 years of Cameroon's independence.

COLONIALISM AND THE ATTAINMENT OF INDEPENDENCE

When the first German colonists arrived in Cameroon in 1884, they found a variety of African communities producing goods for their own use with some surplus for trade. Such trade was largely between the African states, though some existed between coastal communities and European commercial companies. This latter trade was a factor influencing the German decision to colonize Cameroon, but the existing trade was inadequate or inappropriate to German needs in various respects. Certain tropical items desired by the Germans were not available in Cameroon, and some available items were not produced on a sufficient scale to satisfy German needs. Too, there was complaint that German traders lost profit because much of the commerce was handled by African middlemen. In their efforts to solve these problems, the Germans began a process of converting Cameroon's economies to serve German needs (Rudin 1938; Stoecker 1960 and 1968; and Hauser 1970). This process was continued by the French and British who took over the colony in 1916 after Germany's defeat in Cameroon. Rubber, palm oil, cocoa, coffee, bananas, tea, and, later, cotton were the major products desired. These products through sale in Europe became the major source of income of the colony. But the emphasis on the development of these cash (or export) crops meant that other aspects of the Cameroonian economy were ignored. What was produced was essentially an appendix to the French economic system, an appendix based on the production of raw materials for the use of French consumers, industrial and personal. As an appendix, the Cameroonian economy was to remain highly dependent on the French economy; even after political independence was granted, the subordinate position of the Cameroonian economy gave France substantial influence in Cameroon's political system.

In Cameroon during the colonial era, there was almost no industrial development, little infrastructural development, and minimal change in food production. There were, however, rather significant changes in the move from subsistence to cash cropping and in the concomitant commercial developments that took place as the result of the increase in cash cropping and the inflow of products from the factories of France and Europe. With such changes there developed new interests, economic and political, within the Cameroon population. Although many of the roles in these changes were taken by French and other foreigners, there were also significant numbers of Cameroonians who profited financially, socially, and in terms of prestige (Kom 1971; Eily 1971; and Hugon 1968).

Soon after the conclusion of World War II, the new elements in the Cameroon population came into conflict with the French colonial administration and the rather large number of French planters, *commercants* (merchants), and other settlers in the colony. This new Cameroonian elite was not homogeneous in its attitudes toward France, French colonialism, and French capitalism, though there was widespread feeling that the colonial relationship must in some way be changed. The French administrators were thus able in some degree to respond positively to those elements of the elite most favorable to French interests in Cameroon and negatively to those elements most inimical to French interests.

The best organized and most outspoken of these Cameroonian expressions of interest was the Union des Populations du Cameroun (UPC), founded in 1948 by a trade union leader, Ruben Um Nyobe, with some support from Cameroon's trade union movement and the French Communist Party. The UPC had two major goals: true independence from France and the reunification of Cameroon, which had been divided after World War I into British and French sections. The latter goal was closely related to the first, as reunification was used as an alternative to remaining within the French Union, a proposal by France to unite France and its colonies. Support for the UPC within Cameroon came from the rather small working class, the urban areas wherein were concentrated the unemployed, the students, and two ethnic groups—the Bassa and the Bamileke. The UPC was not only the first Cameroonian party to call for independence and a break with France, but it also stood for a reordering of domestic society in favor of the peasant and the worker. It came to stand for a more neutralist position in international affairs, which would have meant a rather clean break with French economic, cultural, and political ties and approached a socialist vision of the society it wished to build.

French authorities were not yet willing to accept independence as a goal, and the UPC was thus subjected to a variety of harassments to prevent its growth. In 1954, a new high commissioner (governor), Roland Pre, was assigned to Cameroon, and he took immediate and strong steps to place controls over the activities of the UPC. Within a few months of Pre's arrival, the UPC leadership had in part gone into exile (first in British Cameroons and later into various "radical" African states) and in part gone underground within Cameroon to lead a campaign of violence against the French administration. Whether the UPC decided to go underground or was forced to do so by Pre's actions is subject to debate (Le Vine 1971; Rubin 1971; Welch 1966; and Joseph 1977), but the effect was that the administration could ban the organization from legal political activity and make it unable to participate in elections. Police and military force could be used to destroy the party apparatus and eliminate its leadership. In the meantime, the administration could put together parties and leaders more amenable to French desires. What followed was a bloody and destructive battle in southern Cameroon that eventually decimated and destroyed the UPC while other Cameroonian parties and leaders accepted and modified UPC goals and became the recipients of independence.

The December 1956 elections were a key event in this process, for the government that came to power from this election was instrumental in negotiating independence from France. Yet, the UPC could not participate in the elections, and thus the party was not represented. The major winners were the Union Camerounaise, a group of northern ethnic and patron parties under the leadership of Ahmadou Ahidjo and the Democrates, representing the central and southern regions under the leadership of Andre-Marie Mbida. Mbida became prime minister, but his government fell from power within a few months, for he failed to comprehend public attitudes on key policy questions—independence, reunification, and amnesty for the UPC. Mbida had put together a coalition government, but as the unpopularity of his policies became clear, Ahidjo's Union Camerounaise withdrew support. The government fell in February 1958, and it became Ahidjo's turn to organize the government. He stayed at the head of government until 1982.

Once in office, Ahidjo made demands on the French for immediate independence and reunification of the two trust territories. The Union Camerounaise had a nationalist orientation, but was less inclined toward radically changing the domestic political and economic situation than the leaders of the UPC. Unlike the independence plank of the UPC, Ahidjo was able to assure the French of continued close cooperation between the two countries and that there would be safety for French investments in an independent Cameroon. No public mention was made concerning a series of agreements he made with France in late 1959 providing for widespread cooperation between the two countries in economic, cultural, political, and military affairs. This came at the same time that changes in attitude occurred in France. Charles de Gaulle had come to power; he offered flexibility to the African states in determining the type of relation that might exist between them and France. It was proposed that Cameroon's trusteeship should no longer continue. France agreed, and the United Nations approved. On January 1, 1960, Cameroon became the independent Republic of Cameroon.

Thus in the process whereby Cameroon became an independent country, the French colonial administration played a critical role in determining who would be the recipients of power in that independent state. Or at the least we may say that the French were able to determine who would *not* be the recipients. By forcing out the UPC—the radical party that called for a strong break with France, a true nonaligned foreign policy, and a socialist system—the French were able to negotiate a very favorable (from their point of view) situation between them and the new government. Too, they were able to put in place a government that was amenable to the type of economic system, essentially a capitalist system, that had been established during the years of colonial rule. And it is assumed that, through the various agreements of cooperation signed by France and the Ahidjo government, France remained in a position to influence strongly Cameroon's domestic and foreign policy for years to come. French troops remained to continue the war against the UPC and to help build a Cameroonian army. Large numbers of Frenchmen remained in influential positions in Cameroon's government and such related agencies as the new university. And French commercial interests remained predominant in business, industry, trade, and other sectors of the economy. In this respect, the boundaries around Cameroonian foreign policy were established by the decolonization process. A capitalist government was in place, and its development policy was oriented toward a capitalist path. The government was heavily indebted to France for its establishment and maintenance, and the government was thoroughly tied into a network of relations with France. Thus circumscribed, the element of choice for Cameroon was essentially how to loosen the French hold and broaden the sources of investment and trade necessary for Cameroon's development, without losing the desired investment and commerce with France in the interim.

GENERAL ASPECTS OF CAMEROON'S FOREIGN POLICY

Throughout the period of independence, Cameroon has enunciated foreign policies similar to those of most African states. Nonalignment; antiimperialism and especially opposition to the racist, white-dominated regimes of South Africa; African solidarity and cooperation; domestic economic growth and development through collaboration with foreign assistance and investment; and the maintenance of national sovereignty are among the standard policies and objectives of most African states. Cameroon has been in agreement with these, though standing on its own definition of them. The maintenance of strong, positive relations with France while gradually extending and intensifying relations with other Western capitalist states, the eventual broadening of relations to include the Eastern bloc and the People's Republic of China (PRC), and attempts to develop significant economic ties with neighboring states in equatorial Africa while maintaining friendly relations with its giant neighbor to the west, Nigeria, have been among the major tactics used. Cameroon has sought foreign aid and has given a warm welcome to foreign investment while attempting to diversify its exports—the major source of domestic funding for its development—and to diversify the customers for its exports and sources of imports in its efforts to bring about the development of a capitalist economic system within the country.

The Foreign Policy Process

From 1958 until 1982, Cameroon was ruled by essentially one man, Ahmadou Ahidjo. He established a highly centralized, authoritarian political system in which the president held very great powers and responsibility. Various provisions of the Constitution are the starting point for this accumulation of power, but Ahidjo followed policies of centralization, coalition building, and repression to enhance the position of the president. The net effect has been to give the president tremendous control over most aspects of politics from the local, village level to the international level.

Centralization was effected through the development of a single party system, the concentration of authority in Yaounde, the ending of the federal system to be replaced by a unitary government, and the use of the Constitution to give the president control over the legislature and over nominations and appointments. Presidential control over the monetary resources of the country gave Ahidjo the wherewithal to build a coalition of local and regional leaders; the bureaucracy and the military; urban dwellers; and a variety of northern-based and Bamileke commercial elements. Coalition building was backed up by the frequent use of force and violence, and abuses of human rights were common. But putting together this patron–client-based coalition required funds, and that depended on Ahidjo's ability to continue the support of the French government and business/commercial/industrial investors who dominate the modern elements of the economy. Such support was maintained through foreign and domestic policies that favored France and foreign business interests. Only with the growth of petroleum exports was Ahidjo able to wean Cameroon away from this dependence and to begin to rely more on domestic and non-French sources of capital and trade.

This concentration of power and responsibility means that foreign policy making in Cameroon is almost entirely the prerogative of the president, and Ahidjo was strongly in favor of capitalist development and close ties to France. Ndiva Kofele-Kale notes that "The foreign policy making process in Cameroon is a highly personalized thing . . . dominated by the style and personality of President Ahmadou Ahidjo" (Kofele-Kale 1981b, p. 197). This concentration of power in the presidency has passed on to Biya, and we can assume that foreign policy making will continue to be largely dominated by the president, will continue to be "a highly personalized thing." This phenomenon is common in African political systems (Aluko 1977, p. 10). Aluko suggests that, because of this powerful personal role of the president in African foreign policy, ". . . changes in governments in Africa have meant changes in the country's external behavior" (Aluko 1977, p. 10). However, this does not seem to be the case in Cameroon, for the transfer of power to Biya did not represent a change in ideology or orientation in leadership. Biya has not altered Cameroon's foreign relations in any significant fashion in his period in office. Biya is a product of the same system that produced Ahidjo, a member of the same establishment, and a president acceptable to France. He is clearly in favor of the economic path followed by the Ahidjo government, and thus the boundaries within which he makes foreign policy are similar to those of the Ahidjo regime. With the input of petroleum revenues his realm of choice within those boundaries is similar to that of Ahidjo's later years. We can expect Biya to continue to diversify Cameroon's foreign contacts and to decrease the proportion of economic ties to France. There has been a marked continuity of foreign relations throughout the more than two decades of Cameroonian independence. This continuity is made obvious by examining Cameroon's relations with France, other major industrialized powers, and African states. This continuity is also clearly seen in Cameroon's policies on foreign investment.

France and the Western States

Cameroon's major and most significant relations were and remain with France, though the strength of this relationship has declined over the years. It should be no surprise that France was at independence the key factor in Cameroonian economic, political, and cultural relations. After all, France had been the predominant colonial and economic power since 1916 and had established a strong network of ties between the two states. And, as we have discussed, France was able to manipulate the independence process so that a highly favorable regime came to power, a regime tied to France through numerous treaties of cooperation. In this manner, France established the limits of choice for Cameroon's foreign policy.

It is the breadth of these treaties that indicates the strength of the French presence at the government-to-government level. Cultural; military; transport and meteorology; technical cooperation; monetary and financial affairs; diplomatic relations; and a variety of legal and technical matters are covered in the ten original agreements. These agreements were renegotiated in 1973 but apparently with only minor changes that in no way reduced France's significant position in Cameroon's affairs (*West Africa,* March 4, 1974, p. 253 and Legum 1976, pp. B443–444). Tunteng argues that the original agreements "provided the juridical framework for this patron–client relationship" between France and its ex-African colonies and that the importance of the revisions was slight (Tunteng 1976, p. 212). Kofele-Kale agrees: "With the possible exception of the diplomatic convention, nothing of substance was accomplished" (Kofele-Kale 1981b, p. 207 and *African Observer,* April–May 1974, p. 3677). These agreements have provided the basis for intensive French cooperation with, collaboration with, and assistance to the Cameroonian government in terms of the provision of financial and technical aid to almost every aspect of the government's activity. French advisors were highly visible and common in various ministry offices. The university, largely paid for with French funds, was administered and largely staffed by French personnel. Numerous French teachers took up positions in Cameroonian secondary schools. The agreements also provided for assistance and protection for French businesses and investors operating in Cameroon. Military assistance included training and equipment, as well as participation by French personnel in the war against the UPC. A joint airline combining several of the ex-French colonies with French capital and expertise was established (Air Afrique).

The monetary system of Cameroon was tightly tied to that of France through the inclusion of Cameroon in the franc zone with its currency pegged to the value of the French franc and controlled through the Banque Centrale des Etats de l'Afrique Centrale. The bank in turn was controlled by France. In such circumstances, a certain stability and respectability is granted to the Cameroonian franc in world affairs, but such qualities depend totally on the world attitude toward the French franc. This arrangement means that Cameroonian currency is easily transferable, and this facilitates foreign—especially French—investment and commerce in Cameroon. However, this monetary tie also means that Cameroon has almost no influence over its currency; Cameroon must devalue (or revalue) whenever the French franc moves. On occasion, what is monetarily wise for France is not appropriate for Cameroonian needs. Cameroon's freedom is in a sense limited by this arrangement, though its position in the Western, capitalist economic system is strengthened.

At independence, France's predominant role in the Cameroonian economy was clearly indicated by import/export statistics. As are the economies of most developing countries, Cameroon's economy is dependent on foreign trade, a factor that only emphasized France's role in that economy. In 1961, France accounted for 59 percent of Cameroonian exports and 55 percent of its imports. These figures appear even more impressive when compared to the second largest partners. The Netherlands purchased 14 percent of exports; West Germany provided 6 percent of imports (International Monetary Fund 1968, p. 118 and Ndongko 1976).

Over the years Cameroon has developed relations with trading partners other than France, and France's relative significance has declined, a great change in Cameroon's relationship with its excolonial ruler. In 1980, France was still the major supplier of Cameroon's imports, but the percentage of imports from France had been reduced to 45 percent, a drop of ten points. West Germany (8.5 percent), the United States (5.5 percent), Japan (5.5 percent), and Italy (5.0 percent) were the next major sources of imports, though none of these compared in magnitude with France. In 1982, France accounted for 44 percent. But substantial change had taken place with respect to exports. The United States replaced France in 1980 as the major purchaser of Cameroon's products, largely the result of a new factor in Cameroon's export make-up—petroleum. France was also challenged by the Netherlands, which had been running a very close second to France for several years (even surpassing France in 1974), which was tied with the United States in 1979, and which remained close to France as the third largest purchaser in 1980. By 1982, the United States was reported to be purchasing 41 percent of all Cameroonian exports, but even this figure may be lower than reality. The U.S. purchased Cameroonian petroleum, and Cameroon consistently under-reported its petroleum exports (Schissel, 1983, p. 2171). These statistics, taking into account imports and exports, indicate a somewhat weakened position for France but also indicate that France remains the most powerful trading partner of Cameroon.

It is important to understand that Cameroonian policies on foreign investment have been designed to encourage and attract such funds to the country. Limits on foreign ownership are slight, and partnerships between Cameroonians and foreign investors are not required. Because of membership in the franc zone the movement of capital into and out of the country is relatively easy, and there are only minimal restrictions on the

Table 8.1 Direction of Cameroon Trade, 1961–1980: Exports (F.O.B.) (by percent)

Nation/Year	*1961*	*1962*	*1963*	*1964*	*1965*	*1966*	*1967*	*1968*	*1969*	*1970*	*1971*	*1972*	*1973*	*1974*	*1975*	*1976*	*1977*	*1978*	*1979*	*1980*
Africa									9.0	8.9	11.5	11.0	10.8	9.4	14.4	12.7	4.6	4.0	6.1	2.8
China					0.0	0.0	0.0	0.0	0.0	0.06	0.01	0.0	0.49	0.42	0.0	0.39	0.82	0.25	1.6	1.7
East Europe									1.3	0.3	0.4	0.1	0.1	0.5	0.7	0.2	0.2	0.1	0.1	0.0
EEC									75.4	71.6	70.4	69.9	70.1	74.8	64.1	67.7	79.0	80.8	61.4	59.7
France	58.9	60.0	56.7	53.8	48.0	40.1	38.3	34.0	32.6	29.6	27.6	29.3	28.5	27.1	26.8	25.4	28.3	33.7	25.1	21.8
Italy	3.6	2.7	3.7	4.1	3.3	4.6	2.9	2.0	3.0	2.1	2.2	3.0	3.9	5.4	3.9	6.3	8.1	7.1	6.8	8.2
Japan	0.2	0.4	0.7	4.1	1.1	1.1	0.6	0.7	1.4	2.9	3.1	3.7	4.6	3.0	2.4	3.9	3.4	2.7	3.2	2.7
Netherlands	14.4	13.1	16.2	13.4	15.9	12.5	18.7	21.2	25.8	23.6	25.4	23.5	24.0	30.6	21.4	22.6	27.3	27.8	20.8	19.2
U.K.	2.1	1.2	1.9	5.8	1.2	1.4	1.4	1.7	1.4	1.9	2.6	1.9	1.1	1.1	2.4	1.7	1.5	1.5	2.3	2.1
U.S.A.	5.6	6.2	5.4	6.9	10.5	15.2	14.0	10.9	5.9	9.7	9.0	9.3	7.5	4.0	2.7	2.8	4.8	5.5	20.8	30.2
U.S.S.R.					0.0	0.0	0.02	0.16	4.5	3.3	1.9	2.0	0.6	3.3	10.5	6.9	3.7	2.5	1.8	0.4
W. Germany	3.6	4.4	5.8	6.1	8.2	7.3	10.9	11.1	9.9	12.3	9.7	9.6	9.9	7.1	7.4	8.8	10.4	7.5	4.3	6.0

Source: United Nations, Statistical Office 1962–1981.

Table 8.2 Direction of Cameroon Trade, 1961–1980: Imports (C.I.F.) (by percent)

Nation/Year	*1961*	*1962*	*1963*	*1964*	*1965*	*1966*	*1967*	*1968*	*1969*	*1970*	*1971*	*1972*	*1973*	*1974*	*1975*	*1976*	*1977*	*1978*	*1979*	*1980*
Africa									10.1	9.3	9.3	9.0	9.0	10.4	8.4	7.8	4.5	8.4	7.0	4.9
China					0.03	0.6	0.5	0.3	0.7	0.7	0.8	1.0	1.8	2.4	0.9	2.3	1.6	3.0	2.0	1.9
East Europe									0.9	1.1	0.9	0.9	0.9	1.1	1.2	0.9	0.4	1.3	0.7	0.7
EEC									74.5	74.0	73.2	68.9	68.6	70.7	71.10	66.6	69.0	65.1	66.4	67.7
France	54.4	54.7	57.0	52.7	58.1	58.1	58.8	51.4	49.0	50.5	49.5	47.6	47.4	47.1	46.3	44.4	45.6	42.3	43.8	44.7
Italy	1.3	1.3	2.0	2.9	3.2	4.8	4.3	3.9	5.1	5.0	6.6	5.5	4.2	5.6	5.7	5.0	5.3	5.1	5.2	5.0
Japan	2.0	3.0	2.9	4.6	2.6	3.0	2.3	2.6	2.4	2.4	2.7	2.4	2.0	2.3	3.9	5.8	6.1	5.7	3.9	5.5
Netherlands	1.9	1.8	1.8	2.5	2.0	2.3	2.1	2.9	3.2	3.5	2.6	2.3	2.3	2.2	3.2	3.1	2.9	2.0	3.7	3.4
U.K.	2.8	2.4	1.8	5.6	1.7	2.0	2.1	4.0	4.3	3.7	4.2	3.3	2.9	3.7	3.8	3.4	4.4	4.6	3.2	2.9
U.S.A.	4.7	5.6	4.9	4.7	6.0	4.6	5.1	6.1	6.0	7.7	7.2	11.2	9.0	6.2	6.6	7.9	7.8	5.2	5.7	5.5
U.S.S.R.					0.1	0.06	0.1	0.7	0.4	0.3	0.2	0.3	0.05	0.4	0.5	0.6	0.7	0.5	0.6	0.5
W. Germany	6.0	5.8	6.0	6.4	7.1	7.2	7.7	9.3	10.1	7.9	7.5	7.7	9.5	9.2	8.4	7.3	7.3	8.0	7.6	8.5

Source: United Nations, Statistical Office 1962–1981.

repatriation of profits. The government provides a variety of benefits, such as tariff and tax exemptions, to entice foreign investors. Probably the major deterrent to potential foreign investment is the government's "Cameroonization" policy. The government has exerted strong pressure on investors to hire and train Cameroonians to replace foreign personnel. In spite of this policy, the environment remains positive. These factors are summarized in a recent U.S. government report: "Political stability, fiscal soundness, a liberal investment code, a nonrestrictive payments policy, a progressive attitude toward private initiative and foreign investment, and an impressive record of growth since independence have contributed to the creation of an attractive business climate in Cameroon" (Michelini 1980, p. 2). This is an area where Cameroon's government has chosen to take a very cautious policy in order to entice foreign investment, even though indigenous investors often complain that their interests take second place to foreigners' interests. Other African states, notably Nigeria, although capitalist in orientation, have been more willing to exert pressure on foreign investors for joint ownerships, less tax concessions and stricter indigenization.

Cameroon remains in the franc zone, and French aid and investment remain significant. But even in the investment sector, French predominance is slowly being weakened. Indigenous, Cameroonian capital (especially from Bamileke, and northern and central government sources) and capital from other Western countries are increasing in relation to French investments. "The number one loser to the Cameroonization of the economy has been French business interests. French interests held in 1973 some 52 percent of the capital. This figure plummeted to only—23.6 percent in 1982—France's percentage of the total capital held by foreigners in the Cameroonian economy has also been dropping: from 77.4 percent in 1973 to 63.1 percent in 1980 to 60.8 percent last year [1982]" (Schissel 1983, p. 2171). Still, relative to other major investors, France holds a predominant position. In 1982, French investment represented 63 billion CFA in the secondary sector; Britain represented 4.3 billion CFA, and Italy 4 billion CFA. United States involvement, especially in banking and petroleum, was rising rapidly and was at about 4 billion in 1982. Both the United States and Cameroon have been striving to increase U.S. trade and investment in Cameroon in recent years. France remains the major source of aid; some 60 percent of bilateral aid received in 1982 was from France (Schissel 1983, p. 2171 and Organization for Economic Cooperation and Development (OECD) 1984, pp. 50–51).

Taking all of these factors together, we conclude that Cameroon's dependent relationship with France in economic matters remains quite strong after more than two decades of independence. That relationship has weakened, and, as France's role has declined, other Western states have taken up the difference. Cameroon has somewhat diffused its economic relationships, but such diffusion has taken place significantly only among the Western states. One suspects that the choice of Cameroon's leaders is to increase the rate of this diffusion. One indication of this is the numerous exchanges of trade and high-level missions between Cameroon and various Western states in recent years. However, the French ties are very strong, not only in the official treaty sense, but also in less discernible ways. French businessmen know how to operate in Cameroon, and the Cameroonian bureaucracy frequently operates to the benefit of French interests and the detriment of other foreign interests. This may be due to individual likes and dislikes of bureaucrats or it may be due to their greater familiarity with the French way of doing things. The net effect is that non-French foreign investors and businessmen frequently feel that there is an invisible but very real pro-French bias among the Cameroonian bureaucracy and that this bias makes it especially difficult for them to operate in Cameroon.

Kofele-Kale notes that "The strange fascination that Cameroon's ruling elite have for metropolitan culture is another factor which explains the assured position France enjoys in Cameroon" (Kofele-Kale 1981b, p. 201). Such a fascination is difficult to document; even more difficult is the attempt to show a relationship between a liking for French culture and foreign policy content. One cannot travel in Cameroonian cities without gaining a sense of the pervasiveness of French culture as an influence on Cameroon. In terms of language, dress, foods, items for sale in shops and stores, and in numerous other ways, one is constantly reminded of France's role. In meeting with and getting acquainted with Cameroonians, except for these from the Anglophone portion of the country, the positive evaluations of French culture greatly outweigh the negative. From the French perspective, there has been a strong attempt to cultivate and increase this liking for things French since Cameroonian independence. This campaign has been most obvious in the Anglophone sector where the French government has played a major role in developing a French language program through the provision of French staff, training, and study in France for Cameroonian staff; a well-conceived French-by-radio program; textbook and curriculum assistance; a language training program for nonschool adults; and the opening of libraries and French cultural centers. Such openness to the spread of French culture is one way in which the Cameroonian government can respond positively to French attempts to maintain close ties with Cameroon, while at the same time Cameroon attempts to expand its economic relations with other states.

Although there has been frequent agreement between France and Cameroon on international issues, there have been some notable cases of disagreement. One of the earliest disagreements was over the question of recognition of the People's Republic of China. Cameroon opposed such recognition in part because the PRC had given support to the UPC. During the period from 1965 to 1970, Cameroon either voted no or abstained on the question of PRC admission to the UN; France favored this admission. But by 1970, the UPC question had been resolved, Cameroon recognized the PRC, and in 1971 Cameroon supported admission of the PRC to the UN (Traxler 1982, p. 136). Cameroon took a very different stand from France on the question of support for Biafra in the Nigerian Civil War (1967–1970), with Cameroon standing firmly behind Nigeria and the OAU and France supporting the Biafrans. In 1971, Cameroon withdrew from the French supported Air Afrique and established an independent national airline. Cameroon has not participated in the annual conferences of Francophone heads of state that France has sponsored, and in 1973 Cameroon dropped out of the French-supported Organisation Commune Africaine, Malgache et Mauritienne, a regional organization for economic, social, and technical cooperation, which for a time was headquartered in Yaounde. And while France has taken a rather mild position against the apartheid policies of the white-dominated government of the Republic of South Africa (and Rhodesia), the Cameroon government has spoken strongly against that government and has assisted the liberation movements through participation in the OAU Liberation Committee and by other means. With the possible exceptions of the Air Afrique and Biafran issues, none of these differences between France and Cameroon were of economic significance for the relationships between the two states. France's interest in Biafra was in part due to the petroleum resources there and in part due to France's long-term belief that Nigeria represented a British-dominated counterpoise to French influence in western Africa. The breakup of Nigeria would have diminished that counterpoise. But for Cameroon the threat of a successful breakaway by Biafra would have presented a bad example for dissident elements within Cameroon society. Too, there was strong fear that a successful Nigeria might take vengeance on neighbors that aided Biafra. Cameroon's self-interest was significantly touched by the war, and it could not afford to follow France's lead. Withdrawal from Air Afrique and the founding of a competitor airline, Camair, was in Cameroon's economic interest, though in recent years mismanagement of Camair has caused financial problems. This only affected French interests indirectly, for France has continued to play a role in Camair (Air France holds 30 percent of the investment, Cameroon 70 percent), and the problems faced by Air Afrique have had little to do with Cameroon's withdrawal.

While Cameroon has developed valuable trade, aid, and even investment relations with the United States, West Germany, and the Netherlands, it is clear that France remains the predominant, still dominating, economic partner of this country. This relationship is buttressed by extensive cultural ties that play a significant, if unmeasurable, role. Disagreements occur between France and Cameroon but generally in areas where no substantial economic interests are affected or where Cameroon's interests are extremely important. This suggests that the realm of choice in Cameroon foreign policy decision making remains limited. Cameroon officials have attempted with some success to expand that realm. These attempts have been aided by the ending of the UPC war and, probably more significantly, by the growth of petroleum exports. The first lessened dependence on French military support; the second lessens dependence on French economic support.

Eastern Europe and the People's Republic of China

Relationships with the Eastern bloc powers and the People's Republic of China took longer to develop than with the Western states, and relations with these states remain relatively minor in importance to this day. As suggested above, one factor influencing such relations was the war with the UPC. In spite of this, Cameroon did send a visiting mission to Eastern Europe as early as 1962, and diplomatic relations opened with the Soviet Union thereafter. However, government attitudes toward the Eastern bloc states seem to have remained negative for several years. Soviet offers of financial assistance were largely unused, and Soviet scholarship offers were viewed with suspicion. Trade with these countries remained insignificant. As late as 1969, Eastern bloc countries represented less than 2 percent of total Cameroonian imports, and Eastern bloc purchase of Cameroon exports represented less than 1 percent of the total. In general, these figures have not increased greatly over the years.

Once the war with the UPC was ended, relations with the PRC were opened and a rather warm relationship between the two states has developed, symbolized most visibly by the PRC's construction of a large cultural center in Yaounde, which now houses, in addition to theaters and halls, the headquarters of the Cameroon political party. The Chinese have been involved in several aid projects, including rural electrification. In recent years, total Chinese trade with Cameroon has surpassed the value of the combined Cameroonian trade of the USSR and Eastern Europe, though the majority of this trade is in imports and is related to Chinese financial assistance programs.

Nonalignment

Cameroon's officials have frequently described their foreign policy as nonaligned. In 1975, Ahidjo stated that "non-alignment . . . is now seen quite simply as an assertion of our personality on the international stage, a desire for independence, that is to say, a desire fully to exercise our free will in international affairs" (Cameroon National Union 1976, p. 132). Similar statements were made throughout his reign, and President Biya has spoken in the same manner. Judgments of the reality of such nonalignment can only be subjective, for the observer is in no position to analyze the motives behind policy decisions. That Cameroon has close and significant relations with France is obvious. That Cameroon and France frequently agree on foreign policy matters is also clear (and will be further evidenced when we discuss Cameroonian–African relations). But that this means that Cameroon's leaders are somehow teleguided from Paris in their behavior is not clear, for it is possible that Cameroonian leaders do agree, not out of coercion, but because of similar views and interpretations of international affairs. It is also clear that on occasion there are disagreements, and Cameroon stands on its own. Kofele-Kale concludes that Cameroon "has pursued a policy of *aligned* non-alignment" (Kofele-Kale 1981b, p. 202). Zartman presents a different perspective, one that relieves us of the polemical aspects of the question, when he suggests that

> we talk of Africa as part of the West . . . The political values for which Africans have struggled, the unfulfilled aspirations they entertain, and the ties they have maintained after achieving independence show the continent to be very much part of the Western world, even if nonaligned in terms of military capabilities and security alliances (Zartman 1984, p. 39).

Cameroon and Africa

Although Cameroon's relationships with Africa are not particularly significant in economic terms, they have a potential significance that may be greater. Unlike some African leaders, Ahidjo dedicated much of his time to domestic affairs and spent relatively little of his efforts and energies in continental or the larger international world. There has been a certain pride in the role Cameroon has played in African affairs, and over the years the country has won the respect of many African leaders both for the quality of its participation in continental relations and for its domestic political stability and economic growth and development. While the major international efforts have been directed toward relations with France and other European and North American states, African affairs have taken a distinct second place in interest and energy. Within Africa, regional and bilateral relations have been more important than continental. It is convenient to consider Cameroon's African relations in three categories—continental, regional, and bilateral with Nigeria.

Continental

There are three major facets to Cameroon policy at the continental level: generalized support for continental unity and cooperation; opposition to continuing colonial rule and white-dominated regimes in Southern Africa; and Cameroon as a model of African unity or as a bridge between French- and English-speaking Africa. However, these goals have not become Cameroonian preoccupations, and no substantial resources have been expended in pursuit of them.

Cameroon leaders have often spoken of the need for African unity, and the country has been an active participant in the Organization of African Unity (OAU). Two Cameroonians have served as its secretary-general, and Ahidjo was its chairman (1969–1970). But as are most states characterized as "conservative," the Cameroonian vision of African unity does not include the formation of some sort of political or economic union at the continental level. Rather, Cameroonians have argued that regional cooperation provides a more effective focus for unity than the continental level. "We believe only that the unity of Africa, to be effective and durable, should be buttressed by concentric circles of solidarity" such as the regional groupings that have arisen (Cameroon National Union 1968, p. 90). As will be discussed, Cameroon has been active in a concrete fashion in regional undertakings.

Cameroon's attitude toward African solidarity was represented by the opening of relations with most African states as they became independent, although representatives were not exchanged in all instances. However, the civil war in Cameroon and the role of the UPC abroad prevented the development of positive relations between Cameroon and several of the so-called "radical" states of the 1960s. Ghana, Guinea, and the United Arab Republic (Egypt) in particular provided various types of support to the UPC. Such problems largely evaporated with the ending of the activities of the UPC in Cameroon.

We have mentioned that Cameroon differed with France on attitudes toward the white-dominated regimes that existed and the one that continues to exist in Southern Africa. Cameroon has taken this stand on its own merits, not merely as a means of symbolizing independence from France. In this respect, Cameroon has taken a much stronger stance than most of the Francophone and many of the Anglophone states. Even while Nigeria was still doing business with Portuguese citizens and allowing them to work in the country, Cameroon was refusing to allow Portuguese to enter their country. Of a more significant nature was Cameroon's refusal to enter into dialogue with South Africa, although France and several Francophone states supported this. Cameroon has consistently followed OAU policies toward South Africa and has been active in the Liberation Committee.

In one sense, Cameroon is a unique country in Africa, for it consists of territories that were ruled by France and Britain. Most African countries suffered under only one colonial ruler. But in other respects, Cameroon can be seen as Africa in miniature, combining a variety of African nationalities as well as a variety of colonial experiences. Because of this background, some have looked to Cameroon as a possible model or at least an example of real African unity and as demonstrating the viability of communication and cooperation between the ex-British and ex-French colonies of Africa. Ahidjo frequently stated that Cameroon "should serve as a bridge between French-speaking Africa and English-speaking Africa, in the exact measure in which Reunification has demonstrated the possibility of a fruitful cohabitation between them" (Cameroon National Union 1968, p. 91). This role for Cameroon has not been the stimulus to any particular action on the part of the government, though it has served as a source of satisfaction and encouragement to the Cameroonian people and, in a limited respect, as a justification for reunification. In general, continental affairs have been relatively unimportant for Cameroonian foreign relations. Of more importance are regional relations where Cameroon sees the possibility of direct economic benefits through regional cooperation.

Regional

While one might agree that Cameroon's continental policy has produced more lip-service than activity, there has been considerable activity at the regional level. This is in keeping with Ahidjo's previously stated view that cooperation and concrete unity are more relevant at this level where similarity of interests, culture, and historical experience lend a more propitious environment for successful cooperation. Such regional undertakings have concentrated on two foci of interaction, the Francophone focus and the equatorial Africa focus (also Francophone but at a smaller scale and consisting of contiguous states).

The Francophone connection produced several organizations of a functional and political nature. These were of more importance in the first decade of independence. Of course, behind many—if not all—of these was a strong influence from France, which felt that such a network of international organizations would facilitate the maintenance of French control over its previous colonies. Soon after independence Cameroon became part of the so-called "Brazzaville group" of states, a collection of Francophone states that essentially was a caucus group in African international politics. This was followed by the Union of African and Malagasy States (UAM) and later the Common Organization of African and Malagasy States (OCAM or OCAMM). The OCAM undertook a variety of cooperative research and scientific undertakings, and Air Afrique was an offspring of the organization. Oyono discusses briefly the variety of structures that emerged during this period, but he goes on to argue that, once Cameroon had ended its civil war and had brought about the end of the federation to form the United Republic of Cameroon, Ahidjo—freed in part from his need to satisfy French policy demands—was able to undertake new foreign policy initiatives. "*Liberes de ces forces centrifuges, les autorites de Yaounde pouvaient desormais donner une orientation nouvelle a leur politique africaine*" ("Liberated from these centrifugal forces, the authorities in Yaounde could henceforth give a new orientation to their African policy") (Oyono 1983, p. 26). This new, independent direction was marked by withdrawal from OCAM and Air Afrique; refusal to participate in the Francophone heads of state conference; changes in status for the French ambassador in Yaounde; and rather strong statements on the perils of nonalignment in today's world. Oyono concludes that, while such political independence was possible, Cameroon remained firmly tied to France in economic matters (Oyono 1983, p. 29). At this widely spread out level of regionalism, there was little gain for Cameroon. The potential of a more localized regionalism where Cameroon—and French—businesses and industries might find room for growth was of much greater interest.

With respect to regional cooperation in equatorial Africa, Cameroon—as well, quite probably, as has France—has its own motivations for fostering cooperation and economic integration. Although the results of such attempts remain rather limited, Cameroon as the leading economic power in the region (consisting variously of Cameroon, Chad, Central African Republic (CAR), Gabon, Congo, and Equatorial Guinea) stands to gain in terms of markets for goods produced in Cameroon; in attracting foreign investment to serve a larger market; and in the transit trade passing through Douala and over the TransCameroon Railway and a new highway into CAR. Granted, the combined population, resources, and market of this region are not great, but cooperation does offer some potential benefit for Cameroon.

The major structure for international cooperation in this region is the Central African Customs and Economic Union (UDEAC), founded in 1966 but relying on a practice of cooperation dating from French colonial control during the twentieth century. At this time, there are five members of UDEAC—Cameroon, Gabon, Congo, the Central African Republic, and Equatorial Guinea—and one other, Chad, had been a member in the past and has reapplied for membership. The members of UDEAC plus Chad are also joined by membership in the Banque des Etats de l'Afrique Centrale (BEAC), which controls the issuance of currency and regulates the members' participation in the franc zone.

The UDEAC has operated mainly as a customs union, though there have been some attempts in recent years at constructing an economic union. As noted in Agbor-Tabi's recent study of UDEAC, the reality is that very little trade occurs between the member states. Each is basically a producer of raw materials for European economies, and the members have little to offer each other (Agbor-Tabi 1984). There is some transit trade especially through Douala into the Central African Republic (and Chad), and there is also a growing trade in foodstuffs from Cameroon to food-deficient Gabon. A large number of Cameroonians find employment in Gabon or are involved there in commerce and transport. The real significance of UDEAC is that in the future it may become a valuable market for Cameroonian goods. Infrastructural development is a key need before that future can begin to take shape. France, among other donor states, has provided substantial assistance for the development of this infrastructure—roads, railroads, port facilities—that improve Cameroon's central position in the region. Douala, with its port and growing industrial, commercial, and banking sectors, is becoming the major pole of development for the entire UDEAC region. Such a development appears to be in the best interests of both Cameroon and France, for it is largely French investors and the Cameroon government that benefit from this role.

Relations within the region have not been entirely cooperative, however. There has been some complaint that Cameroon violated UDEAC agreements by establishing its own oil refinery rather than relying on the refinery in Gabon that was to supply UDEAC countries. Too, it is probable that Gabon would like to see a larger export of Cameroonian food, but Cameroon dampens such trade for fear of causing shortages at home and thus additional increases in food prices. In 1982, there was a period of extreme hostility between the two states stemming ostensibly from a fracas at a soccer match between teams of the two countries. Rioting broke out in Libreville and other cities; Cameroonians were beaten and their property destroyed. Eventually, Cameroon, assisted by France, airlifted over 30,000 of its citizens back to Cameroon. There had been previous conflicts (*West Africa,* December 6, 1977, p. 1877).

Cameroon also has faced difficulties in its relations with Chad, mainly due to the almost continual civil wars there and in recent years due to the obvious intervention of Libya in that strife. The Chad situation has direct impact on Cameroon in several ways, most particularly in terms of the large numbers of refugees that have poured into Cameroon. Many of these have been well cared for in refugee camps near the border, but others have fled to cities and towns, competing with Cameroonians for scarce jobs in the urban sector and elsewhere. Too, the chaos in Chad has had negative effects for Cameroon businesses and traders. For example, the Cameroon Development Corporation's major market for its tea is Chad, but in recent years sales have often been held up for periods of six or more months.

Cameroon would prefer to have stability in Chad, but not stability under Libyan influence or domination. As in most West African states, Colonel Qaddaffi is the cause of paranoia. (A student strike at the University of Yaounde in 1981 was blamed by the government on Libyan influences.) Thus, the government has been very cooperative with the French in their efforts to present a balance against the takeover of Chad by Libya and its allies.

Cameroon's relations with Equatorial Guinea have generally been peaceful and positive. The existence of this small country could be significant for Cameroon in the future. Equatorial Guinea consists of two main parts. One is on the mainland between Cameroon and Gabon; the other consists of a relatively large island and a couple of smaller ones off the coast of Cameroon and Nigeria. Probably the greatest potential of this territory for Cameroon lies in the fact that the off-shore islands could be the basis of, or at least a part of, a dispute with Nigeria, the giant neighbor to Cameroon's west. Elements in both countries have occasionally called for the annexation of these islands, and in view of other disputes between Cameroon and Nigeria this could be a serious issue. In the early 1960s, Ahidjo envisaged the formation of a trilingual federation, joining the English and French Cameroon with the then Spanish colony, now known as Equatorial Guinea. Students at the government's bilingual secondary school at Man O'War Bay received Spanish lessons in preparation for such an eventuality. In this respect, Cameroon was following an old French policy of extending influence over Equatorial Guinea (Liniger-Goumaz 1983, pp. 139–188).

Cameroon also supported the nationalist movement there as part of its general opposition to colonial rule, and Ahidjo welcomed the country's independence in 1968. Even to that point there was widespread support for a takeover, not only of the islands but also of the mainland portion, both of which have strong cultural links with Cameroon peoples. On Equatorial Guinea's independence day, coastal Cameroon was rife with rumors of troop movements, the possibility of war with Gabon, and a takeover of the Spanish territory. Nothing occurred.

Independent Equatorial Guinea has had a difficult political and economic history, and it was ruled for many years by a regime similar to that of the Idi Amin government in Uganda. During this period, Cameroon received and cared for many refugees while attempting to influence the Equatorial Guinean government to follow more reasonable policies. By the time the almost inevitable coup d'etat took place in that country, the economy, polity, and society were in shambles.

The most recent direction in relations between Equatorial Guinea, Cameroon and their neighbors is toward limited economic integration. Although Equatorial Guinea had been a Spanish colony and was tied into the Spanish monetary system, it has now joined the franc zone, becoming a member of the Banque des Etats de l'Afrique Centrale. On December 19, 1983, at the nineteenth summit of UDEAC, it was agreed to have Equatorial Guinea join that organization as a full member (*West Africa,* January 3, 1983, p. 3412; *Africa Research Bulletin-Economic* 1984a, p. 7106). The possibility of petroleum resources makes this small state an attractive partner for UDEAC and a member of the franc zone, all in keeping with France's long-term interests in the region (Liniger-Goumaz 1983).

With Equatorial Guinea's acceptance as a new member and Chad's application for membership expected to be approved in December, 1984, there seems to be some expansion of the UDEAC regional experiment (*Africa Research Bulletin-Economic* 1984, p. 7402).

Regionalism is also under construction on a grander scale in the equatorial zone. Based on the suggestion of President Bongo of Gabon at the 1981 UDEAC summit meeting, representatives of 11 countries (Cameroon, Gabon, Congo, Central African Republic, Zaire, Rwanda, Burundi, Chad, Equatorial Guinea, Sao Tome-Principe, and Angola) met in Libreville in October 1983 to establish the Economic Community of the States of Central Africa (ECSCA) or la Communaute Economique des Etats de l'Afrique Centrale (CEEAC). Of the participants at the meeting, all except Angola agreed to join the new association, a central African counterpart to the Economic Community of West African States (ECOWAS). A common market will be established, leading to economic and monetary integration. Special projects are proposed for land-locked and least-developed members; a regional food security policy is proposed; and cooperation in industrial, transport, and commercial development is intended (*Africa Research Bulletin-Economic* 1983). Although the organization is not expected to become operational until 1985, preliminary investigations and discussions have taken place in 1984 (*Africa Research Bulletin-Economic* 1984c, p. 7285).

As indicated in Table 8.3, CEEAC will provide a much larger economic zone in which Cameroon may operate, though several factors suggest a very difficult future for the organization. Infrastructural linkages in this region are highly undeveloped, but a more significant obstacle to the development of trade between these states is the lack of economic compatibility. In general there is little to be traded between them. Inter-African trade in 1980 for the member states equalled only 7.4 percent of their imports and 8.6 percent of their exports (*Africa Research Bulletin-Economic* 1983, p. 7034). Additional problems include the definition of relations between UDEAC and CEEAC (as well as with the Community of Great Lakes States—Zaire, Rwanda, Burundi). Too, there may be conflict between the four major economic powers involved—Cameroon, Congo, Zaire, and Gabon. This is perhaps the greatest danger from the Cameroon perspective, for in UDEAC it enjoys clear advantages in competition with the other members, but such advantages are lost in CEEAC where Zaire has a much stronger economic potential. A final problem and one that has bedeviled economic integration in Africa is the relative "drag" imposed on the wealthier states by the poorer members.

Table 8.3. UDEAC and CEEAC Members: Comparative Economic Data

Country	*Area(km²)*	*Population (Millions)*	*GNP (Millions of Dollars)*	*GNP per Capita (Dollars)*	*Principal Products*
Cameroon	475,000	8.9	6,642	746.0	Cocoa, coffee, wood, petroleum
Central African Republic	623,000	2.4	646	265.5	Diamonds, coffee, cotton
Gabon	257,000	0.7	2,852	4,181.7	Petroleum, manganese, uranium
Equatorial Guinea	28,000	0.3	—	—	Cocoa, coffee, wood
Congo	342,000	1.7	1,749	1,021.7	Petroleum, wood, agriculture
UDEAC	1,725,000	14	11,889	—	
Burundi	28,000	4.3	986	226.8	Coffee, cotton, tea
Rwanda	26,000	5.5	1,268*	237.1*	Coffee, tea, cassiterite
Sao Tome	1,000	0.1	—	—	Cocoa, copra, coffee
Chad	1,284,000	4.6	321	69.0	Cotton, peanuts, sorghum
Zaire	2,345,000	31	5,161	168.2	Copper, cobalt, coffee
CEEAC	5,409,000	59.5	19,625	—	

*1981 data.

Source: Organization for Economic Cooperation and Development 1984 and *Africa Research Bulletin-Economic* 1983, p. 7033.

It remains to be seen whether CEEAC will move beyond the planning stage into an active role in the economic life of equatorial Africa. Should it do so, it provides Cameroon with an opportunity to expand its economic activities in the region and thus to provide a larger market for its growing industrial and agricultural sectors. Of course, it also opens those sectors to competition. Cameroon may find it more suitable to emphasize the UDEAC connection and to allow CEEAC to remain relatively inert. But for Cameroon, some version of regional cooperation presents the best opportunity for the growth and development of its economic interests. This opportunity is also of benefit to France, for it allows the French government to continue its influence in the region, possibly extending its influence into ex-British colonies, and it gives French business, industrial, and commercial factors the benefits of a larger and wealthier market in which to operate.

Bilateral

Our discussion of regionalism has included much of bilateral nature, but such relations were in the context of regional cooperation. In this section, we shall discuss Nigerian–Cameroonian relations. These two states are linked through one regional organization—the Lake Chad Basin Commission—but the predominant relationships of these two are expressed bilaterally rather than through any regional structure (Ndongko 1976b and Ofoegbu 1978).

As the major economic, political, and military force in the West Africa region, Nigeria remains the single most important entity for Cameroon's Africa policies. Though various writers have described Cameroon–Nigerian relations as "warm," "cordial," "friendly," or "proper," in fact there have been long-term negative aspects to those relations that are more significant than the positive factors. Cameroon–Nigerian relations began from independence with a strong negative feature, and several disputes have joined to continue this conflictual tone. There have been moments of friendliness and cooperation, as during Nigeria's civil war, but the underlying causes of conflict have regularly returned to the forefront.

In 1961 as independence approached for the Anglophone trust territory of Cameroon, plebiscites were conducted there to determine whether the trust would become a part of independent Nigeria or of independent Cameroon. For purposes of determining the outcome, the votes were counted separately in the two administrative divisions of the territory (Welch 1966, pp. 224–243). As a result, Southern Cameroons became a part of the Federal Republic of Cameroon, but Northern Cameroons became a part of the Federal Republic of Nigeria. This latter result caused an official outcry in Cameroon against the British and against Nigeria. The complaint was taken to the United Nations and to the International Court of Justice, where Cameroon received no satisfaction. It was to take several years for the Cameroon government to overcome its anger, and during this period the anniversary of the plebiscite was celebrated as a national day of mourning in Cameroon. Such was the start of Cameroonian–Nigerian relations.

The more significant source of conflict between the two states is the undelineated nature of their border, especially in the swampy southern coastal and adjacent offshore areas. Here there have been numerous small jurisdictional conflicts over such issues as tax collection and law enforcement. In part, this is related to an attitude among commercial elements in the Nigerian city of Calabar that this area is in their economic hinterland, but of a more serious nature are the implications of the exact location of the border in determining which state has access to offshore fishing and offshore/inshore petroleum resources. The uncertainty of the border and the potential value of the resources of the area have led to a series of skirmishes and conflicts, the most serious of which almost led to a war in 1981. Cameroon forces killed five Nigerian soldiers somewhere in the border area. As tensions grew, military forces were called to each side of the border. Nigerian planes buzzed over Cameroon's new oil refinery. Calabar radio and the Nigerian press called for war. A mob in Lagos attacked the Cameroonian embassy (*West Africa,* June 6, 1981, p. 1317 and Irele 1984). During the crisis, France reportedly rushed weapons and advisers to strengthen Cameroonian defenses. Shortly after this, a second problem arose in the northern border area. Nigeria claimed that Cameroon was diverting waters from the Kalia River that should have flowed into Nigeria. The lack of water was reportedly having negative effects on Nigerian farmers (*Africa Research Bulletin,* March–April, 1982, p. 6367). Other projects on the Benue and Chari Rivers are potential causes of conflict (*New Nigerian,* May 28, 1981, p. 32 and June 11, 1981, pp. 1 and 13).

Commercial and trade relations are another area of concern for the two states. Smuggling is of great concern to Cameroon, for goods coming illegally from Nigeria undercut Cameroonian industries and lower the receipts from import taxes that are so important to the Cameroonian budget. Nigeria would like to increase its trade with Cameroon, seeing its population as a logical market for Nigerian-produced goods. Cameroon fears that such competition would undermine its struggling industrial sector and thus does not wish to see an increase in this trade. It is widely assumed that this is the cause of Cameroon's failure to improve the miserable highway links between the two states. Cameroon could benefit from an increased sale of foodstuffs to Nigeria, which suffers a severe food deficit situation, but such an increase might cause higher food prices in Cameroon and might give Nigeria reason to insist on opening the Cameroon market to Nigerian goods. As a result of these considerations, smuggling continues at a high but unmeasured rate, and legitimate trade remains small. Cameroon's long term interest lies in developing links with its UDEAC partners and preventing the spread of Nigerian economic ties to the area. France, although developing strong economic links with

Nigeria, prefers to see Cameroon—and France—remain the major economic influence in the UDEAC area, too.

There have been periods of good relations between these two countries as during and after the Nigerian civil war when Cameroon stood firmly in support of Nigerian policies and assisted in settling differences between Nigeria and those states that had supported Biafra during the war. Perhaps out of gratitude for this support, the military ruler of Nigeria, General Gowon, met with President Ahidjo in Maroua in 1975 to discuss the land and maritime borders, trade, the Lagdo Dam proposals, and relations in general. The two leaders settled the border issues—for the time being (*West Africa,* June 9, 1975, p. 670 and June 16, 1975, p. 700). This was the highpoint of positive relations between the states, but, as we have discussed, there was a rapid decline in the next few years. Some observers argue that the civilian government that came to power in Nigeria in 1979 was dismayed by the Maroua agreement, felt that General Gowon had given away too much, and so purposely moved toward a crisis situation in order to bring about renegotiation of the border (*The Punch,* June 1, 1981, pp. 8 and 12). We can expect a low level of conflict, with the possibility of serious problems at some time, continuing between Cameroon and Nigeria. The Cameroon economy could be engulfed by this powerful western neighbor should trade and commercial relations become too open. For Cameroon, the wiser choice is to develop its regional ties to the east, with its UDEAC partners, while maintaining a correct, but distant, relationship with Nigeria.

In general, Cameroon views regional ties as the most significant aspect of its Africa policies. In this, there is considerable congruence between Cameroonian and French interests and policies. We have seen that France has been very supportive of Cameroon's regional African policies, from assistance in the Nigerian crisis of 1981 to aid in developing a UDEAC infrastructure with Douala as its hub. Cameroon is a useful asset in its attempt to maintain and expand its economic domination of equatorial Africa. But such expansion also benefits the attempts of Cameroon to develop its economy.

CONCLUSIONS

Some years ago I. William Zartman wrote that

> Eur-African relations are a matter of continuity and change, but judgments of them vary considerably. . . . To some, the successor of colonialism is neocolonialism and dependency; for others, what is taking place is gradual disengagement, and the multilateralization of ties to the developed nations (Zartman 1976, p. 325).

The latter approach Zartman called "decolonization," "an evolutionary process, as various forms of bilateral, metropolitan influence are replaced with multilateral relations" (Zartman 1976, p. 326). It is decolonization that seems to best describe the history of Cameroon foreign relations. There has been a gradual disengagement from France, most easily observable (and measurable) in economic relations. Over the years Cameroon has begun to diversify its trading and investment partners. Although France does remain the most powerful partner, Cameroon has developed significant economic relations with other states, often in opposition to French economic interests. Most of this multilateralization has been within the Western, capitalist world, though diplomatic and economic relations have extended to the communist bloc as well.

It is in this respect that we see the limits of choice within Cameroon foreign relations; however, a dilemma remains if we attempt to explain those limits. In our introduction we suggested that such limits are a result of the Cameroonian political economy, that the choice of a capitalist mode of development oriented Cameroon toward the opening of more intensive relationships with countries of a similar economic system. The development of relations with Britain, the Netherlands, West Germany, the United States, and Italy makes sense both from the point of view of Cameroonian decision makers and from the points of view of the named states. That France might oppose such multilateralization in an attempt to maintain its significant economic benefits also seems logical. Young presents an alternative explanation in his comparison of the foreign policies of African capitalist, populist socialist, and Afro-Marxist regimes. In essence, he argues that the Eastern bloc states have little to offer in terms of trade, aid, and investment and that therefore all African states must remain primarily tied economically to the West (Young 1982, pp. 253–296). To this can be added the argument that, for some African states, choice is even more limited by their relative lack of attraction for Western or Eastern bloc interests. Those that produce export crops, have significant mineral resources, or are strategically located are in a better position to attract outside interest. But such "attractiveness" is increased or decreased by policy decisions made by African leaders. Cameroon's decision, whether or not prompted by France's mode of departure from its colonial status, to follow a capitalist development policy set the boundaries of its foreign policy options, and the succeeding decisions to implement policies of openness to foreign investors and trade have greatly increased its attractiveness. So, too, government policies with respect to its budget, to the control of foreign debt, and its general monetary and financial policies have increased its attractiveness. That is, there is a role for leadership in African politics. Decisions are made, policies are chosen, and these factors do influence events. But the role of such influence is limited or bound by the political economy in which Cameroon exists, and that is a product of the colonial and independence processes the country has undergone. Concepts of dependency and economic determinism leave little room for this leadership variable, but the success of Cameroon's foreign policy suggests that it is, indeed, important.

9

A BIBLIOGRAPHY OF CAMEROON

Diego Ungaro

Abalu, G.I. 1974. "Capital Shortage Illusion: A Case Study of Commercial Agriculture in Western Cameroon." *Journal of Rural Economy and Development* (Ibadan) 9 (2): 107–118.

Abdi Sheik-Abdi. 1981. "Ideology and Leadership in Somalia." *Journal of Modern African Studies* 19: 163–172.

Adelman, I. and Robinson, S. 1978. *Income Distribution Policies in Developing Countries.* Stanford: Stanford University Press.

African Business (London), 1982.

Afrique agriculture (Paris). 1979–1983.

______. 1982. "L'Agriculture dans le Ve Plan 1982–1986." Parts 1 and 2. (March 1; April 1).

Afrique-Asie. 1983. "Manoeuvres au Cameroun: en combat feutre." August 1, 1983, pp. 26–28.

Afrique Information (Paris) 1981–1983.

Agbor-Tabi, Peter. (n.d., c. 1985) "Effectiveness of AID in Reaching Its Intended Beneficiaries, i.e., the Rural Poor in AID Project Areas." Quarterly Progress Report 1. Office of Agriculture and Rural Development. Yaounde: U.S. Agency for International Development.

______. 1970. *The Customs Union of Central African States.* Doctoral dissertation, University of South Carolina. Agriculture and Rural Development, USAID/Yaounde.

______. 1984. "Cameroon and the UDEAC." Paper presented at the 1984 African Country Day Conference, School of Advanced International Studies, Washington, D.C.

Ahidjo, Ahmadou. 1964. *Contribution a la construction nationale.* Paris: Presence Africaine. 136 pp.
Ahidjho's speeches for the UNC's congress in 1962 about domestic, foreign, and economic policy; social and financial issues; and "auto-decolonisation."

______. 1968a. *The Political Philosophy of Ahmadou Ahidjo.* Monaco: Paul Bory.

______. 1968b. *Ahmadou Ahidjo par lui-meme.* Yaounde: Republique Federale du Cameroun.

______. 1968c. *As Told by Ahmadou Ahidjo.* Monaco: Paul Bory. 102 pp.

______. 1973. *Pour la revolution verte. For the Green Revolution.* Speech given at the opening of the Agricultural Show, Buea, March 9, 1973.

______. 1976. *Fondements et perspectives du Cameroun nouveau.* Aubagne-en-Provence: St. Lambert. 181 pp.

______. 1980. "General Policy Report." Presented by the National President of the Cameroon National Union, President of the United Republic of Cameroon, Bafoussam, February 13, 1980.

Ajami, Fouad. 1981. *The Arab Predicament: Arab Political Thought and Practice Since 1976.* Cambridge: Cambridge University Press.

Aletum, M.T. 1975. *Political Conflicts within the Traditional and Modern Institutions of the Bafut, Cameroon.* Louvain: Vauder.

Alexandre, Pierre. 1970a. "The Problems of Chieftancies in French-Speaking Africa." In *West African Chiefs,* edited by M. Crowder and O. Ikime, pp. 24–78. New York: Africana.

______. 1970b. "Chiefs, Commandants and Clerks: Their Relationships from Conquest to Decolonisation in French West Africa." In *West African Chiefs,* edited by M. Crowder and O. Ikime, pp. 2–13. New York: Africana.

Allaya, Mahmoud. 1979. "Etudes des marches et des perspectives d'echanges cerealiers des pays de l'Afrique de l'Ouest: Senegal, Mali, Haute Volta, Cote d'Ivoire, Ghana, Nigeria, Cameroon." Document no. ITC/DTC/135. Geneva: International Trade Center. 99 pp.

Aluko, Olajide, ed. 1977. *The Foreign Policies of African States.* London: Hodder and Stoughton.

Anguile, A.G. and David, J.E. 1965. *L'Afrique sans frontieres.* Monaco: Paul Bory.

Ansprenger, Franz. 1961. *Politik im Schwarzen Afrika: Die modernen politischen Bewegungen im Afrika franzosischer Pragung.* Cologne and Opaladen: Westdeutscher Verlag.

Ardener, Edwin O. 1967. "The Nature of the Reunification of Cameroon." In *African Integration and Disintegration,* edited by A. Hazelwood, pp. 285–334. London: Oxford University Press.

Ardener, Shirley, Ardener, E.W., and Warmington, W.A. 1960. *Plantation and Village in the Cameroons.* London: Oxford University Press.

______. 1968. *Eyewitness to the Annexation of Cameroon.* Buea: Government Printer.

Arkhipoff, Oleg. 1971. "Le probleme de la synthese economique: un exemple, le traitement sur ordinatateur de la comptabilite nationale camerounaise." *Revue economique de Madagascar* (Tananarive) (January–December): 319–355.

Arouna, N. 1977a. *Secteur refugie et developpement economique au Cameroun.* Yaounde: Office Nationale de Recherche en Science et Technologie. 50 pp.

______. 1977b. *Offre et demande des produits viviers dans la region de Yaounde.* Yaounde: Office Nationale de Recherche en Sciences Economiques et Sociales. 77 pp.

Atayi, E.A. and Knipscheer, H.C. 1980. "The Marketing of Food Crops in the Eastern Province of Cameroon." In International Institute of Tropical Agriculture, Ibadan, Agricultural Economics Discussion Paper, no. 11, pp. 1–27.

Austen, Ralph A. 1977. "Duala versus Germans in Cameroon: Economic Dimensions of a Political Conflict." *Revue francaise d'histoire d'outre-mer* 64:477–497.

Azarya, Victor. 1976. *Dominance and Change in North Cameroon: The Fulbe Aristocracy.* New York: Sage Publications. 72 pp. A study of the distribution of power, wealth, and prestige among the Fulbe before, during, and after the colonial period.

Badibanga, Andre. 1980–1981. "Je suis le 'Pere de la Nation.'" *Revue francaise d'etudes politiques africaines* 16:103–116.

Baeschlin-Raspail, Beat C. 1968. *Ahmadou Ahidjo: Pionnier de l'Afrique moderne.* Monaco: Paul Bory. 119 p.

Bahoken, J. and Engelbert, Atangana. 1976. *La politique culturelle en Republique Unie de Cameroun.* Paris: Les Presses de l'Unesco. 93 pp.

Bakvis, Herman. 1978. "French Canada and the 'Bureaucratic Phenomenon.'" *Canadian Public Administration* 21:103–124.

Bala-Mbarga, Henri. 1970. *J'aime mon pays: le Cameroun—Manuel d'Instruction Civique et d'Education Nationale.* Yaounde: Les Presses du Centre d'Edition et Production. 264 pp.

Banoun, David Samuel. 1980. *La gestione du patrimonie de l'etat en Republique Unie du Cameroun.* Yaounde: CLE.

Barbier, J.C., Courade, G.J., and Tissandier, J. 1980. *Complexes agro-industriels au Cameroun.* Paris: ORSTOM. 281 pp.

Bayart, Jean Francois. 1970. "L'Union Nationale Camerounaise." *Revue francaise de science politique* 20 (4): 681–718.
The emergence of single party government in Cameroon.

______. 1971. "Cameroun: l'illusion du parti unique." *Revue francaise d'etudes politiques africaines* 65: 41–49.

______. 1972. "Les rapports entre les eglises et l'Etat du Cameroun de 1958 a 1971." *Revue francaise d'etudes politiques africaines* 80: 79–104.

______. 1973a. "Presse ecrite et developpement politique au Cameroun." *Revue francaise d'etudes politiques africaines* 88: 48–63.

______. 1973b. "One-party Government and Political Development in Cameroon." *African Affairs* 72 (287): 125–44.

______. 1974. "Les categories dirigeantes au Cameroun." *Revue francaise d'etudes politiques africaines* 9 (105): 66–90.

______. 1978a. "Regime de parti unique et systemes d'inegalite et de domination au Cameroun: esquisse." *Cahiers d'etudes africaines* 18, 1–2 (69–70): 5–35.

______. 1978b. "The Political System." In *Gaullist Africa: Cameroon under Ahmadou Ahidjo,* edited by Richard Joseph, pp. 43–90, Eungu (Nigeria) Fourth Dimension Press.

______. 1979. *L'Etat au Cameroun.* Paris: Presses de la Fondation Nationale des Sciences Politiques. 298 pp.

______. 1980a. "One-Party Government and Political Development in Cameroon." In *An African Experiment in Nation Building: The Bilingual Cameroon Republic since Reunification,* edited by Ndiva Kofele-Kale, pp. 159–187. Boulder: Westview Press. (Also in *African Affairs* 72: 125–144.)

______. 1980b. "Paroles imperiales et voix du peuple en Centrafrique (1979)." *Politique africaine* 1:88–101.

Beauvilain, Alain. 1980. "Eleveurs et agriculteurs-eleveurs dans le bassin de la Benoue (Nord Cameroun): une exploitation du recensement general de la population et de l'habitat d'avril 1976." *Revue de geographie du Cameroun* 1 (2): 119–143.

Bederman, Sanford H. 1968. *The Cameroons Development Corporation: Partners in National Growth.* Bota: Cameroon Development Corporation.

Behrman, Lucy C. 1970. *Muslim Brotherhoods and Politics in Senegal.* Cambridge: Harvard University Press, 1970.

Belinga, E. 1976. *Cameroun: la revolution pacifique du 20 mai.* Yaounde: Lamaro. 198 pp.

Benjamin, Jacques. 1971a. "Dix ans de federalisme Camerounais 1961–1970." In *Federalisme et nations,* edited by Roman Serbyn, pp. 279–290. Montreal: Universite du Quebec.

______. 1971b. "Le federalisme camerounais: l'influence des structures federales sur l'activite economiques ouest-camerounaise." *Canadian Journal of African Studies* 5 (3): 281–306.
An article on the application of the federalist scheme in Cameroon and its effects on the minority groups.

______. 1972. *Les camerounais occidentaux: la minorite dans un etat bicommunautaire.* Montreal: Les presses de l'Universite de Montreal. 250 pp.

______. 1980. "The Impact of Federal Institutions on West Cameroon's Economic Activity." In *An African Experiment in Nation Building,* edited by Ndiva Kofele-Kale, pp. 191–226. Boulder, Colorado: Westview Press.

Benjamin, N. and Devarajan, S. 1983. "Une matrice de comptabilite sociale du Cameroun, 1979–80." Washington, D.C.: West Africa Country Programs Department, World Bank.

______. 1984. "Oil Revenues and Protectionism in Cameroon: Experiments with a Computable General Equilibrium Model." Typescript.

Bernard, Philippe J. 1977. "Pour une generalisation de l'etude des facteurs sociaux et culturels du developpement." *Tiers Monde* 18 (70): 339–351.

Beti, Mongo. 1972a. "Le Cameroun d'Ahidjo." *Temps Modernes* (November): 812–841.

______. 1972b. "Les proces du Cameroun: autopsie d'une decolonisation." *Partisans* (March): 111–132.

______. 1977. *Main basse sur le Cameroun: Autopsie d'une decolonisation.* Paris: Editions F. Maspero. 270 pp.

______. 1981. "Les oppositions africaines et nous." *Peuples noirs—Peuples africains* 4 (24): 66–83.
Correspondence between Mongo Beti and the leaders of the "Comite pour defendre et assister les prisonniers politiques au Cameroun" (CDAPPC). The author denounces the Stalinist behavior of the "Comite revolutionnaire" of the UPC, which controls the CDAPPC and the MANIDEM.

______. 1982. "Cameroun: le Pinochet noire, premiere victime du national-tiers mondisme." *Peuples noirs—Peuples africains* 30:1–12.
Ahidjo's regime succeeded in defeating opposition but not in controlling the country. His overthrow has been decided in Paris.

Biarnes, Pierre. 1968. "Cameroun: Le poids de la function publique." *Revue francaise d'etudes politiques africaines* 30–31: 12–14.

Bidias, Benjamin. 1971. *Les finances publiques et l'economie financiere de la Republique Federale du Cameroun.* Yaounde: Imprimerie Nationale. 411 pp.

Billard, Pierre. 1968. *Le Cameroun Federal,* 2 vols., Lyon: Imprimerie de Beaux Arts.

Binder, Leonard, ed. 1966. *Politics in Lebanon.* New York: Wiley.

Binet, J. 1961. "Les cadres au Cameroun." *Civilisations* 12: 21–38.

Biya, Paul. 1968. *Les institutions et la vie politique du Cameroun depuis l'independence.* Unpublished thesis, Faculte de Droit, Paris.

Bockel, Alain. 1971. *L'Administration camerounaise.* Nancy: Berger-Levrault. 62 pp.

Bonnal, Albert. 1977. "Remarques sur la planification camerounaise." *Revue francaise d'etudes politiques africaines.* August–September: 66–68.

Boulet, J. 1975. *Magoumaz: pays mafa (nord Cameroun).* (Etude d'une territoire de montagne). Paris: ORSTOM, and La Haye: Mouton. 92 pp.

Bourdon-Higbee, H. 1976. "The Besieged Media of Cameroon." *Montana Journalism Review* 19: 11–19.

Brain, Robert. 1972. *Bangwa Kinship and Marriage.* New York: Cambridge University Press. 200 pp.

Breton, Jean-Marie. 1972. "Le controle superieur de l'etat au Cameroun." *Bulletin de Institut International d'Administration Publique* (Paris) 23: 543–605.

______. 1973. "Le controle superieur de l'etat en Republique Unie du Cameroun." *Revue camerounaise de droit* (Yaounde) 4: 118–145.

______. 1979. "De le tutelle a la Republique unie: reflections sur la dynamique unitaire dans l'evolution institutionelle du Cameroun independant." *Revue juridique et politique* 33: 184–215.

Briere, Eloise. 1981. "Resistance a l'acculturation dans l'oeuvre de Mongo Beti." *Canadian Journal of African Studies* 15 (2): 181–199.
A consideration of the writings of Mongo Beti, tracing the development of "the theme of resistance to acculturation."

Buo, S.K. 1976. "How United is Cameroon?" *Africa Report* (New York) 21 (6): 17–20.

Burfisher, Mary E. 1984. "Food Import Trends in Cameroon." Prepared for the Africa and Middle East Branch, International Economics Division, U.S. Department of Agriculture.

Burnham, Philip C. 1979. "Permissive Ecology and Structural Conservatism in Gbaya Society." In *Social and Ecological Systems,* edited by P.C. Burham and R.F. Ellen, pp. 185–202. London: Academic Press.

______. 1981. *Opportunity and Constraints in a Savanna Society: The Gbaya of Meiganga, Cameroon.* New York: Academic Press. 324 pp.

Cameroon. 1972. "Constitution of the United Republic." *Official Gazette of the United Republic of Cameroon.* Supplement 12 (4): 33–42.

Cameroon Chamber of Commerce. 1965. *The Cameroon Federal Republic: 1963–64.* Douala: Cameroon Chamber of Commerce.

Cameroon, Commission Nationale du Comite Agro-Pastoral. 1981. *Comite Agro-Pastoral de Bertoua du 5 au 8 fevrier.*

Cameroon Development Bank (BCD) 1982. *Annual Report.* Yaounde: BCDO.

Cameroon, Federal Republic of. 1961. *Premier Plan Quinquennal de Developpement Economique et Social.* Yaounde: Ministry of Planning. 272 pp.

Cameroon, Ministry of Agriculture. 1980a. *Bilan diagnostic du Secteur Agricole de 1960 a 1980.* Yaounde: Ministry of Agriculture.

______. Direction des Etudes et Projets. 1980b. *Perspectives de Developpement pour l'An 2000 (Esquisses). Sous-Secteur Agriculture.* Yaounde: Ministry of Agriculture.

______. 1981. *Veme Plan Quinquennal de Developpement. Plan Semencier National: Resume: Couts d'Ensemble.* Mission FAO TCP/CMR 8.904 (1).

Cameroon, Ministry of Economic Affairs. 1981a. *Note de Synthese du Plan Alimentaire a Long Terme.* Yaounde: Ministry of Economic Affairs.

______ and Planning. 1981b. *The Fifth Five-Year Economic, Social and Cultural Development Plan 1981–1986.* Yaounde: National Printing Press.

Cameroon, Ministry of Industrial and Commercial Development. 1972. *Investor's Guide.* Yaounde: United Republic of Cameroon Printing Press.

Cameroon, Ministry of Planning and Territorial Development. 1972. *Third Five-Year Economic and Social Development 1971/72–1975/76.* Yaounde: Ministry of Planning and Territorial Development.

Cameroon National Union. 1967. *First National Council (Premier Conseil National) Held at Yaounde from the 5th to the 8th November 1967.* Yaounde: National Printing Press. 229 pp.

Cameroon National Union, Political Bureau. 1968. *As Told by Ahmadou Ahidjo.* Monaco: Paul Bory. 102 pp.

______. 1969. *First National Congress: General Policy Report* (Presentation of A. Ahidjo, National President). Geneva: CNU.

______. 1976. *Ahmadou Ahidjo from A to Z: CNU 10th Anniversary.* Yaounde: Cameroon National Union.

Cameroon, Office National de Commercialisation des Produits de Base (ONCPB). 1980. *Budget 1980/81.* Yaounde: ONCPB.

Cardoso, F.H. 1972. "Dependency and Development in Latin America." *New Left Review* 74: 83–95.

Carson, G. and Chau, Ta-Ngoc. 1981. *Disparites regionales dans le developpement de l'education: diagnostic et politiques de reductions.* Paris: UNESCO. Cameroon is one of the case studies on the subject.

Catrisse, Benoit. 1981. "Le Cameroun a l'aube du Ve plan." *Afrique Industrie Infrastructures* (March 1): 36–115.

Chaffard, Georges. 1965. *Les carnets secrets de la decolonisation. Tome I.* Paris: Editions Calmann-Levy.

Chaliand, Gerard. 1969. *Armed Struggle in Africa: With the Guerrillas in "Portuguese" Guinea.* New York: Monthly Review Press. 142 pp.
It contains an analysis of the UPC failure.

Chambliss, Mary T. 1968. *Cameroon's Agricultural Economy in Brief.* Report no. 215. Washington: USDA, Economic Research Service Foreign Report.

Champaud, Jacques. 1970. "Mom (Cameroun), ou le refus de l'agriculture de plantation." *Etudes Rurales* (Paris) 37–38: 299–311.

______. 1972. "Genese et typologie des villes du Cameroun de l'ouest." *Cahiers ORSTOM Serie Sciences Humaines* 9(3): 325–336.

Chazan, Naomi. 1978. "Political Culture and Political Socialization: A Ghanaian Case." *Review of Politics* 40: 3–31.

Christy, Ralph D. 1976. *Potentials for Cameroon's Agriculture in Economic Development.* Baton Rouge: Southern University and A & M College, Unemployment and Underdevelopment Institute. 4 pp.

Chumbow, Sammy Beban. 1980. "Language and Language Policy in Cameroon," pp. 281–311. In Kofele-Kale 1980a.

Clarke, John I. 1969. "Population Distribution and Dynamics in Cameroon." In *Geography and a Crowding World,* edited by R.M. Prothero, L. Kosinski, and W. Kelinsky, pp. 348–362. New York and London: Oxford University Press.

______. 1972. "Cameroon." In *Africa South of the Sahara 1972,* pp. 189–208. London: Europa Publications.

Clignet, Remi and Jordan F. 1971. "Urbanization and Social Differentiation in Africa: A Comparative Analysis of the Ecological Structures of Douala and Yaounde." *Cahiers d'etudes africaines* 2: 261–297.

______. 1972. "Quelques remarques sur le role des femmes africaines en milieu urbain: Le cas du Cameroun." *Canadian Journal of African Studies* 6 (2): 303–315.

______. 1975a. "The Impact of Educational Structures and Processes on National Integration in Cameroon." In *The Search for National Integration in Africa,* edited by D.R. Smock et al., pp. 139–158. New York: Free Press.

______. 1975b. "Education, emploi et succes professional au Cameroun." *Canadian Journal of African Studies* 9 (2): 193–212.

______ and Stark, M. 1974. "Modernisation and Football in Cameroon." *Journal of Modern African Studies* 12 (3): 409–421.

______. 1976. *The Africanization of the Labor Market: Educational and Occupational Segmentation in the Cameroon.* Berkeley: University of California Press. 275 pp.

An analytical survey of labor market; bargaining power of wage earners and employers; labor policies; and education in Cameroon.

______. 1977a. "Educational and Occupational Differentiation in a New Country: The Case of the Cameroon." *Economic Development and Cultural Change* 25 (4): 731–746.
The author argues that there is no relation between education and skills required in the labor market in Cameroon.

______. 1977b. "Social Change and Sexual Differentiation in the Cameroon and the Ivory Coast." *Signs* 3: 244–260.

______. 1980. "Teachers and National Values in Cameroon: An Inferential Analysis from Census Data." In *Values, Identities and National Integration,* edited by J.N. Paden, pp. 321–366. Evanston: Northwestern University Press.

Cohen, Abner. 1974. *Two-Dimensional Man: An Essay on the Anthropology of Power and Symbolism in Complex Society.* Berkeley and Los Angeles: University of California Press.

Cohen, William B. 1970. "The Colonized as Child: British and French Colonial Rule." *African Historical Studies* 3: 427–431.

Comte, Gilbert. 1973. "Treize annees d'histoire." *Revue francaise d'etudes politiques africaines* 8: 39–57.

Conway, P. and Gelb, A. 1984. "Oil Windfalls in a Controlled Economy: A 'Fix-price' Equilibrium Model of Algeria." Washington: Development Research Department, World Bank.

Cooksey, Brian. 1981. "Social Class and Academic Performance: A Cameroon Case Study." *Comparative Education Review* 25: 403–418.

______. 1982. "Education and Sexual Inequality in Cameroon." *The Journal of Modern African Studies* 20 (1): 167–177.

Courade, Georges and Courade, Christiane. 1978. "L'ecole du Cameroun anglophone: de l'ecole coloniale a l'ecole nationale." *Tiers-Monde* (October–December): 743–769.

______. 1980. "Les plantations d'Unilever au Cameroun (Plantations Pamol du Cameroun limited) ou la croissance d'une firme multinationale dans une region marginale." In *Complexes agro-industriels au Cameroun,* Paris: ORSTOM. 281 pp.

Coustou, Alain. 1971. "Transport et developpement economiques du Cameroun." *Annales de la Faculte de Droit et des Sciences Economiques de Yaounde* 2: 43–58.

Crozier, Michel. 1964. *The Bureaucratic Phenomenon.* Chicago: University of Chicago Press.

Cruise O'Brien, Donal B. 1971. *The Mourides of Senegal.* Oxford: Clarendon Press.

David, Nicholas. 1980. "History of Crops and Peoples in North Cameroon to A.D. 1900." In *West African Culture Dynamics,* edited by B.K. Swartz and R.E. Dumett, pp. 139–182. The Hague: Mouton.

______ and Voas, David. 1981. "Societal Causes of Infertility and Population Decline Among the Settled Fulani of North Cameroon." *Man* (London) 16 (4): 644–664.

Decraene, Phillipe. 1979. "Cameroon: Ahidjo's Quest for Unity." *The Guardian.* February 25, 1979, p. 12.

DeGarine, Igor. 1978. "Population, Production and Culture in the Plains Societies of the Northern Cameroon and Chad: The Anthropologist in Development Projects, Comments." *Current Anthropology* 19 (1): 37–65.

______. 1980. "Approaches to the Study of Food and Prestige in Savannah Tribes: Massa and Mussey of Northern Cameroon and Chad." *Social Science Information/Information sur les sciences sociales* (London) 19 (1): 39–78.

DeGastines, Francois. 1978. "L'enseignement des langues nationales au College Libermann de Douala." *Recherche, Pedagogie et Culture* (Paris) 6: 18–21.

DeLancey, Mark W. 1973. *Changes in Social Attitudes and Political Knowledge Among Migrants to Plantations in West Cameroon.* Ph.D. dissertation. Bloomington: Indiana University Press. 412 pp.

______. 1977. "Credit for the Common Man in Cameroon." *Journal of Modern African Studies* (June): 316–322.

______. 1978. "Institutions for the Accumulations Redistribution of Savings among Migrants." *Journal of Developing Areas* 12: 209–224.

______. 1980. "Cameroon National Food Policies and Organizations: The Green Revolution and Structural Proliferation." *Journal of African Studies* 7 (2): 109–122.

DeLancey, Virginia. 1978. "Women at the Cameroon Development Corporation: How Their Money Works." *Rural Africana* 2: 9–33.

______. 1981. "The Impact of Cameroon Agricultural Policies on the Production of Food Crops." Study prepared for USAID/Yaounde.

______. 1983. "Strategies for Maintaining Food Self-Sufficiency in Cameroon." Paper presented at the Annual Meeting of the African Studies Association, Boston.

______. 1984. "Agricultural Extension for Women in Cameroon: A Case Study." International Center for Research on Women, for the WID Office of USAID.

Delavignette, Robert. 1962. *L'Afrique noire et son destin.* Paris: Editions Gallimard.

Delpech, B. 1977. *Un essai de prospective sociale: esquisse d'une communaute pionniere par de jeunes ruraux sud camerounais.* Yaounde: Office National Recherche Science et Technologie, Institute de Science Humaines, Centre de Sciences economiques et sociales. 66 pp.

Delpey, Roger. 1981. *La manipulation.* Paris: Jacques Granchier.

Demol, Erik and Nihan, Georges. 1982. "Le secteur non structure 'modern' de Yaounde." *Revue internationale du travail* 121 (1): 79–91.

Derrick, Jonathan. 1972. "Cameroon: East Meets West." *Africa (Africa Journal Ltd.,* London) (June): 24–26.

______. 1980. "The 'Germanophone' Elite of Douala Under the French Mandate." *Journal of African History* 21 (2): 255–267.

Dervis, K., de Melo, and Robinson. 1982. *General Equilibrium Models for Development Policy.* Cambridge: Cambridge University Press.

Dillon, Richard G. 1977. "Ritual, Conflict and Meaning in an African Society." *Ethos* 5 (2): 151–173.

______. 1979. "Limits to Ritual Resolution in Meta Society." *Paideuma* 25: 35–39.

______. 1980. "Violent Conflict in Meta Society." *American Ethnologist* 7 (4): 658–673.

Direction de la Statistique. 1982. "Statistiques du commerce exterieur du Cameroun." Yaounde: Government of Cameroon.

Djeudjan, G-L. 1978. "Le role des societes dans le developpement economique de la Republique Unie du Cameroun." *Revue juridique et politique, independence et cooperation* 32 (1): 223–230.

Domar, E.D. 1946. "Capital Expansion, Rate of Growth and Employment." *Econometrica* 15: 137–147.

Dongmo, Jean-Louis. 1973. "Typologie de l'agriculture camerounaise." *Annales de la Faculte de Lettres et Sciences Humaines* (University of Yaounde) 2 (5): 19–40.

______. 1980. "L'attraction migratoire nationale des deux capitales camerounaises Douala et Yaounde." *Cahiers d'outre-mer* 33 (129): 49–64.

______. 1981. *Le Dynamisme Bamileke (Cameroun) Vol. 1: La maitrise de l'espace agraire* and *Vol. 2: La maitrise de l'espace urbaine.* Yaounde: Universite de Yaounde. 424 and 293 pp.

Dos Santos, T. 1973. "The Crisis in Development Theory and the Problem of Dependence in Latin America." In *Underdevelopment and Development,* edited by H. Bernstein, pp. 57–80. Harmondsworth (UK): Penguin.

Dsamou, Martin. 1974. "Historique et objectifs du Trans-camerounais." *Banque des Etats de l'Afrique Centrale, Etudes et Statistiques, Bulletin Mensuel* (October): 570–589.

Dumont, Rene. 1970. "The Beginnings of Intensification and Poverty in the North Cameroons." In *Types of Rural Economy,* edited by Rene Dumont, pp. 83–89. New York: Praeger.

Eckebil, Jacques-Paul. 1983. "Cameroon: Recent Examples of Areas of Priority in Research." *The Courier* 82 (November–December): 86–88.

Eckstein, Harry. 1966. *Division and Cohesion in Democracy: A Study of Norway.* Princeton: Princeton University Press.

______. 1980. *The Natural History of Congruence Theory.* Monograph Series in World Affairs 18 (2). Denver: University of Colorado.

______ and Gurr, Ted R. 1975. *Patterns of Authority: A Structural Basis for Political Inquiry.* New York: Wiley.

Economist Intelligence Unit Ltd. 1975. *Forest Industries Development in the Federal Republic of Cameroon.* London. 458 pp.

EDIAFRIC. 1971. *L'economie camerounais.* Numero special du *Bulletin de l'afrique noire.* Paris: EDIAFRIC. 230 pp.

______. 1972. *Les Plans de Developpement des pays d'Afrique noire: Mauritanie, Mali, Niger, Togo, Senegal, Cote d'Ivoire, Cameroun, Gabon.* Paris: EDIAFRIC. 325 pp.

______. 1976. *Les elites camerounaises: Qui est qui au Cameroun.* Numero special du *Bulletin de l'Afrique noire.* Paris: Ediafric, La Documentation africaine. 233 pp.

Eguchi, Paul Kazuhisa. 1980. *Fulfulde Tales of North Cameroon II.* African Language and Ethnography no. 13. Tokyo: Tokyo University of Foreign Studies, Institute for the Study of Languages and Cultures of Asia and Africa. 605 pp.

Eily, F. Etoga. 1971. *Sur les chemins du developpement: Essai d'histoire des faits economiques du Cameroun.* Yaounde: Centre d'Edition de Production de Manuels et d'auxiliaires de l'Enseignement. 521 pp.

Ejedepang-Koge, S.N. (n.d.) *Tradition and Change in Peasant Activities: A Study of the Indigenous People's Search for Cash in the South-West Province of Cameroon.* Published by the author. 328 pp.

______. 1972. "The Tradition of a People, Bakossi: A Historico-Socio-Anthropological Study of One of Cameroon's Bantu Peoples." Unpublished paper. 354 pp.

Ekaney, N. 1976. "Radio and National Development in Cameroon: A Descriptive Analysis." *Gazette* 2: 115–128.

Elongo, Lovett. 1966. "Cameroon: Unification and Beyond." *SAIS Review* 10 (3): 24–29.

Enonchong, H.N.A. 1967. *Cameroon Constitutional Law.* Yaounde: Centre d'Edtion et de Production de Manuels et d'auxiliaires de l'Enseignement.

Epale, S.J. (n.d.) "The Impact of Early English Christian Missionary Contact on Economic Growth in Cameroon 1800–1884." In *Symposium Leo Frobenius,* edited by Deutsche UNESCO-Komission, pp. 37–66. Koln: Deutsche UNESCO–Komission.

______. 1978. "The Mobilisation of Capital in a Rural Milieu: The Example of the Bakweri of the South West Province of Cameroon." *Rural Africana* (Fall): 69–88.

Essang, S.M. and Oben, D.H.E. 1975. "Labour Absorption in Large Scale Agriculture: A Case Study of the Cameroon Development Corporation Plantations." *Malayan Economic Review* 20 (2): 22–32.

Etonga, Mbu. 1980. "An Imperial Presidency: A Study of Presidential Power in Cameroon," pp. 133–157. In Kofele-Kale 1980a.

Europe outremer. 1975. *Cameroun: les perspectives des cinq prochaines annees.* Paris: Europe outremer 52 (548). 66 pp.

Eyinga, Abel. 1971. *Le pouvoir de decision au Cameroun.* Unpublished thesis, Faculte de Droit, Paris.

______. 1978a. *Introduction a la politique camerounaise.* Paris: Editions Anthropos. 365 pp.

______. 1978b. *Mandat d'arret pour cause d'elections: de la democratie au Cameroun.* Paris: Editions l'Harmattan.

Eyongetah, Tambi and Brain, Robert. 1974. *A History of Cameroon.* London: Longman. 192 pp.
A brief outline of the precolonial history of Cameroon and the impact of French and English colonization on the present conditions, written by a historian and an anthropologist.

Fao-Unrsid. 1970. "Some Old and New Basse Cooperative Experiences in Cameroon." In *Rural Cooperatives and Planned Change in Africa: Case Materials,* edited by R.J. Apthorpe, pp. 59–93. Geneva.

Faraut, Francois. 1972. "Les populations Mburu de l'Adamaoua (Cameroun)." *L'Homme* 12 (2): 141–144.

Fichier Industriel de l'Afrique Noire (Paris) 1981–1983.

Floyd, B. and Tandap, L. 1980. "Intensification of Agriculture in the Republique Unie du Cameroun." *Geography* 65 (289): 324–327.

Fonlon, Bernard. 1966. *The Task of Today.* Victoria: Cameroon Printing and Publishing Company, Ltd.

Forje, John W. 1977. *Planning for Development: Cameroon's Five-Year Development Plan.* Lund: Bokforlaget Doxa. 143 pp.
Reprint from an essay of the Department of Economic History, University of Lund, 1973.

_____. 1981. *The One and Indivisible Cameroon: Political Integration and Socio-Economic Development in a Fragmented Society.* Lund: Department of Politics, University of Lund. 191 pp.

Fouman, Akome J. 1979. "Les grandes etapes de la construction juridique au Cameroun de 1958 a 1978." *Penant* 88 (764): 188–196.

France, Secretariat d'Etat aux Affaires Etrangeres. 1970. *Actualites Cooperation: Special Dossier Cameroun.* Report no. 8. Paris: Bureau d'Information sur la Cooperation.

Frank, Andre Gunder. 1969. *Latin America: Underdevelopment or Revolution.* New York: Monthly Review Press.

Franqueville, Andre. 1972. "Les relations ville-campagne sur la route au Nord de Yaounde." *Cahiers ORSTOM, Serie Sciences Humaines* 9 (3): 337–387.

_____. 1979. "Croissance demographique et immigration a Yaounde." *Les cahiers d'outre-mer* (October–December): 231–234.

Furtado, Celso. 1970. *Economic Development of Latin America: A Survey from Colonial Times to the Cuban Revolution.* Cambridge: Cambridge University Press.

The Futures Group. (n.d.) *Cameroon: The Inter-relation of Population and Development.* Washington, D.C.: Resources for the Awareness of Population Impacts on Development (RAPID) Project-USAID. 64 pp.

_____. 1983. *Cameroon.* Washington, D.C.

Gardinier, David. 1969. *Le Cameroun.* Paris: Editions Nouveaux Horizons.

Geary, Christian. 1979. "Traditional Societies and Associations in We (North West Province, Cameroon). *Paideuma* (Wiesbaden) 25: 53–72.

Geschiere, Peter. 1975. "Traditional Elders, Colonial Chiefs and Modern Intellectuals: Leadership and Changes in the Maka Villages (South East Cameroon)." *Kroniek van Afrika* (Leiden) 2: 89–119.

_____. 1978. "The Articulation of Different Modes of Production: Old and New Inequalities in Maka (South East Cameroon)." *African Perspectives* (Leiden) 2: 45–68.

_____. 1982. *Village Communities and the State: Changing Relations Among the Maka of South East Cameroon Since the Colonial Conquest.* London: Kegan Paul International. 512 pp.

Gillis, Malcolm, et al. 1983. *Economics of Development.* New York: W.W. Norton.

Godfrey, Martin and Langdon, Steven. 1976. "Partners in Underdevelopment? The Transnationalization Thesis in a Kenyan Context." *Journal of Commonwealth and Comparative Politics* 14 (1): 42–63.

Gondidec, Pierre Francois. 1961. "Les institutions politiques de la Republique Federale du Cameroun." *Civilisations* 11 (4): 370–395.

______. 1962. "Les institutions politiques de la Republique Federale du Cameroun." *Civilisations* 12 (1): 13–26.

______. 1969. *La Republique Federale du Cameroun.* Paris: Editions Berger-Levrault. 88 pp.
An introduction to Cameroonian politics and political institutions.

Gondolo, Andre. 1979. "Evolution economique de la ville de N'Gaoundere (Cameroun)." *Les cahiers d'Outre-Mer* (April–June): 179–193.

Goode, W.J. 1963. *World Revolution and Family Patterns.* New York: The Free Press.

Green, Reginald Herbold. 1969. "The Economy of the Federal Republic of Cameroon." In *The Economies of Africa,* edited by R. Robson and D.A. Lury, pp. 236–286. London: Allen and Unwin.

Groupement interprofessionel pour l'Unite et de la Coordination des interets economiques au Cameroun (GICAM). 1984. *L'economie camerounaise: bilan de l'exercise 1982–1983.* Douala et Yaounde.

Guermann, M. 1974. "L'organisation judiciaire de la Republique Unie du Cameroun." *Revue camerounaise de droit* (Yaounde) 5: 10–14.

Guyer, Jane I. 1978. "The Food Economy and French Colonial Rule in Central Cameroon." *Journal of African History* 19 (4): 577–598.

______. 1980a. "Head Tax, Social Structure and Rural Incomes in Cameroon, 1922–1937." *Cahiers d'etudes africaines* 20 (3): 305–329. (Also Brookline, Massachusetts: African Studies Center, Boston University, working paper NS no. 3.)

______. 1980b. "Female Farming and the Evolution of Food Production Patterns Amongst the Beti of South-Central Cameroon." *Africa* 50 (4): 341–356.

______. 1981. "The Depression and the Administration in South Central Cameroon." *African Economic History* 10: 67–79.

Gwan, E.A. 1976. "Types, Processes and Policy Implications of Various Migrations in Western Cameroon." In *International Program for Population Analysis. The Dynamics of Migration,* vol. 1, edited by Washington, D.C., pp. 1–40.

Gwei, Solomon Nfor. 1975. "Education in Cameroon: Western Precolonial and Colonial Antecedents and the Development of Higher Education." Ph.D. dissertation, Department of Education, University of Michigan.

Hagen, E.E. 1962. *On the Theory of Social Change.* Homewood, Illinois: Dorsey.

Haggblade, Steve. 1978. "Africanisation from Below: The Evolution of Cameroonian Saving Societies into Western-style Banks." *Rural Africana* (Fall): 35–55.
The integration of the traditional "njangi" credit system with the chartered bank system produced saving associations for the urban societies called "urban njangi."

Harrod, H.R.F. 1948. *Toward a Dynamic Economics.* London: MacMillan.

Hata, N. 1976. "The Village Community of the Domon Society in Nord Cameroun." *Kyoto University African Studies* 10: 273–293.

Hauser, Karin. 1970. *Deutscher Kolonialherrschaft in Afrika.* Freiburg: Atlantis.

Hewitt, Adrian. 1979. "The European Development Fund as a Development Agent: Some Results of EDF Aid to Cameroon." *ODI Review* 6: 41–56.

Horner, George R. 1962. "The Bulu Response to European Economy." In *Markets in Africa,* edited by Paul Bohannan and George Dalton, pp. 170–189. Evanston: Northwestern University Press.
This essay is not included in the paperback edition of the book.

Horner, N.A. 1956. "Protestant and Roman Catholic Missions Among the Bantus of Cameroun." Ph.D. dissertation, The Hartford Seminary Foundation.

Hudson, Michael C. 1968. *The Precarious Republic: Political Modernization in Lebanon.* New York: Random House.

Hugon, Philippe. 1968. *Analyse du sous-developpement en Afrique noire, l'exemple de l'economie du Cameroun.* Paris: Presses Universitaires de France. 325 pp.
A detailed study of the economic and socioeconomic aspects of the Cameroonian case. Includes recommendations for development plans with a focus on the restraints of economic growth, the causes of disequilibrium, and a strategy for growth.

Hurault, Jean. 1962. *La structure sociale des Bamileke.* Paris and The Hague: Mouton.

______. 1970. "Essai de synthese du systeme social des Bamileke." *Africa* 40: 1–24.

Illy, Hans F., ed. 1974. *Kamerun-Strukturen und Probleme der Sozio-Okonomischen/Entwicklung.* Mainz: v. Hase and Koehler Verlag.

______. 1978. "How to Build in the Germs of Failure: Credit Cooperatives in French Cameroon." *Rural Africana* (Fall): 57–67.

Imbert, Jean. 1973. *Le Cameroun.* Paris: Presses Universitaires de France. 126 pp.

Institut d'Etude du Developpement Economique et Social. 1968. *Introduction au Cameroun 1968.* Paris: Institut d'Etude du Developpement Economiques et Social. 164 pp.
A general survey of Cameroon that contains chapters devoted to geography, history, institutions, demography, economy, health, education, and the labor force in the country.

International Bank for Reconstruction and Development. 1955. *The Economic Development of Nigeria.* Baltimore, Maryland: Johns Hopkins University Press. 686 pp.
The book includes Southern (West) Cameroons, then administered through Nigeria, and also deals with the Cameroons Development Corporation on pp. 182–191.

______. 1963. *The Economy of the Federal Republic of Cameroon.* Report prepared by G.C. Billington and M.J.W.M. Pajimans. Department of Operations, Africa. 39 pp.

______. 1980. *United Republic of Cameroon Agricultural Projects Reconnaissance Mission-Main Report.* Washington, D.C.: IBRD.

International Development Association. 1981. "Report and Recommendations of the President of the IDA to the Executive Directors." Report P-3074-CM.

International Monetary Fund. 1968. "Cameroon." In *Surveys of African Economies Vol. I: Cameroon, Central African Republic, Chad, Congo (Brazzaville) and Gabon.* pp. 54–123. Washington, D.C.: International Monetary Fund.

International Union for Child Welfare. (n.d.) Application to the Agency for International Development for an Operational Grant for the United Republic of Cameroon: Center for Training Farm Families.

Irele, Modupe. 1984. *Nigeria and Cameroun.* Lagos: Libriservice.

Isambert-Jamati, Viviane. 1965. "L'autorite dans l'education francaise." *Archives europeennes de sociologie* 6: 149–166.

Jackson, Robert H. and Rosberg, Carl G. 1982. *Personal Rule in Black Africa: Prince, Autocrat, Prophet, Tyrant.* Berkeley, Los Angeles, London: University of California Press.

Jacquot, H. 1974a. "La planification economique au Cameroun." *Revue camerounaise de droit* (Yaounde) 5: 15–30.

______. 1974b. "Les aspects institutionnels de la planification economique au Cameroun." *Institut International d'Administration Publique, Bulletin* (April–June): 295–331.

Johansen, L. 1960. *A Multi-sectoral Study of Economic Growth.* Amsterdam: North-Holland.

Johnson, W.R. 1965. "The Cameroon Federation: Political Union Between English and French-speaking Africa." In *French-speaking Africa,* edited by W.H. Lewis, pp. 205–220. New York: Walker.

______. 1970a. *The Cameroon Federation: Political Integration in a Fragmentary Society.* Princeton: Princeton University Press. 426 pp.
A description of the United Kingdom and French colonial legacies that imposed a fragmented and bilingual society on the traditional cultural patterns. The author describes the process of national integration through the organization of the unification movement. Power organization of the federation lacks a sense of political community.

______. 1970b. "The Union des Populations du Cameroun in Rebellion: The Integrative Backlash of Insurgency." In *Protest and Power in Black Africa 1886–1966,* edited by Robert T. Rotberg and Ali A. Mazrui, pp. 671–692. New York and London: Oxford University Press.
The positive features of the UPC rebellion.

Joseph, Richard A. 1974. "Ruben Um Nyobe and the 'Kamerun' Rebellion." *African Affairs* 73 (293): 428–444.

______. 1975. "National Policies in Post-War Cameroun: The Difficult Birth of the U.P.C." *Journal of African Studies* 2 (2): 201–239.
A radical national party was created in Cameroon as a reaction against French repression of independent movements.

______. 1977. *Radical Nationalism in Cameroun: Social Origins of the U.P.C. Rebellion.* Oxford: Clarendon Press. 383 pp.

______, ed. 1978. *Gaullist Africa: Cameroon under Ahmadou Ahidjo.* Eungu: Fourth Dimension Publishers.

______. 1980. "Church, State and Society in Colonial Cameroun." *The International Journal of African Historical Studies* 13 (1): 5–32.

Jouve, Edmond. 1977. "Cinq ans d'Etat unitaire." *Revue francaise d'etudes politiques africaines* (August–September): 42–65.

Kale, P.M. 1967. *Political Evolution in the Cameroons.* Buea: Government Printer.
The author presents the West Cameroon political story from the perspective of a key participant.

Kamajou, Francois and Baker, C.B. 1980. "Reforming Cameroon's Government Credit Program: Effects on Liquidity Management by Small Farm Borrowers." *American Journal of Agricultural Economics* (November): 709–718.

Kamerun National Democratic Party. 1964. *10th Annual Convention Working Papers.* Kumba: Kamerun National Democratic Party. 76 pp.

Kaptue, Leon. 1979. "L'administration coloniale et la circulation des indigenes au Cameroun: le laissez-passer, 1923–46." *Afrika Zamani* (Yaounde) 10–11: 160–184.

Kamarck, Andrew M. 1967. *The Economics of African Development.* New York: Praeger.

Kebzabo, Saleh. 1978. "Ahidjo 20 ans apres." *Demain l'Afrique* (February): 53–68.

Kendrick, Robin. 1976. *A Survey of Labor Relations in Cameroon.* Ann Arbor: University of Michigan, Center for Research on Economic Development. 19 pp.

______. 1979. "Survey of Industrial Relations in Cameroon." In *Industrial Relations in Africa,* edited by U.G. Damachi et al., pp. 73–105. New York: St. Martin's Press.

Keohane, Robert and Nye, Joseph. 1977. *Power and Independence.* Boston: Little, Brown and Company.

Kimble, David. 1963. *A Political History of Ghana: The Rise of Gold Coast Nationalism.* Oxford: Clarendon Press.

Kingue, Abel and Ntumazah, Ndeh. 1982. "La verite sur le Comite revolutionnaire." *Peuples noirs—Peuples africains* 5 (25): 12–47.
The "Comite revolutionnaire" has constantly sabotaged the UPC activities.

Kleis, Gerald W. 1980. "Confrontation and Incorporation: Igbo Ethnicity in Cameroon." *African Studies Review* 23 (2): 89–100.

Kofele-Kale, Ndiva. 1978. "Patterns of Political Orientations Toward the Nation: A Comparison of Rural-Urban Residents in Anglophone Cameroon." *Africa Social Research* (Lusaka) 26: 469–488.

______. 1980a. *An African Experiment in Nation Building: The Bilingual Cameroon Republic Since Reunification.* Boulder, Colorado: Westview Press. 369 pp.
The first chapter is devoted to the search for a Cameroonian identity and chronicles the rise and evolution of Cameroon nationalism. The second and third chapters deal with the political and economic institutions and the distribution of political power, wealth, and services of the federal state's economy. Also analyzes the Cameroon's social development and the policies of bridging gaps between French- and English-speaking areas and between rural and urban people.

______. 1980b. "The Impact of Environment on Ethnic Group Values in Cameroon." In *Values, Identities and National Integration,* edited by J.N. Paden, pp. 121–150. Evanston, Illinois: Northwestern University Press.

______. 1981a. *Tribesmen and Patriots: Political Culture in a Polyethnic African State.* Washington, D.C.: University Press of America. 359 pp.

______. 1981b. "Cameroon and Its Foreign Relations." *African Affairs* 80 (319): 197–217.
Self-reliant development and national unity are the main national interests. The dependence on France is the major obstacle to the achievement of these goals.

______. 1983. "Cameroon: Checks and Balances." *West Africa* (December): 2871–2872.

______. Forthcoming. "Class, Status, and Power in Post-Reunification Cameroon: The Rise of an Anglophone Bourgeoisie, 1961–1980." In *Studies in Power and Class in Africa,* edited by I.L. Markovitz.

Kom, David. 1971. *Le Cameroun: Essai d'analyse economique et politique.* Paris: Editions Sociales. 334 pp.

Kouo, Felix. 1979. "Les repercussions de la crise economique de 1929 au Cameroun." *Afrika Zamani* (Yaounde) 10–11: 100–131.

Kouomegni-Kontchou, Augustin. 1979. "Le droit public camerounais, instrument de construction de l'unite nationale." *Revue juridique et politique* (October–December): 415–441.

Kwast, Lloyd E. 1971. *The Discipling of West Cameroon: A Study of Baptist Growth.* Grand Rapids, Michigan: Erdmans. 205 pp.

Laburthe-Tolra, Philippe. 1981. *Les seigneurs de la foret: essai sur le passe historique l'organisation sociale et les normes ethiques des anciennes Beti du Cameroun.* Paris: Publications de la Sorbonne. 490 pp.

La Gazette (Douala). 1984. "Les dix-sept mois qui ont ebranle le Cameroun." May 29, 1984. Special issue.

Laye, Camara. 1968. *A Dream of Africa. (Dramouss)* Translated by James Kirkup. London: Collins.

Lebegue, Jean. 1967. "L'evolution economique du Cameroun." *Promotions* (Paris) 80: 57–71.

Legum, Colin, ed. 1976. *Africa Contemporary Record.* New York: Africana.

Lenglart, J. 1972. *Les zones d'actions prioritaires integrees (ZAPIS) de l'Est Cameroun.* Paris. 470 pp.

Lerner, D. 1958. *The Passing of Traditional Society.* New York: The Free Press.

Levine, Michael D. 1980. "Export Crops and Peasantization: The Bakosi of Cameroon." In *Peasants in Africa,* edited by M.A. Klein, pp. 221–241. Beverly Hills, California: Sage.

Le Vine, Victor T. 1961a. "The New Cameroon Federation." *Africa Report* VI, 2: 7, 8, 10.

______. 1961b. "Unifying the Cameroons." *West Africa* (July): 774–775.

______. 1963. "The Cameroon Federal Republic." In *Five African States,* edited by G. Carter, pp. 263–360. Ithaca, New York: Cornell University Press.

______. 1964a. "Cameroon Political Parties." In *Political Parties and National Integration in Tropical Africa,* edited by J.S. Coleman and C.G. Rosberg, pp. 132–184. Berkeley: University of California Press.

______. 1964b. *The Cameroons from Mandate to Independence.* Los Angeles: University of California Press.
A political history of preindependent Cameroon.

______. 1968. "Political Elite Recruitment and Political Structure in French-speaking Africa." *Cahiers d'etudes africaines.* 8 (3): 369–389.

______. 1970. "A Contribution to the Political History of Cameroon: The United Nations and the Politics of Decolonization—The Termination of British Cameroons Trusteeship." *Abbia* 24: 65–90.

______. 1971. *The Cameroon Federal Republic.* Ithaca, New York: Cornell University Press. 205 pp.
A general introduction to politics and government of the only case of union between French- and English-speaking countries in Africa; contemporary political organization; personalities; structures and institutions of Cameroon on federal and state levels. Background of social and economic systems is covered. The emphasis is on the cooptation policy of Ahidjo's presidency.

______ and Nye, Roger P. 1974. *Historical Dictionary of Cameroon.* Metuchen, New Jersey: Scarecrow Press. 198 pp.

______. 1975a. "Leadership Transition in Black Africa: Elite Generations and Political Succession." *Munger Africana Library Notes* 30: 1–67.

______. 1975b. "Political Integration and the United Republic of Cameroon." In *The Search for National Integration in Africa,* edited by D.R. Smock et al., pp. 270–284. New York: Free Press.

______. 1979. "Parliaments in Francophone Africa: Some Lessons from the Decolonization Process." In *Legislatures in Development,* edited by Joel Smith and Lloyd D. Musolf, pp. 125–154. Durham, North Carolina: Duke University Press.

______. 1980. "Perspectives on Contemporary Politics in Cameroon." Washington, D.C.: Department of State (unpublished paper).

______. 1983. "Cameroon: The Politics of Presidential Succession." *Africa Report* 28: 22–26.

Lewis, I.M. 1980. *A Modern History of Somalia: Nation and State in the Horn of Africa.* London and New York: Longman.

Lewis, W.A. 1955. "Is Economic Growth Desirable?" *Theory of Economic Growth.* Homewood, Illinois: Irwin.

______. 1963. "Economic Development with Unlimited Supplies of Labour." In *The Economics of Underdevelopment,* edited by A.N. Argawala and S.P. Singh, pp. 400–409. London: Oxford University Press.

______. 1966. *Politics in West Africa.* New York: Oxford University Press.

Limagne, J. 1972. "Cameroun: de l'unification a l'unite." *Revue francaise d'etudes politiques africaines* 80: 10–13.

Liniger-Goumaz, Max. 1983. *De la Guinee Equatoriale nguemiste.* Geneva: Editions du Temps.

Lippens, Philippe. 1968. "Democratie economique et democratie sociale au Cameroun." *Revue des etudes cooperatives* 151: 25–40.

______. 1973. "Les relations entre les populations et les pouvoirs publics dans la ville de Douala." *Bulletin de l'Institut International d'Administration Publique* (Paris) 27: 481–499.

Lloyd, P.C. 1966. *The New Elites of Tropical Africa.* London: Oxford University Press.

______. 1967. *Africa in Social Change.* Baltimore: Penguin.

______. 1971. *Classes, Crises and Coups.* London: MacGibbon and Company.

Lockard, Kathleen G. 1980. "Religion and Politics in Independent Uganda: Movement Toward Secularization." In *Analyzing Political Change in Africa:*

Applications of a New Multidimensional Framework, edited by James R. Scaritt, pp. 40–73. Boulder, Colorado: Westview Press.

Loginova, V.P. 1976. *United Republic of Cameroon.* Studies on Developing Countries no. 87. Budapest: Institute for World Economics of the Hungarian Academy of Sciences. 88 pp.
Cameroon enters its second decade of independence.

Mainet, Guy. 1976. "Douala, le port et la ville." *Les cahiers d'outre-mer* (January–March): 49–69.
Port activity, localization, and economy of Douala.

______. 1979a. "Le role de la femme dans l'economie urbaine a Douala." *Annales de le Faculte des Lettres et des Sciences Humaines,* 8: 187–204.

______. 1979b. "Mobilite residentielle et dynamique urbaine a Douala." *Les cahiers d'outre-mer* (April–June): 139–157.

______. 1980. "New Bell: Population, emplois et moyens d'existence." *Revue de geographie du Cameroun* 1 (1): 64–93.

Makinen, Marty. 1981. *A Benefit-Cost Analysis of Measles Vaccination in Yaounde, Cameroon.* Discussion Paper no. 96. Ann Arbor: University of Michigan, Center for Research on Economic Development. 20 pp.

Marches Tropicaux et Mediterraneens. "A Basic Economic Survey: Cameroon 1960–1980." October 29, 1976. 160 pp.

Marches Tropicaux et Mediterraneens. (MTM). Paris, 1976–1983.

Margerie, Olivier de. 1978. *Economie appliquee aux problemes de developpement du Cameroun.* Yaounde: Ecole Nationale d'Administration et de Magistrature. 152 pp.

Marguerat, Yves. 1974. "Reflexions provisoires sur la decadence des villes secondaires au Cameroun." In *Kamerun—Strukturen und Probleme der Sozio-Okonomischen Entwicklung,* edited by H.F. Illy, pp. 131–136. Mainz: v. Hase & Koehler Verlag.

Markovitz, Irving L. 1977. *Power and Class in Africa.* Englewood Cliffs, New Jersey: Prentice-Hall.

Marticou, H. 1973. "Les freins a la penetration du progres technique dans l'agriculture camerounaise." *L'agronomie tropicale* (May): 518–536.

Martin, Jean-Yves. 1975. "Inegalites regionales et inegalites sociales: l'enseignement secondaire au Cameroun septentrional." *Revue francaise de sociologie* 16 (3): 317–334.
Empirical research conducted in northern high schools of Cameroon.

______. 1980a. "Social Differentiation and Regional Disparities: In Educational Development in Cameroon." In *Regional Disparities in Educational Development: Diagnosis and Policies for Reduction,* pp. 21–113. Paris: UNESCO, International Institute for Educational Planning.

______. 1980b. "Unequal Access to School Education in Northern Cameroon." *African Environment* 14–16: 61–88.

Mawhood, Philip. 1971. "Rural Local Government in Tropical Africa: Examples from Tanzania and Cameroon." *Cahiers de l'administration africaine/African Administrative Studies* (Tangier) 6: 109–124.

Mbarga, Emile. 1973. "Evolution politique du Cameroun en 1972: le referendum du 20 mai 1972 et la formation de la Republique Unie du Cameroun." *Revue juridique et politique, independence et cooperation* 27 (3): 363–394.

______. 1982. *Les institutions politiques du Cameroun.* Yaounde: Imprimerie Nationale. 210 pp.

Mbome, Francois. 1978. "Les empechments du president de la Republique du Cameroun." *Revue francaise d'etudes politiques africaines* 152–153: 50–58.

______. 1981. "Reflexions sur le reforme constitutionnelle du 9 juin 1979 au Cameroun." *Penant* 773 (July–September): 34–47.
Procedures to be applied in case of vacancy in the presidency.

McClelland, D.C. 1964. "A Psychological Approach to Economic Development and Cultural Change." *Economic Development and Cultural Change* 12: 320–324.

McCulloch, Merran; Littlewood, Margaret; and Dugast, I. 1954. *Peoples of the Central Cameroons.* London: International African Institute. 174 pp.
An important survey ande compilation of research on Tikar, Bamum, Bamileke, Banur, Bafia, and Bolom ethnic groups of Cameroon.

Medard, Jean-Francois. 1979. "L'etat sous-developpe au Cameroun." *Foi et vie* (December): 56–109.
The state of Cameroon is underdeveloped even if it is effectively strong. In reality, it is weak because, according to the author, it lacks "social discipline," which is rooted in patrimonialism.

______. 1982. "La regulation socio-politique." In *Etat et bourgeoisie en Cote d'Ivoire,* edited by Y.-A. Faure and J.-F. Medard, pp. 61–88. Paris: Karthala.

Meillassoux, Claude. 1973. "The Social Organization of the Peasantry: The Economic Basis of Kinship." *Journal of Peasant Studies* 1: 81–90.

______. 1981. *Maidens, Meal, and Money: Capitalism and the Domestic Community.* Cambridge: Cambridge University Press.

Meisel, James H. 1982. *The Myth of the Ruling Class: Gaetano Mosca and the "Elite."* Ann Arbor: University of Michigan Press.

Melone, S. 1972. *La parente et la terre dans la strategie du developpement (l'experience camerounaise: etude critique).* Paris: Klincksieck, and Yaounde: Universite Federal du Cameroun. 201 pp.

Merton, Robert K. 1973. *The Sociology of Science.* Chicago: University of Chicago Press.

Metuge, S.E. 1976. *An Input-Output Study of the Structure and Resource Use in the Cameroon Economy.* Lund: University of Lund, Department of Economy. 184 pp.

Michelini, Philip. 1980. *Marketing in Cameroon.* Washington, D.C.: U.S. Department of Commerce, International Trade Administration, OBR 80-26. 33 pp. Foreign trade outlook for Cameroon.

Ministere de l'Economie et du Plan, April 1981. "Rapport d'execution des quatre premieres annees du quatrieme Plan." Direction de la Planification, Yaounde.

Ministry of Industrial and Commercial Development. 1972. *Investor's Guide.* Yaounde: United Republic of Cameroon Printing Press.

Mohammadou, Eldridge, ed. 1979. *Ray on Rey-Bouba: Tradition transmise par Alhadji Hamadjoda Abdoullaye. Traditions historiques des Foulbe de l'Ad*amawa (Les Villages de la Benoue.) Garoua: Musee Dynamique du Nord Cameroun. Paris: CNRS, 348 pp.

Mongory, J. 1976. "Genese et contradictions du syndicalisme camerounais." *Revue francaise d'etudes politiques africaines* 11 (132): 74–89; 12 (133): 56–83; 12 (134): 90–118.

Morel, Yves. 1978. *Tableaux de l'economie du Cameroun.* Douala: College Libermann. 232 pp.

Mortimer, Edward. 1969. *France and the Africans 1944–1960.* London: Faber and Faber.

Mosima, Fritz M. 1979. "The Social and Economic Impact of the Cameroon Plantations." *Annales de la Faculte des Lettres et Sciences Humaines* 217–230.

Mveng, Englebert. 1963. *Histoire du Cameroun.* Paris: Presence africaine. 533 pp.
A long and analytical collection of sources for a Cameroonian historiography up to the independence of Cameroon, discussed in a sociological manner.

_____ and Beling-Nkoumba, D. 1974. *Manuel d'histoire du Cameroun.* Yaounde: Centre Edu. et Prod. Man. et auxiliares de l'enseignement. 284 pp.
A text for primary and secondary school use. It is divided into 50 lessons.

Mvodo, V. Ayissi and Faou, R. Le. 1973. "Influence of International Labour Standards on the Legislation of Cameroon." *International Labor Review* 108: 163–185.

Mvodo Nyina, Barthelemy. 1976. "L'enseignement dans la politique coloniale francaise au Cameroun de 1916 a 1938." *Etudes d'histoire africaine* (Lubumbashi) 8: 199–213.

Nassara, P. 1975. "Aspects de la domination politique au Cameroun." *Revue francaise d'etudes politiques africaines* (May): 88–112.

Naweri, Joseph Komla. 1983. "The Beginnings of Freedom." *West Africa.* November 7, 1983.

Ndi, J.B. 1978. "Repression contre le mouvement etudiant camerounais: l'interdiction de l'Union Nationale des Etudiants du Kamerun (UNEK) en France." *Peuples noirs—Peuples africains* 1 (2): 167–172.

Ndongko, Wilfred A. 1974a. "Regional Economic Planning in Cameroon." *Intereconomics, Monthly Review of International Trade and Development* (May): 154–157.

______. 1974b. *Regional Economic Planning in Cameroon.* Uppsala: Scandinavian Institute of African Studies.

______. 1974c. "A Comparative Analysis of French and British Investment Policies in Cameroon." *Pan African Journal* (New York) 8 (1).

______. 1975a. *Planning for Economic Development in a Federal State: The Case of Cameroon 1960–1971.* Munchen: Weltforum Verlag. 214 pp.

______. 1975b. "Revenue Allocation in Cameroon Under the Federal System." *Ikenga* (Noukka) 3 (1–2): 18–27.

______. 1976a. "The External Trade Pattern of Cameroon: 1957–72." *Africa Quarterly* (New Delhi) 16 (1): 76–87.

______. 1976b. "The Economic Implication of Multimembership in Regional Groupings: The Case of Cameroon and Nigeria." *Afrika Spectrum* 11 (3): 319–323.

______. 1977. "The Financing of Economic Development in Cameroon." *Africa Development* (Dakar) 2 (3): 59–76.

______. 1979. "Financing Economic Development: The Cameroon Experience." *Quarterly Journal of Administration* (Ife) 14 (1): 29–53.

______. 1980. "The Political Economy of Regional Economic Development in Cameroon." In *An African Experiment in Nation Building: The Bilingual Cameroon Republic Since Reunification,* edited by Ndiva Kofele-Kale, pp. 227–250. Boulder, Colorado: Westview Press.

Nelson, Harold D. 1974. *Area Handbook for the United Republic of Cameroon.* Washington, D.C.: U.S. Department of the Army, American University, Foreign Areas Studies Division. 335 pp.
An exhaustive introduction to history, social structure, ethnic composition, political development, and security issues of Cameroon.

Ngayap, Pierre Flambeau. 1983. *Cameroun: Qui governe? De Ahidjo a Biya, l'heritage et l'enjeu.* Paris: l'Harmattan. 352 pp.

Nicod, M. 1983. "Prospects for Oil and Gas Production and Reserves through 1990 in the United Republic of Cameroon." Geneva: Petroconsultants, S.A.

Njiawue, Nicanor. 1972. "Some Lessons from the History of The Cameroonian Revolution." *PanAfricanist* (Evanston) 4: 1–16.

Njoya, A.N. *Le Cameroun dans les relations internationales.* Paris: Librairie general de Droit et de Jurisprudence. 414 pp.

Nkuete, Jean. 1980. *Monnaie et finances comme moteur de developpement: le cas du Cameroun.* Yaounde: CLE. 263 pp.

Nkwi, Paul Nchoji. 1976. *Traditional Government and Social Change: A Study of the Political Institutions Among the Kour of the Cameroon Grassfields.* Fribourg: University Press. 233 pp.

_____. 1977. *Grassfield Kings and Chiefs and Modern Politics.* Yaounde: Office National Recherche Science et Technologie, Institute de Sciences Humaines, Centre de Sciences economiques et sociales. 27 pp.

_____. 1979a. "Cameroon Grassfield Chiefs and Modern Politics." *Paideuma* (Wiesbaden) 25: 99–115.

_____. 1979b. *Zapi de l'Est: a Socio-Economic Analysis (Zones d'actions prioritaires integres).* Yaounde: Department of Sociology, University of Yaounde. 368 pp.

_____ and Warnier, Jean Pierre. 1982. *Elements for a History of the Western Grassfields.* Yaounde: Department of Sociology, University of Yaounde. 236 pp.
The precolonial history of the western grassfields region in Cameroon, especially in the nineteenth century. Trade and political organization patterns with specific analysis.

Nwabuzor, Elone. "Ethnic Value Distance in Cameroon." In *Values, Identities and National Integration,* edited by J.N. Paden, pp. 205–229. Evanston, Illinois: Northwestern University Press.

Nurske, Ragnar. 1958. *Problems of Capital Formation in Underdeveloped Countries.* Oxford: Basil Blackwell.

_____. 1976. "The Case for Balanced Growth." In *Leading Issues in Economic Development,* edited by G.M. Meier, pp. 640–643. New York: Oxford University Press.

Nwosu, H.N. 1976. "The Concepts of Nationalism and Right to Self-Determination: Cameroon as a Case Study." *African Quarterly* (New Delhi) 16 (2): 1–26.

Nzouankeu, Jacques M. 1968. *La pensee politique d'Ahmadou Ahidjo.* Monte Carlo: Paul Bory. 100 pp.

_____. 1969. "Remarques sur la constitution camerounaise." *Civilizations* (Brussels) 19 (2): 216–225.

Ofoegbu, Mazi Rae. 1978. "The Chad Basin Commission." In *Nigeria and the World,* pp. 82–95. Edited by A.B. Akinyemi. Ibadan: Oxford University Press.

Onambele, Xavier. 1970. "Les problemes de la distribution cooperative au Cameroun." *Revue des etudes cooperatives* 49 (162): 383–389.

ONAREST. (n.d.) "Le Nord-Cameroun. Bilan de dix annees de recherches." No. 16, Vol. I and II. Travaux et documents de l'I.S.H., Yaounde.

Organization Camerounaise de Lutte pour la Democratie. 1982. *Dossier noir du petrole camerounais.* Paris: 70 pp.

Organization for Economic Cooperation and Development (OECD), Business and Industry Advisory Committee. 1966. *Rapport sur les investissements prives dans l'economie du Cameroun. Conclusions et recommendations du BIAC sur l'encouragement de investissements prives au Cameroun.* Paris: OECD. 104 pp.

______. 1984. *Geographical Distribution of Financial Flows to Developing Countries.* Paris: OECD.

O'Sullivan, John. 1972. "Union des Populations du Cameroun (U.P.C.): A Study in Mass Mobilization." *Ufahamu* (Los Angeles) (Spring): 53–71.
The liberation struggle waged by UPC. It is an excellent case study of successful African mobilization.

Osuntokun, J. 1977. "Great Britain and the Final Partition of the Cameroons 1916–1922." *Afrika Zamani* (Yaounde) (December): 53–71.

Oumarou, Aminou (presente par). (n.d.) "IIIeme congres ordinaire de l'UNC, Befoussam 1980: rapport d'activites du Secretariat a l'organization." Photocopied. 25 pp.

Owona, Adalbert. 1969. "A l'aube du nationalisme camerounais: le curieuse figure de Vincent Ganty." *Revue francaise d'histoire d'outre-mer* 56 (204): 199–235.

______. 1979. "Les debuts de l'experience communale au Cameroun d'expression francaise." *Annales de la Faculte de Lettres et des Sciences Humaines* 9: 239–243.

Owona, Joseph. 1973. "Le nouvelle constitution camerounaise du 20 mai 1972: de l'Etat federal a l'Etat unitaire." *Revue juridique et politique* 27 (1): 3–39.

______. 1975a. "L'institutionalisation de la legalite d'exception dans le droit public camerounais." *Revue juridique et politique* (January–March): 3–49.

______. 1975b. "La reforme politique et constitutionelle de la Republique Unie du Cameroun." *Revue juridique et politique, independance et cooperation* 29 (4): 486–510.

______. 1983. "La querelle de l'etat et du parti." In *Le Renouveau camerounais: certitudes et defis,* edited by Un Groupe de citoyens. Yaounde: Editions ESSTI, University of Yaounde.

Oyono, Dieudonne. 1983. "Introduction a la politique africaine du Cameroun." *Le mois en Afrique* 18 (207–208): 21–30.
The autonomy implemented since 1973 with the withdrawal from the Franco-African summits is undermined by the reliance on the franc-area economy. Presents efforts to coordinate independence and cooperation.

Pabum, Anthony S. 1976. "Engel's Law: The Case of Cameroon, West Africa." Baton Rouge: Unemployment and Underemployment Institute. 12 pp.

Paden, John N. 1973. *Religion and Political Culture in Kano.* Berkeley and Los Angeles: University of California Press.

Peter, Jean E. 1971a. "Situation et perspective du Cameroun dans le cadre du plan quinquennal." *Revue juridique et politiques* 25 (2): 211–246.

______. 1971b. "Bilan et perspectives de l'industrie camerounaise en 1970." *Revue juridique et politique* 25 (1): 211–246.

Philombe, Rene. *Le livre camerounais et ses Auteurs: Une contribution a l'histoire litteraire du Cameroun avec notice biobibliographique.* Yaounde: Editions Semences africaines. 304 pp.

Platon, Pierre. 1980. "Le marche camerounais 1980." *Marches tropicaux et mediterraneens* (November): 1717–1938.
An economic survey of Cameroon.

Podlewski, Andre. 1975. "Cameroun." In *Population Growth and Socio-Economic Change in West Africa,* edited by John Caldwell et al., pp. 543–564. New York: Columbia University Press.

Population Reference Bureau. 1984. *1983 World Population Data Sheet.*

Prebisch, R. 1950. *The Economic Development of Latin America and Its Principal Problems.* New York: United Nations.

Price, Robert. 1974. "Politics and Culture in Contemporary Ghana: The Big-Man Small-Boy Syndrome." *Journal of African Studies* 1: 173–204.

Prouzet, Michel. 1974. *Le Cameroun.* Paris: Librairie Generale de Droit et de Jurisprudence. 377 pp.

Quinn, Frederick. 1980a. "Charles Atangana of Yaounde." *Journal of African History* 21 (4): 485–495.

______. 1980b. "Beti Society in the Nineteenth Century. *Africa* (London) 50 (3): 293–304.

Remy, G. 1972. "De la montagne a la plaine: aspects, et problemes d'un mouvement de colonisation au Nord-Cameroun." *Cahiers d'etudes africaines* 12–13 (47): 500–511.

Renard, J.J. 1981. "L'industrie du papier dans les pays en voie de developpement." *Industrie et Travaux d'Outre Mer,* pp. 508–518.

______. 1983. "La Cellucam apres deux annees de fonctionnement." *Industrie et Travaux d'Outre Mer,* 344–345.

Robert, Jacques-Henri. 1980. *Le droit des societes commerciales de l'ex-Cameroun oriental.* Yaounde: CLE. 187 pp.

Rosenstein-Rodan, Paul. 1943. "Problems of Industrialization of South and Eastern Europe." *Economic Journal* 53: 205–211.

Rostow, W.W. 1960. *The Stages of Economic Growth: A Non-Communist Manifesto.* Cambridge: Cambridge University Press.

______. 1963. *The Economics of Take-Off into Sustained Growth.* London: MacMillan.

Rubin, Neville N. 1971. *Cameroun: An African Federation.* New York: Praeger, and London: Pall Mall. 259 pp.
A political economy approach to Cameroon's underdevelopment and colonial history that led to the federation.

Rudin, Harry R. 1938. *Germans in Cameroon, 1884–1914.* New Haven: Yale University Press.

Sabean, David Warren. 1983. "The History of the Family in Africa and Europe: Some Comparative Perspectives." *Journal of African History* 24: 163–171.

Sahlins, Marshall D. 1977. "Poor Man, Rich Man, Big-Man, Chief: Political Types in Melanesia and Polynesia." In *Friends, Followers, and Factions,* edited by Steffen W. Schmidt et al., pp. 220–231. Berkeley, Los Angeles, London: University of California Press.

Scalabre, Camille. 1977. "Notes sur l'Islam, le Christianisme et l'Animisme au Cameroun." *Revue francaise d'etudes politiques africaines* (August–September): 69–92.

Schamp, E. 1978. *Industrialisierung in Aquatorialafrika.* Munchen: Weltforum.

Schaetzen, Yves de. 1982. "La place du secteur prive dans l'industrie camerounaise." *Afrique industrie* 13 (266): 44–73.

Schatz, Sayre P. 1977. *Nigerian Capitalism.* Berkeley: University of California Press.

Schatzberg, Michael G. 1979. "Conflict and Culture in African Education: Authority Patterns in a Cameroonian Lycee." *Comparative Education Review* 23 (1): 52–65.
The coexistence of different cultures causes administrative problems in Cameroon's high schools.

______. 1985. *Politics and State in Zaire: The Mechanics of Coercion in Lisala.* Unpublished manuscript.

Schissel, Howard. 1983. "Cameroon's Economy: Myth or Reality." *West Africa* (September 12): 2107–2108.

Schonfeld, William R. 1976. *Obedience and Revolt: The French Behavior toward Authority.* Beverley Hills, California and London: Sage.

Schultz, Theodore W. 1961. "Investment in Human Capital." *American Economic Review* 51: 1–17.

Sennett, Richard. 1980. *Authority.* New York: Vintage Books.

Shaw, Timothy M. and Grieve, Malcolm J. 1977a. "Dependence or Development: A Review Article on International and Internal Inequalities in Africa." *Development and Change* 8: 377–408.

______. 1977b. "Inequalities and the State in Africa." *Review of Black Political Economy* 8: 24–42.

Shaw, Timothy M. and Aluko, Olajide, eds. 1984. *The Political Economy of African Foreign Policy: Comparative Perspectives.* New York: St. Martins.

Sissom, Andrew B. and Ahlers, Theodore H. June 1981. "The Socio-Economic Impact of SEMRY I: Economic Aspects." Research Report No. 1. Yaounde: Centre de Recherches Economiques et Demographiques.

Sklar, Richard L. 1963. *Nigerian Political Parties: Power in an Emergent African Nation.* Princeton: Princeton University Press.

______. 1975. *Corporate Power in an African State: The Political Impact of Multinational Mining Companies in Zambia.* Berkeley and Los Angeles: University of California Press.

Slageren, Jaap Van. 1969. *Histoire de l'Eglise Afrique (Cameroun).* Yaounde: Editions CLE. 149 pp.
A history of Christian churches in Africa with a special section on Cameroon. This is a text for school use.

Sobgui, Gabriel Alexis. 1976. *Planification economique et Projections spatiales au Cameroun.* Paris: Nouvelles Editions Debresse. 225 pp.

Societe Nationale d'Investissement (SNI). 1979. "Rapport d'activite de l'exercice 1977—1978." Yaounde: Government of Cameroon.

______. 1981. "Rapport d'activite de exercice 1979–1980." Yaounde: Government of Cameroon.

______. 1983. "Societe nationale de Raffinage (SONARA), Fiche No. 10.0.A." Yaounde: Government of Cameroon.

Soen, D. and Comarmond, P. 1971. "Savings Associations Among the Bamileke: Traditional and modern Co-operation in South West Cameroon." *Journal de la societe des africanistes* (Paris) 41 (2): 189–201.

Soyinka, Wole. 1973. *Collected Plays I.* London: Oxford University Press.

Stanford Research Institute. 1964. (Project directed by F.L. Turner). *The Economic Potential of West Cameroon. Priorities for Development.* Menlo Park: Stanford Research Institute. 7 volumes.

Stark, Frank M. 1976. "Federalism in Cameroon: The Shadow and the Reality." *Canadian Journal of African Studies* 10 (3): 423–443. Also In *An African Experiment in Nation Building,* edited by Ndiva Kofele-Kale, pp. 101–132. Boulder, Colorado: Westview Press, 1980.

______. 1980. "Persuasion and Power in Cameroon." *Canadian Journal of African Studies,* 14 (2): 273–293.

Stoecker, Helmuth. 1960 and 1968. *Kamerun unter Deutscher Kolonialherrschaft.* Berlin: Rutten and Loening and Berlin: Deutscher Verlag.

Sunkel, Osvaldo. 1969. "National Development Policy and External Dependence in Latin America." *Journal of Development Studies* 6: 23–48.

_____ and Fuenzalida, Edmundo. 1974. "Transnationalization, National Disintegration and Reintegration in Contemporary Capitalism." IDS Working Paper No. 18. Brighton: Institute for Development Studies.

Sween, Joyce and Clignet, Remi. 1974. "Urban Unemployment as a Determinant of Political Unrest: The Case Study of Douala, Cameroon." In *Kamerun—Strukturen und Probleme der Sozio-Okonomischen Entwicklung,* edited by H.F. Illy, pp. 145–172. Mainz: v. Hase & Koehler Verlag.

Tardits, Claude. 1973. "Parente et pouvoir politique chez les Bamoum (Cameroun)." *L'Homme* (Paris) 13 (1–2): 37–49.

_____. 1979. "L'organisation politique traditionnelle du Royaume Bamoum (Cameroun)." *Paideuma* (Wiesbaden) 25: 73–87.

_____. 1980. *Le royaume Bamoum.* Paris: Colin. 1078 pp.

Taylor, L.E. et al. 1980. *Models of Growth and Distribution for Brazil.* London: Oxford University Press.

Tchala, Abina. 1982. "The State, the Bureaucracy and Farmers in Rural Development: A Case-Study of the Social Relations of Production in Selected Development Corporations." Ph.D. Thesis. Ithaca, New York: Cornell University.

Thijs, M. and Willame, J.C. 1983. "Transferts de technologies et Industrialisation au Cameroun." Bruxelles: Centre d'Etude et de Documentation Africaines (CEDAF).

Tixier, Gilbert. 1973. "Etude comparee des politiques economiques du Cameroun et de la Cote d'Ivoire." *Revue juridique et politique* 27 (1): 91–178.

Toure, A. 1982. "Paysans et fonctionnaires devant la culture et l'etat." In *Etat et bourgeoisie en Cote d'Ivoire,* edited by Y.-A. Faure and J.-F. Medard, pp. 231–251. Paris: Karthala.

Traxler, E.E. 1982. "French Relations with Francophone Africa." Ph.D. dissertation, University of South Carolina.

Trepanier, Ginette. 1970. "La paysanne camerounaise entre I emancipation et l'alienation." *Canadian Journal of African Studies* 4 (3): 321–332.

Tunteng, P-Kiven. 1976. "External Influences and Subimperialism in Francophone West Africa." In *The Political Economy of Contemporary Africa,* pp. 212–231. Edited by Peter C.W. Gutkind and Immanuel Wallerstein. Beverly Hills and London: Sage.

UNCTAD/GATT, International Trade Center. 1969. *Cameroon—The Market for Selected Manufactured Products from Developing Countries.* ITC/MR/2/101/F. Geneva. 128 pp.

Cameroon's foreign trade, government economic policies, and market information. It contains a list of major businesses in the country.

Union des Populations du Cameroun. 1960. *La Revolution Camerounaise: ses objectifs, sa signification et ses repercussions dans le continent africain.* Cairo: Union des Populations du Cameroun. 80 pp.

______. 1971. *L'U.P.C. parle. . . .* Paris: Maspero. 116 pp.

United Nations, Food and Agriculture Organization. 1982. *1981 FAO Production Yearbook.* Vol. 35. Rome: Food and Agriculture Organization.

______. 1983. *1982 FAO Production Yearbook. Vol. 36. Rome: Food and Agriculture Organization.*

United Nations Institute for Training and Research. 1971. *The Brain Drain from Five Developing Countries: Cameroon, Columbia, Lebanon, Philippines and Trinidad and Tobago.* New York: United Nations Institute for Training and Research (UNITAR): 173 pp.

United Nations, Statistical Office. 1962–1981. *Yearbook of International Trade Statistics.* New York: United Nations Statistical Office.

United States, Agency for International Development. 1981. "CDSS Substitute." Yaounde: U.S. Agency for International Development.

______. 1982. *Country Development Strategy Statement FY1984, Cameroon.* Washington, D.C.: U.S. Agency for International Development (USAID).

United States, Department of Agriculture. (n.d.) Data bank figures for Cameroon.

United States, State Department. 1981. *Country Reports on Human Rights Practices.* Washington, D.C.: U.S. Government Printing Office.

Vansina, Jan. 1980. "Lignage, ideologie et histoire en Afrique equatoriale." *Enquetes et documents d'histoire africaine* 4: 133–155.

______. 1982. "Mwasi's Trials." *Daedalus* 111:49–70.

______. 1983. "The Peoples of the Forest." In *History of Central Africa, I,* edited by David Birmingham and Phyllis M. Martin, pp. 75–117. London and New York: Longman.

Vaughan, James H., Jr. 1964. "Culture, History and Grass-Roots Politics in a Northern Cameroons Kingdom." *American Anthropologist* 66 (5): 1078–1095.
The formation of political parties and voting behavior in northern Cameroon.

Vaughn, Megan. 1983. "Which Family? Problems in the Reconstruction of the History of the Family as an Economic and Cultural Unit." *Journal of African History* 24: 275–283.

Vernon-Jackson, H.O.H. 1967. *Language, Schools and Government in Cameroon.* New York: Teachers College Press.

Vincent, Jeanne-Francoise. 1972. "Donnees sur le mariage et la situation de la femme Mofu (massif de duvanger et de Wasan, Cameroun du Nord)." *Cahiers ORSTOM Serie Sciences Humaines* 9 (3): 309–324.

______. 1979. "Place et pouvoir de la femme dans les montagnes Mofu (Nord Cameroon)." *Cahiers d'Etudes africaines* (Paris) 19 (1–4): 225–251.

Walker, Sheila S. 1980. "From Cattle Camp to City: Changing Roles of Fulbe Women in Northern Cameroon." *Journal of African Studies* (Spring): 54–63. The modernized women living in town consider those living in nomadic-pastoralist areas as the true representatives of the Peul people.

Warnier, Jean-Pierre. 1979. "La polarite culture–nature entre le chef et Takangos a Mankon." *Paideuma* (Wiesbaden) 25: 21–33.

Weekes-Vagliani, Winifred et al. 1976. *Family Life and Structure in Southern Cameroon.* Paris: Organization for Economic Cooperation and Development (OECD). 88 pp.

Weinreich, U. 1953. *Languages in Contact: Findings and Problems.* The Hague: Mouton.

Weinstein, Brian. 1966. *Gabon: Nation-Building on the Ogooue.* Cambridge: MIT Press.

Weladji, C. 1974. "The Cameroon–Nigeria Border." *Abbia* (Yaounde) 27–28: 152–172.

Welch, Claude E. Jr. 1966. *Dream of Unity.* Ithaca: Cornell University Press.

World Bank. 1980a. "The United Republic of Cameroon. Economic Memorandum." No. 2877-CM. Washington, D.C.: World Bank.

______. 1980b. "Cameroon: Energy Issues and Options." Unpublished paper. Washington, D.C.: World Bank.

______. 1980c. *United Republic of Cameroon Agricultural Projects Reconnaissance Mission. Main Report.* Washington, D.C.: World Bank.

______. 1981. *Accelerated Development in Sub-Saharan Africa: An Agenda for Action.* Washington, D.C.: World Bank.

______. 1983. *World Development Report 1983.* New York: Oxford University Press for the World Bank.

______. 1984. *World Development Report 1984.* New York: Oxford University Press for the World Bank.

Young, Crawford. 1976. *The Politics of Cultural Pluralism.* Madison: University of Wisconsin Press.

______. 1982. *Ideology and Development in Africa.* New Haven: Yale University Press.

Zachariah, Kunniparampil Curien and Julien, Conde. 1981. *Migration in West Africa: Demographic Aspects.* New York: Oxford University Press for the World Bank. 130 pp.

Zartman, I.W., ed. 1976. "Europe and Africa: Decolonization and Dependency." *Foreign Affairs* 54: (January): 325–343.

______, ed. 1983. *The Political Economy of Nigeria.* New York: Praeger.

______. 1984. *"Africa and the West: The French Connection." In African Security Issues,* edited by Bruce Arlinghaus, pp. 39–58. Boulder, Colorado: Westview Press.

______ and Christopher Delgado, eds., 1984. *The Political Economy of Ivory Coast.* New York: Praeger.

Zolberg, Aristide. 1969. *One-party Government in the Ivory Coast* (revised edition). Princeton: Princeton University Press.

Index

Index

About the Editors and Contributors

About the Editors and Contributors

MICHAEL G. SCHATZBERG is Associate Professor of Comparative Politics and African Studies at The Johns Hopkins School of Advanced International Studies. He received his doctorate in political science from the University of Wisconsin at Madison. He is author of *Politics and Class in Zaire* and editor of *The Political Economy of Zimbabwe* in the Series of SAIS Studies on Africa. His articles on various aspects of African politics and society have appeared in numerous scholarly journals and edited volumes. He is a recipient of a National Endowment for the Humanities grant to study patterns of authority and governance in Kenya.

I. WILLIAM ZARTMAN is Professor of International Politics and Director of the African Studies Program at The Johns Hopkins School of Advanced International Studies in Washington, D.C. He is the author of *International Relations in the New Africa, The Politics of Trade Negotiations between Africa and the European Communities, Ripe for Resolution: Conflict and Intervention in Africa* (for the Africa Project of the Council on Foreign Relations), and co-author of *Africa and the United States* and *Africa in the 1980s.* Dr. Zartman is also editor of the series of SAIS African Studies published by Praeger, including *The Political Economy of the Ivory Coast, The Political Economy of Nigeria, The Political Economy of Morocco,* and *The OAU After Twenty Years.* He received his M.A. from The Johns Hopkins University and his Ph.D. from Yale University.

NANCY C. BENJAMIN is a doctoral student in the Economics Department at the University of California at Berkeley. From 1982 to 1984, she was a Researcher in the West Africa Department of the World Bank, developing a social accounting matrix and computable general equilibrium model of Cameroon. She has worked on other World Bank projects in sub-Saharan Africa and was a summer intern in the United States Treasury Department. Ms. Benjamin received her B.A. and M.A. degrees in economics from the University of California at Berkeley.

MARK W. DELANCEY is a Professor in the Department of Government and International Studies at the University of South Carolina. He obtained his M.A. and Ph.D. in Political Science and African Studies at Indiana University. He has spent some eight years in Nigeria, Cameroon, and Somalia teaching and conducting research. His fields of interest include international relations, rural development, cooperatives and credit unions, and agricultural policy. Dr. Delancey is author of a forthcoming book on Cameroonian political economy and several essays on Cameroonian rural development, Nigerian foreign policy, and the international relations of South Africa.

VIRGINIA DELANCEY is a Research Associate with the Institute of International Studies, University of South Carolina. She received her M.B.A. from Indiana University and her Ph.D. from the University of South Carolina. Dr. Delancey, who specializes in population, agricultural, and private enterprise issues, has spent five years in Cameroon, completing her doctorate and teaching at the University of Yaounde. She has conducted research in Africa under the auspices of the World Bank, which recently published her book *Consequences of High Fertility and Close Child-Spacing in Africa,* and with grants from Fulbright, Social Science Research Council, and UNESCO. She is completing work on a report "Women and Agriculture: An Extension for Third World Women."

SHANTAYANAN DEVARAJAN is an economist at the Development Research Department of the World Bank. He is on leave from the John F. Kennedy School of Government at Harvard University, where he is an Associate Professor of Public Policy. Mr. Devarajan received his A.B. degree in mathematics from Princeton University and his M.A. and Ph.D. degrees in economics from the University of California at Berkeley. His research is in the areas of natural resource economics, project evaluation, and economy-wide models of developing countries. Since 1975, Mr. Devarajan has been a consultant to the World Bank on projects in Malaysia, Cyprus, Cameroon, and Hungary.

NDIVA KOFELE-KALE received his Ph.D. and J.D. from Northwestern University. He is presently Director of International Studies and Professor of Political Science at Governors State University in Illinois. He is the author of *Comparative Political Culture & Socialization, An African Experiment in Nation-Building: The Bilingual Cameroon Republic Since Reunification,* and *Tribesmen and Patriots: Political Culture in a Polyethnic African State.*

VICTOR T. LE VINE is Professor of Political Science at Washington University in St. Louis. He received his Ph.D. from the University of California at Los Angeles. Dr. Le Vine has been a student of Cameroonian politics since 1959 and has authored three books on Cameroon: *The Cameroons from Mandate to Independence, The Cameroon Federal Republic,* and *Historical Dictionary of Cameroon,* with Roger Nye. Dr. Le Vine is currently working on a study of the political economy of oil in three Central African countries.

WILFRED A. NDONGKO is Professor and Director at the Institute for Human Sciences, University of Yaounde, specializing in economic planning, regional integration, international trade, and financial policy concerns. He received his doctorate from Carleton University, Ottawa. He is a frequent contributor to economic and African studies journals and is the author of *Planning for Economic Development in a Federal State: The Case of Cameroon, 1960–1971* and editor of *Economic Cooperation and Integration in Africa.*

DIEGO UNGARO received his M.A. from The Johns Hopkins School of Advanced International Studies in African Studies and is now working with NOMISMA in Italy, completing research on Mozambique and Angola.

JEAN-CLAUDE WILLAME is Acting Director of the Centre d'Etudes et de Documentation Africaines (CEDAF) in Brussels. He obtained his Ph.D. from the University of California at Berkeley. As Acting Director of CEDAF, he has been associated with several evaluation missions for the Commission Market and the Belgian Public Aid Agency for Development in Zaire, Zambia, and Cameroon. Dr. Willame is the author of *Patrimonialism and Political Change in the Congo.*